Capital of Cultures
Istanbul

Capital of Cultures

Istanbul

İlhan AKŞİT

Archaeologist

AKŞİT KÜLTÜR VE TURİZM YAYINCILIK

Contents

I. Topography of Istanbul, the Capital of Three Empires   9

II. Founding of Istanbul, Byzantion   17

III. Capital of the Roman Empire: Constantinopolis   23

IV. Capital of the Byzantine Empire: Constantinopolis   29

City Walls of Istanbul   39

Byzantine Palaces   45

Roads, Squares and Monuments   51

Byzantine Cisterns   63

Byzantine Churches and Monasteries   69

Hagia Eirene   77

Hagia Sophia   79

Chora Monastery   87

V. Ottoman Period in Istanbul   97

Ottoman Mosques in Istanbul   111

Süleymaniye Mosque   127

Sultanahmet Mosque (Blue Mosque)   133

Tombs of the Sultans   139

Aqueducts, Fountains and Baths   145

Castles, Towers and Fortresses   152

Ottoman Palaces   159

Topkapı Palace   167

Dolmabahçe Palace   185

Kiosks and Summer Palaces   197

Waterside Mansions by the Bosphorus   205

Inns and Bazaars   215

Museums of Istanbul   219

Istanbul Archaeological Museums   225

Museum of Turkish and Islamic Arts   233

VI. Istanbul in the 21st Century   239

Editing: Necdet Akşit

English Translation and Editing: Ayşegül Eryılmaz Williams, Jason Ryan Williams.

Graphic & Design: Hasan Basri Özsu

Photographs: İzzet Keribar, Kadir Kır, Lütfi Özgünaydın, Güngör Özsoy, Hasan Basri Özsu, Akşit Ltd. Şti. Arşivi

Color Separation: Seval Grafik, Tel: (+90.212) 526 01 30

Printed by & Bookbinder: Ömür Matbaacılık A.Ş.
Beysan San. Sitesi Birlik Cad. No:20 34524 Haramidere / Istanbul
Tel: (+90.212) 422 76 00
Fax: (+90.212) 422 46 00
www.omur.com.tr

Preface

Lamartine says,

"God and human, nature and art cooperated to create this marvelous and matchless piece of nature on earth": Istanbul

Indeed, there is no other city in the world with such a rich and generous nature, which is molded with such diverse cultures. This location, admired and inhabited by people for thousands of years, started its long historical time line with the Palaeolithic Age and served as the home and capital of three of the world's biggest empires. Having not only cherished as if mature wine with the cultural deposition accumulated over the years, it also caught up with the modernism of the 21st Century, and continues to mesmerize its onlookers today with its mystic beauty blending the old and new.

Having served as the capital city of the Roman, Byzantine and Ottoman Empires whose territories spanned Asia, Europe and Africa, Istanbul evolved into a center where very diverse regional and religious cultures interconnected, with works of art being brought here from different places adding up to its own riches. The obelisk from the Temple of Karnak in Egypt and the Serpentine Column from the Temple of Apollo in Delphoi which were brought to decorate the city, the world-renowned Hagia Sophia which remains to be important even today, and the Sultanahmet Mosque (Blue Mosque) can all be seen in the same snapshot, representing a fine example for showing the richness of Istanbul's cultural mosaic.

Istanbul, which was the natural capital city of the world for many centuries, has been honored in being designated as the 'European Capital of Culture for 2010'. This decision is important for Istanbul-a city which has humbly accepted thousands of praises and honors it received from the past to the present-for sharing with the world its cultural accumulation as well as its unique nature and dynamism of life in all its colors. Istanbul, which is going through an assertive development not only in tourism but also in art, entertainment, trade and shopping, has become a metropolis today making a name for itself with these qualities.

On the occasion of Istanbul's designation as the 'European Capital of Culture for 2010', we wanted to contribute in the efforts to further familiarize the world with our seven-hilled city where the old and new are intertwined together like ivy. I extend my thanks to everyone who put forth efforts in the publication of our work, including Ayşegül Erylmaz Williams and Jason Ryan Williams who performed diligent translation of the book.

With all my respect...

Archaeologist

Ilhan Akşit

AKŞİT KÜLTÜR VE TURİZM YAYINCILIK

Cağaloğlu Yokuşu Cemal Nadir Sokak Nur İşhanı 2/4 34440 İstanbul / TÜRKİYE
Tel : (+90.212) 511 53 85 - 511 67 82
Fax: (+90.212) 527 68 13

www.aksityayincilik.com
info@aksityayincilik.com
Publication Place, Date: İstanbul-2009

ISBN: 978-975-7039-63-1

KISIRKAYA

KİLYOS

Sazlıdere
Baraj
Gölü

Alibeyköy
Baraj
Gölü

İKİTELLİ

BAHÇEŞEHİR

...KÇEKMECE

EYÜP

ORTAKÖY

BEŞİKTAŞ

KUZGUNC...

TAKSİM

KABATAŞ

Haliç

ÜSKÜDAR

BEYLİKDÜZÜ

TOPKAPI

FATİH

EMİNÖNÜ

SARAYBURNU

HAREM

BÜYÜKÇEKMECE

AYASOFYA
S. AHMET

KÜÇÜKÇEKMECE

CANKURTARAN

YENİKAPI

HAYDARPAŞA

KÜÇÜKÇEKMECE

KADIKÖY

YEDİKULE

AMBARLI

AVCILAR

FLORYA

ATAKÖY

ZEYTİNBURNU

MODA

YEŞİLYURT

FENERBAHÇE

YEŞİLKÖY

SEA   OF   MARMARA

BLACK SEA

İRCİKÖY

RUMELİ
FENERİ

ANADOLU
FENERİ

ÇAYAĞZI
(RİVA)

POYRAZ
KÖYÜ

RUMELİKAVAĞI

ANADOLUKAVAĞI

ARIYER

ARABYA

BEYKOZ

YENİKÖY

PAŞABAHÇE

KANLICA

A.HİSARI

KANDİLLİ

Elmalı
Baraj
Gölü

Ömerli
Baraj
Gölü

AN

SUADİYE

BOSTANCI

DRAGOS

Topography of
Istanbul,
the Capital of
Three Empires

Topography of Istanbul

Istanbul, which Lamartine revealed his admiration by saying, "There, God and human, nature and art created together the most marvelous scene which the human eye can see on earth," is situated on a peninsula surrounded by the Istanbul Strait (Bosphorus)-the only waterway linking the Black Sea and Mediterranean cultures-the Marmara Sea and the Golden Horn Estuary (Haliç).

As if justifying Napoleon Bonaparte, who said "If the world was just one country, the capital would be Istanbul", Istanbul is the only city on earth which served in its history as the capital of three great empires; the Roman, Byzantine and Ottoman. Standing out in the world as the only city established over two continents, Istanbul is also the largest and the most impressive city of modern-day Turkey in terms of population, trade, industry, education and culture with its location suited for sea and land trade, acclaimed natural beauties, ideal climate and geographical features. In regards to population, it ranks third in the world and first in Europe. Having passed down from Byzantion to Rome, from Rome to Byzantion, and then to the Ottomans, Istanbul is a European capital of culture today with its nature, history, and cultural accumulation.

Many theories are assumed of the formation of the land site on which Istanbul is situated. The most convincing among these is the formation of the strait as a result of the rises and compressions in the Mesozoic Era and Cenozoic Era. More accurately, the furrows deepened as a result of the ruptures in the Bosphorus and the Golden Horn, which were old river valleys, and were flooded with the rise of the seas in the Quaternary Era. In this location, which thus formed with the land sites surrounding it and which came to be inhabited, the Bosphorus-the most beautiful strait of the world-came into existence. The widest part of the 29.9 km long strait measures 3600 m, between the Anatolian Lighthouse (Anadolu Feneri) and the Rumelian Lighthouse (Rumeli Feneri), whereas the narrowest part measures 698 m, between the Anatolian Fortress (Anadolu Hisarı) and the Rumelian Fortress (Rumeli Hisarı). The average depth of the strait is 50 m, whereas the deepest part measures 120 m and is located between Kandilli and Bebek.

Lying from north east to south west, the strait is referred to as the Bosphorus in Western sources. This name meaning 'ox passage' was given based on the following legend: King Inachos of Argos had a daughter named Io. When Io grew up, she became a nun at the Temple of Hera in Argos. The philanderer chief god Zeus saw and admired this beautiful nun and had intercourse with her. Hera, the jealous wife of Zeus, discovered this and became greatly outraged. Zeus wanted to protect his beloved from the wrath of Hera, thus he transformed her into a white calf and took oaths that he had a no relationship with her. Hera wanted the calf for herself. She took Io with her and left Argos the "thousand-eyed" to stand guard with her. In the meanwhile, Zeus was looking for ways to save his

beloved. He commissioned the messenger god Hermes to assassinate the guard Argos. Hermes killed Argos by casting a spell on him, consequently saving Io. This time, Hera set a gadfly to pester the white calf. Io scurried from one continent to the other, in an effort to escape the gadfly with no success. Around this time she swam across the Istanbul Strait. This legend is said to have been the reason why the strait was given the name Bosphorus.

The Golden Horn Estuary, which stretches inland for about 7.5 km from the sea and is 300 m wide, forms an important natural port and today is referred to as "the Golden Horn". Denysos of Byzantion stated that Io gave birth to Ceroessa-her daughter from Zeus-at Semistra, which is located at the end of the estuary. Perhaps the estuary was named after Ceroessa as Keras, meaning horn.

The strait served as a stage for various mythological scenes, and with the rocky area at its section opening to the Black Sea, the strait was also involved in the mythological legend of the Argonauts. The legend has it that, when Jason-the protagonist of the Argonauts' Voyage-grew up, he reclaimed the throne which his uncle took from his father. His uncle said that he would give him the throne if he brought back the Golden Fleece which was taken to Georgia. Jason prepared for the journey, gathering around himself the most distinguished gallants of the time. First, he had a ship built with 55 oars, by the famous master Argos and set sail for this journey of countless adventures from Thessalia. The gallants setting sail for this voyage, also including Heracles, belonged to the generation preceding the heroes of the Troian War. For the ship to sail through the Dardanelles Strait and proceed across the Marmara Sea, afterwards setting out to the Black Sea, it had to sail through the Bosphorus. The Argo sailors had quite an adventure in the Marmara Sea at Kyzikos. Afterwards, they arrived in the land of Bebrycs, which was located in Kadıköy (Chalcedon) and ruled by King Amycos". As they were about to defeat the Bebrycs and sail through the Bosphorus, a night storm threw them off course. They arrived in the land of King Phineus the prophet, who was the blind son of Poseidon. Phineus and his people were given no respite by the Harpies, which had bird-shaped bodies and woman-shaped heads. The Argonauts saved the king from these creatures which kept stealing their food, and in return, the king guided them as to how they could cross the clashing rocks at the exit of the strait. If the dove they were to release into the rocks could make it across, they would also be able to make it across. The dove they released glided between the rocks at the last minute, leaving behind the long feathers of its tail, and as the rocks were retreating, the Argonauts made it across before the rocks could close back. They then set out for the Black Sea, following the advice of the king. The tremendous pointed rocks located in front of the Rumelian Fortress today are believed to be those same clashing rocks. These rocks were daunting for sailors at all times, and in the Roman

Istanbul, which sits in natural wonder meticulously created by God, separates Asia and Europe with the strait running through it. Ruled by many cultures over its long history, the city now has a wide spectrum of works exhibited all together irrespective of their time. A history of thousands of years across two continents, as well as newly-constructed modern buildings and bridges, all intertwined together, form the panorama of the city.

While the Istanbul Bosphorus seperates Asia from Europe, the Bosphorus and Fatih Sultan Mehmet Bridges

Period, a column named the Column of Pompeius was erected over them. Known as the "Distaff Rock" (Öreke Taşı) in the Ottoman Period, these rocks were visited by all travelers coming to Istanbul. In its general appearance, Istanbul is characterized as a plateau. This plateau has been broken into pieces with high flat areas and rivers. The highest hill here is Büyük Çamlıca Hill measuring 262 m high, and Yuşa Hill measuring 201 m high. The rivers within the provincial borders are in the form of small streams. The major ones are the rivers of Riva, Küçüksu and Göksu on the Asian side, and Alibey, Kağıthane, Sazlıdere, Karasu and Trança on the European side. The largest lake of Istanbul is Lake Terkos, which meets the water demand of the city.

Settlement in Istanbul and the Islands

Sub-provincial districts lined up along both sides of the Bosphorus and along the Golden Horn have been divided into smaller districts over time, proportionately to the increase in their population, and increased in number. On the European side, along the Bosphorus lie the districts of Sarıyer, Beşiktaş and Eminönü from north east to south west. To the west of Beşiktaş is Şişli and towards the south lies Beyoğlu, which forms one bank of the Golden Horn. The districts of Eyüp and Fatih form the other bank of the Golden Horn. Lying along the Bosphorus on the Anatolian side are the districts of Üsküdar, and also Beykoz which is close to the Black Sea. Another district opening to the Black Sea

is Şile. Şile and its affiliated town Ağva stand as a decent sanctuary of relaxation both for Istanbulites and the city's guests. The Belgrade Forest to the north of the city served as the main water basin of Istanbul throughout history, and important ponds, dams and water passages have been constructed here since the Roman Period. This water was connected to Istanbul via aqueducts, each of which still stands today as works of art.

Along the Marmara shores of Istanbul, the nine islands off the shore of Bostancı and Dragos Hill are known as the Islands of Istanbul. The Islands, which are located to the south of Istanbul, face the Anatolian side and are about 20 km from Sarayburnu. Some of them are among the most beautiful

resorts of Istanbul today. During Byzantine times, these islands were places of exile or imprisonment for princes and emperors and thus were named as the Princes' Islands. They were also known as Papadonisia (Priests' Islands) due to the monks who lived in this neighborhood in seclusion.

The Islands are a part of the Kocaeli Peninsula and they were formed around the beginning of the Quaternary Era together with the straits, during earth crust movements. Among them, Big Island (Prinkipo), Heybeliada (Khalki), Burgazada (Antigone), Kınalıada (Proti) and Sedefadası (Antherovitos) are those which are open to settlement. There is no settlement on Yassıada (Plati), Kaşıkadası (Pita), Sivriada (Ohia) and Tavşanadası (Neandros).

connect the two continents. The Bosphorus Bridge is seen in the foreground.

13

These islands, which comprise hills of various heights, were eventually filled with mansions and became a holiday resort for Istanbulites, but now they can be inhabited in winter too. On these islands of rich and assorted vegetation are the piney woods and Judas trees exhibiting a distinct beauty.

Apparently Christian monasteries were established over the Roman temples on the islands. During Byzantine times, in 567, Emperor Justin II commissioned a palace known as Megale on Büyükada. The islands served as the place of exile for many princes, patriarchs, even dethroned emperors. Constantinos (or Constantine) VI and Empress Irene commissioned the Women's Monastery (Hagia Irene) to be built over the remnants of the Megale Palace, and his young son who engaged in a battle of throne with him enclosed there Constantine VI after having his eyes blinded with hot iron. When the empress was dethroned in 802 with a coup, she too was exiled to this island. At the time of fierce conflicts during the Byzantines, especially during the account settlement between the iconoclasts and iconophiles, St. Theodoros, in 809, Empress Theodosia and her son Vasilius, in 820, were exiled to the Hagia Triada Monastery in Heybeliada, the famous clergyman Metodios was exiled to Burgazada in 835, and Patriarch Ignatios was exiled to Sedefadası in 857, and afterwards many palace members were exiled to the islands. On his way back to Istanbul, following his defeat in Malazgirt, Romanos Diogenes was blinded by those who seized the power and was imprisoned in the Hristos Monastery, which he himself had commissioned in Kınalıada. At the time of the Ottoman rule, the

Bebek Cove.
Lined up along the Bosphorus, coves such as Istinye, Tarabya and Kanlıca create sheltered waters for yachts and boats.

Aerial view of the Bosphorus.
Connecting the Marmara Sea and Black Sea, the Bosphorus forms two streams running in opposite directions, one on top and the other at the bottom.

patriarchate was entrusted with the rights of utilizing the soil and ownership on the islands. Around the mid-19th Century, scheduled ferry trips to the islands began, and in the 20th Century, the islands became popular not only among Turks, but also Greek, Armenian and Jewish citizens. Büyükada is the largest of the islands, where churches, church schools and monasteries, most of which were built after the second half of the 19th Century are still remarkable in their architectural structure. On the island, on top of the Hagia Yorgi Hill measuring 203 m is a monastery of the same name and a new church; on the second high hill is the Greek Orphanage, which is a massive wooden house. Furthermore, on the island, there is a Greek church and monastery (Hagios Nicolaos), Armenian Catholic churches and Jewish synagogues, together with four mosques. Heybeliada, which is the second largest island, served as the major ecclesial education center for the Greek population, following the conquest of Istanbul. Heybeliada Clergy School, Makarios Monastery and Hagia Yorgi on Ümit Hill are the major religious buildings of the island.

Kınalıada, which is the closest island to Istanbul, is intensively populated by the Armenian community. The only Armenian church on the islands is the Surp Krikor Lusavoriç Church. Located on Manastır Hill is the Greek Orthodox Hristos Monastery. The mosque on the shore has a remarkable modern outlook. On Burgazada, which is a very green island, Hagios Ioannis, Hagia Yorgi and the monastery church Hristos on the hill are the three Greek Orthodox churches which still survive on the island today.

Heybeliada (Khalki) as seen from the Büyükada district of Istanbul.

Aerial view of the Golden Horn-one of the most sheltered natural ports of the world.

Founding of
Istanbul,
Byzantion

Founding of Istanbul, Byzantion

Previous page:
Aerial view of Istanbul with
the Sultanahmet Mosque in
the foreground and the Hagia Sophia
Museum in the background.

Istanbul
1.Topkapı Palace
2.Hagia Eirene
3.Hagia Sophia
4.Sultanahmet Mosque (Blue Mosque)
5.Museum of Great Palace Mosaics
6.Small Hagia Sophia
7.Basilica Cistern
8.Museum of Turkish and Islamic Arts
9.Hippodrome
10.Cistern of a Thousand and One
Columns (Binbirdirek Sarnıcı)
11.Theodosios Cistern
12.Istanbul Archaeological Museums
13.Yenikapı
14.The Marmara Walls
15.Sepetçiler Summer Palace
16.Cityline Ferry Port
17.New Mosque
18.Egyptian Bazaar
19.Sirkeci Rail Station
20.Rüstempaşa Mosque
21.Istanbul Chamber of Commerce
22.Süleymaniye Mosque
23.Grand Bazaar
24. Bayezıd Mosque
25.Constantine Column
26.Istanbul University
27.Shehzade (Crown Prince) Mosque
28.The Aqueduct of Valens
29.Galata Bridge

A.G.de Busbecq says " It's as if Istanbul was created by nature to be the capital of the world." Appraised by everyone throughout its long past, the neighborhood of this beautiful city had been chosen as a dwelling by people even before the founding of the city.

Studies in Yarımburgaz Cave to the north of Küçük Çekmece show that this place was inhabited by people even in the Palaeolithic Era. Settlements which are the continuation of this period have been encountered in Pendik and Fikirtepe. During studies of the sunken Byzantine ruins conducted at the Port of Theodisios in Yenikapı, along with nearly 30 Byzantine boats, Neolithic-Era remnants were found six meters below the sea level.

Having set out on their journey around 686 BC and after a long exploration, the Megarians arrived at the hill where the Topkapı Palace is situated today. This place was so beautiful that the Megarians fell in love with it. Seen on the opposite shores were the settlements of the colonies which had arrived before them. The Megarians recalled the oracles who had said "Establish a homeland opposite the land of the blind", before they set out on their journey to establish a homeland for themselves. The Megarians deemed the people on the opposite side "blind" for having settled there instead of this miraculous place which they were standing on and thought that place was the "land of the blind" referred to in the prophecy. Thus they built their homes and settled there.

The Megarians named the new city they founded after their leader as Byzantion and surrounded it with a rampart. These city walls made of massive rocks seem to have had two gates and seven towers. They also surrounded the seaside and had 27 towers on that side. Hence, the city of Byzantion became the most powerful city, with the strongest city walls along with those of Rhodes.

The Temples of Apollon, Artemis and Aphrodite are thought to have been situated on the acropolis where the modern-day Topkapı Palace is. Evidently, the Temple of Poseidon and the holy area of Athena must have been situated on the coast to the north of the peninsula.

The city had two ports; one was in today's Sirkeci and was secured by two towers which could sometimes be closed with a chain, and the other was on the Marmara coast to the south, at Çatladıkapı (the Cracked Gate). Near these ports were the Temples of Demeter and Kore. Outside the city, by the Golden Horn was the Temple of Hera, which Darius set fire to in 512 BC, at the time of the Campaign to Greece. Around the same place was the Temple of Pluto, which was demolished in 340 BC. There was a bronze sculpture of Helios-the solar god on the city's acropolis, at the Thrakion Square. It also had a rectangular agora with a portico, like those of the

ancient cities. Buildings such as gymnasion, augusteon and strategion were being built and thus the city was rapidly developing. Around the 6th and the 5th Centuries BC when Byzantion was established, many Ionian cities in the Aegean were erecting tremendous temples for their gods, as if competing with one another. In newly established Byzantion too, temples built in the name of many gods started to emerge one after another. Having dedicated their city to the mother goddess Rhea, who gave birth to Zeus, the people of Byzantion accepted her as their guardian. They were also constructing holy areas for Helios and Selena.

At the outset of the 5th Century BC, the Persians suppressed an uprising of Ionian cities led by Aristagoras the Tyrant of Miletos. Meanwhile, many cities were ravaged by the Persians. Byzantion was among them. Byzantion is known to have joined the Campaign to Greece organized by King Xerxes of Persia in 481 BC, with around 100 ships.

The Spartan commander Pausanius, who inflicted defeat on the Persians in Plataea in 487 BC, seized Byzantion the following year and the city remained in his dominion until 477 BC. Pausanius had the city repaired and decorated it with new buildings in this period.

After Pausanius, Byzantion fell to the Athenians. Meanwhile, Byzantion became the base of the Athenian navy. Byzantion joined the Attica-Delos Union formed by around 300 city states led by Athens, and later sided with the Athenians at the Peloponnesian War in 431 BC, which broke out due to the rivalry between Athens and the Spartans. However, following the failed campaign initiated by Athens against Syracuse in 413 BC, Byzantion gained its freedom and left the Athens union together with many cities and switched to the Spartan side. In return, Alkibiades I of Athens launched a campaign to Byzantion in 409 BC and conquered the city. However, in 405 BC, the Spartans defeated the Athenians in Hellespontos, ending the lengthy Peloponnesian Wars, at the same time repossessing Byzantion. According to what we learn from 'Anabasis' of Xenophon, ten thousand Greek mercenary troops, which had joined the campaign against the Persian King in 400 BC, arrived in Byzantion defeated and distraught. Seemingly, Byzantion minted its own money towards the end of the 5th Century BC.

In 378 BC, Byzantion became a member of the second Attica-Delos Union and joined wars as a member of this union. Around this time, previously-established Chalcedon became a part of Byzantion as well. The city continued its life for a while maintaining good relations with its close neighbors such as Selimbria in Silivri. Byzantion appears to have participated in operations against Athens, starting from 364 BC. Around this time in Macedonia, Philippos II held the Macedonian throne. Byzantion was allies with Philippos, yet the King's invasion of Thrace in 341 BC caused Byzantion to act in opposition to him. They united with Athens and other cities and

GOLDEN HORN

HALİÇ

engaged in defense preparations against him. In return, Philippos II sieged Byzantion in 340 BC. This siege lasted until the spring of 339 BC. The King dispensed with sieging Byzantion in the spring but did not withhold from ravaging every corner. The people of Byzantion managed to overcome this great destruction in a short time, due to their fertile lands, and the commerce of tuna fish and wheat.

After lifting the siege of Byzantion, Philippos II was killed during a wedding. Alexander, who had just turned 20 and whom history named Alexander the Great, ascended to the throne after him. Despite his young age, Alexander took over a strong army as well as experienced administrators from his father, and was also taught by great philosophers such as Aristotle. With his venturesome and audacious spirit, he immediately suppressed the rebellions that had broken out due to his succession to the throne, and seized wide territories in Europe.

Having overcome the disarrays, Alexander could now set his eyes to the east and realize his dreams. Setting out for that purpose in spring 334 BC, Alexander crossed the Dardanelles Strait and struck the first blow at the Persians by the River Granikos. Alexander quickly went down into the south without stopping by Byzantion. Now the world seemed to lie before him: Vast lands to be conquered were ahead of him, the cities were opening their gates to him. Alexander had started a new age by striking the last blow at the Persians. In this period which is known as the Hellenistic Age, Byzantion maintained its independence.

Byzantion did not become involved in the conflicts between Alexander's generals, after Alexander's death at a young age in 323 BC, and managed to remain unbiased during the battles between Lysimachos and Antigonos. However, even though it accepted Antigonos's dominion later on, it maintained its independence in its internal affairs. At the time, the city controlled maritime trade from the Black Sea to Egypt, and ensured trading between Europe and Anatolia.

This period of welfare was distorted by the Galatians who invaded the region in the 3rd Century BC. Starting from 278 BC, Byzantion had to pay annual taxes to the Galatians, who plundered Chalcedon. Despite these high taxes, Byzantion continued its development. Meanwhile, the Kingdom of Bithynia was founded, and Byzantion was faced with pressure from them and the Kingdom of Macedonia. Byzantion persevered through this pressure with the help of Ptolemaios II. Philadelphos reigning over Egypt, and that of its neighbors.

Around this time, Byzantion's territories reached as far as Rhegion in Thrace and as far as Bithynia on the Anatolian side, which is near Yalova. They were on good terms with King Nicomedes of Bithynia, their neighbor in the east. However, when they also had to pay customs duties in addition to the taxes they already paid to the Galatians, Byzantion encountered difficulty. Around 220 BC, Rhodes and its ally Prusias I began to threaten the city. However, they were not the only ones who threatened this developed city. The city was now faced with the threat from King Philippos V of Macedonia. In addition, Byzantion was not strong enough to stand up to these great threats. Therefore it called for the help of Rome and then continued to live under the auspices of Rome, at a time when the glory of Rome burned bright.

An aerial view of the Hagia Eirene.

Capital of
the Roman Empire:
Constantinopolis

Capital of the Roman Empire: Constantinopolis

The torch of Rome was burning in the world now, and Roman troops made their presence felt both in Europe and Anatolia. Around this time Kingdom of Macedonia captured the territories in Thrace and Western Anatolia, after which the Kingdom of Pergamon called for the help of Rome. During the war fought in 197 BC, the Romans inflicted defeat on King Philippos of Macedonia. Later on, King Antiochos III of the Seleucids wanted to revive his old kingdom but he was defeated by the Romans near Manisa and had to leave the territories in Anatolia to Rome as a result of the signed treaties. Rome considered that it was still early for it to become the owner of Anatolia. Therefore, it left the territories it acquired to Rhodes and the Kingdom of Pergamon, who were allies in this war. While the territories of Caria and Lycia were left to Rhodes, the territories all the way to Antalya were given to the Kingdom of Pergamon. Thus the Kingdom of Pergamon, which was established with the treasure of Lysmachos, was becoming a kingdom that was assuming important roles in Anatolia. Byzantion became annexed to Rome from 146 BC and sided with Rome both during the pirate wars and its wars with Mithridates. Despite this, Rome still did not want to become the owner of Anatolia. Afterwards, Rome formed a union with the Kingdoms of Pergamon, Galatia and Bithynia but this union was dissolved with the provocation of Carthaginian Hannibal. When King Attalos III of Pergamon died and left his territories to Rome in 133 BC, Rome became the owner of Anatolia.

When King Nicomedes of Bithynia, too, died and left his territories to Rome in 74 BC, all of Anatolia came under the control of Rome. During the period of Vespasianus (69-79), the city lost the special status it held until then, due to the uprisings which broke out in the eastern provinces. It was made liable to pay taxes to the Roman governor. The economic status of the city was still good. It measured 70 hectares, and temples were built here dedicated to the Egyptian deities Serapis and Isis, as well as a stadion near the port and a theatre by the side of the acropolis. The city had two main squares to the west of the strategeron. Main roads by the Golden Horn lay all the way up to the necropolis on the hills. The water demand of the baths was met with the waterways which were commissioned by Emperor Hadrianus. The city was now larger, and became wider to include both sides of the Golden Horn. Little villages were formed along the Bosphorus, and temples of Zeus Urios and Cybele were built around this area. Furthermore, a castle was built at the narrowing point of the Bosphorus, which was to retain its importance until the Middle Ages. Following the death of Emperor Commodus at the end of the 2nd Century, a battle for the throne began between Pescennius Niger, the governor of Syria, and Septimus Severius, who were the two candidates for emperor. Here, Byzantion made a big mistake by supporting the losing side. As punishment, Septimus Severius blockaded the city for three years. The city fell in 196 and was devastated. The city walls were demolished and many people were killed. Furthermore, its right of urbanization was abolished and it was annexed to Perinthos (Marmara Ereğlisi) with a village status. Septimus Severius's son

Antonius Bassianus Caracalla understood the strategic importance of Byzantion; therefore, he put pressure on his father and requested that the city be repaired. In 197, the rights of the city were restored, and Severius reconstructed the city larger, expanding it twice as much, and named the city Antonia after his son. Caracalla (211-217), who had replaced his father on the throne, continued the settlement activities. However, the construction of the hippodrome and the Zeuksippos baths was left incomplete. In the 4th Century, when the Roman Emperor Diocletianus informed that he had withdrawn from the state administration, Rome was faced with an internal crisis. Constantinos, who took the lead at a young age after his father's death, was declared the sovereign of this land in 306 as one of the four Kaisers of Rome. Constantinos surmounted the Alps with an army of 40,000 at his command, defeated the Roman Kaiser Maxentius, and headed east. Having also defeated Licinius the Kaiser of the East, who was his brother in law at the same time; he reigned as the sole dominant power of Rome until 337.

Constantinos had seen that it would be hard to govern the vast territories from Rome, and therefore started looking for a new capital. Constantinos deemed Byzantion suitable for the capital city he had in mind and he relocated the center of the empire from Rome to Byzantion, and declared this place the new governmental center. In accordance with that decision, he first expanded the Septimus's Walls 3 km to enlarge the city. The emperor, who was to accept Christianity later on, was favorable towards Christians. Thus, besides old pagan temples in the city, Christian churches also began to ascend. In order to eliminate the differences in the religion, Constantinos invited patriarchs and assembled the First Ecumenical Council in Iznik (Nicaea). The aim of the emperor was to resolve the disagreement between Arius the Patriarch of Alexandria and his Patriarch on 'whether Jesus was of the same substance as God the Father or not'. This is because Arius the Patriarch of Alexandria defended that the Son and Father are not of the same substance. The Council of Nicaea rejected Arius's proposition, but Arianism began to spread among the people rapidly. The Emperor was awarded the title of "guardian of Christian churches" due to his services. The city was comprised of main streets spreading out on the foot of the seven hills and large streets cutting across them. The fora on these streets were made utilizing the rugged structure of the city. While the large main street Mese, Augusteion and Forum Constantinos, as well as a large palace complex, Episcopal Church, Hagia Irene, and Temples of Rhea and Tykhe were being built, the construction of edifices such as the Hippodrome and Zeuksippos Bath, which were initiated by Septimus Severus, were completed. Also, the construction of the official buildings such as the Senate, Praetorium and Capitol were completed. The Million Stone, which is enclosed within a deep chasm located between the Basilica Cistern (Yerebatan Sarnıcı) and Hagia Sophia, and which was accepted as the starting point of all the roads leading to Rome, was built during this period. A monumental cemetery began to be constructed on a hill at the northern end of the city,

in connection with the Church of the Holy Apostles (Havariyyun Kilisesi). The opening ceremony of the new capital city was held on May 11, 330 with a spectacular religious ceremony. Now Byzantion was left in the distant past, and the new city was named "Nea Roma". Before long, this new capital, which far exceeded the fame of old Rome, was named Constantinopolis after its founder. The city was administrated by a governor entitled proconsul. After 359, administrators known as 'Praefectur', who were entitled governor-mayor, were in service. Names of governor-mayors are observed on some of the epigraphs found in Istanbul today. Constantions had Forum Constantinos built, which was a great rounded square in the city center. In the middle of this forum, he had a monument made from red porphyry erected, which is known as Çemberlitaş (Constantine Column) today. He had his sculpture placed on top of the monument, which was in the form of 'Apollon saluting the sun'. Later on, he had a palace built on the slopes facing the Marmara Sea and encouraged the notables of Rome for the development of the new capital. While he was having the Cistern of a Thousand and One Columns (Binbirdirek Sarnıcı) built, he also had another palace built near it, only the remnants of which can be seen today near the Court House. Emperors who assumed leadership after Emperor Constantinos continued the development activities. The water demand was met by carrying water to the urban area through the pipes installed underground, from outside the city walls. The Valens Aqueducts at Unkapanı, which were commissioned by Emperor Valentinianus around 368-373, retain their magnificence even today. These aqueducts were later repaired by Architect Sinan and were used during the Ottoman time with new additions. Towards the end of the 4th Century, the city spread over the foot of the seven hills just as in Rome and was separated into 14 regions interconnected with regular roads. The square before Hagia Sophia was named Augusteion and the Severius Portico leading to Çemberlitaş was renewed. Mese Street, which was the porticoed road continuing from the forum in the Bayezid Square, went down to Aksaray, and then to Cerrahpaşa. These porticoes were two-storey each and on the lower floors were stores. There were promenade areas on the second floors which were accessed via stairs. Obelisks were being brought to various places of the empire to decorate the squares. The obelisk depicting the victories of Tutmosis II was brought from the Temple of Karnak in Egypt, but this was not put into its place. The Serpentine's Column (Burmalı Sütun), which was brought from Greece, was erected in the middle of hippodrome.

Theodosios I (378-395), who assumed the throne after Emperor Valens (364-378) was a devout Orthodox, and he appointed Gregorius of Nazianzos as the patriarch, who was also like him. In 381, he attempted to ensure unity in the religion by assembling the 2nd Ecumenical Council in Hagia Irene. This council reaffirmed the decisions taken at the Council of Nicaea and rejected Arianism once again. Emperor Theodosios severely prohibited Pagan and Arian positions, trying to establish the Orthodox understanding. In the meantime, he turned today's Bayezid Square into the largest forum of the city, decorated it with monuments and called it the Theodosios Square. The monument erected in the name of the emperor here stood intact until the earthquake in 1509. This emperor, who was worn out with religious issues, died in 395, after which Rome separated into two and turned into two new empires.

The Million Stone.
This monument, which was accepted as the epicenter of the capital of the Eastern Roman Empire, can bee seen near the water gauge before the Basilica Cistern.

The Aqueduct of Valens. This aqueduct was begun by the emperor Valentinus in 368 AD., and was restored by the architect Sinan during the Ottoman period. The aqueduct, which stretches between Sarachane and Zeyrek was originally 1 km in length, although only a section 800 m in length now stands. It is 18.50 m in height. It is locally known as the Bozdoğan aqueduct.

Capital of
the Byzantine Empire:
Constantinopolis

Capital of the Byzantine Empire: Constantinopolis

Created with marvelous beauty by God, Constantinopolis was now living up to its splendor thanks to mankind.

In 395, Emperor Theodosios died, leaving vast territories behind which were shared by his two sons, leading to the emergence of two empires as Eastern and Western Rome. The Western Roman Empire was left to his son Honorius and its center was Ravenna, while his other son Arcadios became the emperor of the Eastern Roman Empire, the center of which was Byzantion. This separation was taken advantage of by King Alaric of the Western Goths who were residing in Macedonia and Greece. When he marched on Eastern Rome, the Emperor Arcadios assigned him as the commander of the Balkans, thus avoiding the threat. However, Western Rome failed to do the same and was forced to fall with the pressure from the Goths.

After Arcadios died in 480, Theodosios became emperor at the age of 7 and his sister Pulcheria was appointed as the deputy of the emperor. The reign of this emperor was to last 42 years, during which Istanbul went through the greatest change and the main features of the city, as it reached to this date, was first given. The Huns emerged as a new and notably dangerous enemy of the Byzantine Empire. The Byzantines warded off this threat in return for money; however, they still decided to surround the city with durable walls. Anthemios, who was the commander of the eastern territory, was assigned to this task. These walls built by Anthemios were damaged by an earthquake in 447, and then commander Constantinos assigned by Theodosios II secured the city by having both the damaged walls repaired and an additional rampart and dike built in front of these walls which were extended 1200 m.

Religious trends continued during Theodosios II and new ones emerged, thus the 3rd Ecumenical Assembly was convened to resolve them. Following the strenuous discussions during this meeting, the doctrine which holds that Mother Mary gave birth to her son Jesus as the son of God was affirmed. This time however, monophysitism emerged which holds that Jesus had only one and a divine nature, in other words that Jesus was of the same essence as God. When Theodosios II died in 450, without leaving any children behind, his sister's husband, General Marcianos replaced him. Marcianos assembled the Council of Chalcedon in 451 to resolve the religious discrepancy. At the end of the lengthy discussions during this meeting, it was decided that the Constantinopolis Patriarch was to be deemed equal to the Pope. This set the first step for the separation of churches as east and west.

Now the Germanic communities permeated Constantinopolis, where religious turmoil took place, and they became very influential on the Aspar administration and thanks to him, Leon I of Illiria became the emperor instead of Marcianos. Later on, to discard Aspar, the emperor brought the Isaurians, who resided in upper Antalya, to Constantinopolis. The commander leading the forces which came here took control of the city in 474 and before long, by the name of Zenon, he declared his empire. Following the death of Zenon, his wife married Anastasios-one of the palace guards-and ascended him to the throne. Anastasios was a Monophysit, whereas the people in the capital were Orthodox. Therefore the mayhem increased even further. When Anastasios died without leaving behind an heir, the palace guards selected their commander as the heir to the throne. Thus in 518, Commander Justinos, who was a Thracian peasant, assumed the Byzantine throne. Because the new emperor was an Orthodox, he made peace with the Pope, ending the disagreement between the eastern and western churches. Justinos had no children and thus he designated his nephew Justinianos (or Justinian) as the heir to the throne. Having become the Counsel in 521, Justinianos derived his strength from the Blues, who represented the Orthodoxy and large landowners. This relationship resulted in him being detested by the Greens representing Monophysitism, as well as merchants and artisans. In 522, he met Theodora who was the daughter of a bear tamer, and wanted to marry her. Due to the opposition against this marriage, he waited until he took the throne. Eventually in 527, Justinianos replaced the emperor when he died and thus Theodora became the empress, which introduced the second bright period of the Byzantine history. What stood as a land mark during this period was the fact that Theodora gained prominence with her intelligence and became a queen, the ruler of the regency, despite being the daughter of a bear tamer.

Defending the eastern borders against the Sassanids, and the Danube borders against the Slavs and Bulgarians, the emperor had to introduce new taxes to this end. All of this led to the formation of the two hostile fronts between the Monophysitist Greens and the pro-government and religious Blues. These conflicts transformed into anarchy and resulted in an uprising-the Nika Revolt, in 532. The rebels controlled the city for a week, devastating every place including the religious buildings such as Hagia Sophia and Hagia Irene. Now everything seemed to have ended for the Orthodox Blues and Justinianos. Even though the Emperor considered running away, Theodora prevented this attempt and a counterattack was launched. Around this time, Commander Belisarios, who was returning from the Iranian border, assisted by deploying his troops over the rebels who had gathered in the Hippodrome, killing 30,000 rebels and suppressing the riot. After the empire regained its strength, Justinianos carried out a reform in the state and made a breakthrough by compiling all of the laws introduced since Hadrianus in 10 volumes. This regulation which is also known as "Justinianos's Laws" abolished the duties vested in the aristocrats, establishing bureaucracy. Those who retained their pagan beliefs were killed and pagan schools were closed.

The emperor was reconstructing the burnt city and Hagia Sophia on one hand, while working on reuniting the empire on the other hand, which was his greatest dream. Therefore, taking advantage of the chaos in the Ostrogothic Kingdom in Italy, he conquered Sicily in 535. Afterwards, Rome as well

Previous page:
View of Hagia Sophia at night.

Constantine is presenting a model of the city to Mary.
The inscription behind the Emperor says, "Constantine, a great saint and sovereign".
The Emperor is wearing ceremonial attire.

as Ravenna, which was the capital city of the Ostrogoths, were both taken in 540. Barely one year passed following this victory, when a plague epidemic from the Mediterranean decimated the great families, artisans, and clergymen in the capital, affecting even the emperor. Then, before the sorrows of this disaster could finally subside, the Ostrogoths rose in riot, and the Sassanids waged war against Byzantion. Having always supported Emperor Justinianos during these hard days, Empress Theodora died in 550. At the end of the wars, Byzantion had become prevalent in all of the Mediterranean. However, the never-ending wars consumed not only the state's treasury but also the strength of Byzantion.

By 559, the dome of Hagia Sophia was demolished, followed by another plague epidemic. With disasters coming one after the other, there was yet another wave of catastrophe approaching the capital. Scarcely was the plague epidemic gone when the Western Huns came as close as to the neighborhood of Byzantion. The emperor, who had turned 77 then, left the capital to find a way out of the situation and made peace with the Huns in return for money, after which he returned to the city with triumphal processions.

The period of Justinianos was a period when Byzantine culture completed its formation. Cherished with political accomplishments, this culture was now gaining its true identity. Antique Greek culture, Roman culture and Eastern culture were melted in the pot of Christianity, forming a new art. Hagia Sophia became the best example of this culture. This building, a Roman basilica, had a dome which was constructed with inspiration from the East and the church was formed with the combination of the East and West. Furthermore, the mosaics, and icons specific to the Byzantine culture, emerged as a result of this cultural combination.

The level of civilization reached during the period of Justinianos reversed the relations that had existed between Rome and Byzantion before. Now it was not Rome that was the center of art and culture but Constantinopolis. Mosaic decorations of the Byzantine-era buildings in Rome and Ravenna clearly prove this. After Justinianos, the periods of Justinos II, Tiberius and Mauricius were spent combating against the Lombards, Franks and Slavs from the West and the Sassanids from the East. These conflicts lasted until 591, after which Phocas assumed the throne. During his reign, religious and political conflicts began in the capital, with state trying to strike a balance by supporting the Blues at times, and the Greens at other times.

By the 7th Century, the religion of Islam was born in Arabia. This religion surpassed the borders of the Arabian Peninsula and resulted in the Islamic armies forcing the gates of Byzantion. Even though the Byzantine walls managed to stop each of these attacks, some characteristics of this new religion were to surmount the walls and influence Byzantion. When Leon III ascended to the throne (717-741), chaos was prevalent in the country. Monasteries were increasing and becoming richer with each passing day, establishing great authority over the people. Having first stopped the Arab raids, the Emperor was then inspired by the ban of pictures in Islam and prohibited the worship of the icons, and representations of Jesus, Mary and saints on the walls. This was the period of Iconoclasm, which was

Icon of St. Eudoxia.
The icon is inlaid with precious, colored stones, and dates from the Byzantine period.
Istanbul Archaeological Museum.

Justinian in ceremonial attire handing a model of Hagia Sophia to Mary.
Next to Justinian is the inscription, "The exalted sovereign Justinian."

Gold Medallion.
On both sides of the medallion scenes from
the life of Jesus are depicted in three bands.
On the observe , we see the Annunciation
and the Adoration in the upper band, the
Birth of Christ and the Flight to Egypt
in the middle, and the Adoration of
the Magi in the lower. On the reverse
the Miracles of Jesus take place. This
side is surrounded by busts of
saints placed within the curves of
branches. Around the outer edge of
the medallion there is a bead band.
Material: Gold Provenance: Adana
Period: 6th Century AD.
Diameter: 8.2 cm Weight: 22.83 gr.

Silver Tray.
In relief and partly gilded, the
tray depicts Christ and his
Apostles. On the right and left
of a table, under the lamp
suspended from the center of a
ciborium, six apostles, with
haloes around their heads, have
been worked. On either side of
the table, there are two Christs
back to back, facing the apostles.
On the back of the tray, there is the
stamp of the workshop. Around the
edge of the tray there are inscriptions
partly worn off. Material: Silver
Provenance: Aleppo (Stuma), Syria
Period: 6th Century AD.
Diameter: 36.5 cm Weight: 836.60 gr.

to last for about a hundred years, and the Christian elders were represented with cross only. This decision, which was remarkable for the religious culture, was applied for a certain while and ended in the 9th Century. In this Century, Basileious, who was a Macedonian stableman living in Constantinopolis, had the emperor suffocated and declared himself as the emperor in 867. Thus the period of Macedonian Emperors started between 867-1081. In this period, new laws which suited the conditions were introduced and implemented. They were published under the name 'Basilica'. Also, merchants and artisans in the territories of the whole empire became organized in the form guilds. The noble class was given the possibility to buy the land of the peasants, initiating the process of feudalism. This resulted in new emerging problems, the sporadic discontent would eventually turn into an uprising, forcing many emperors to fight against it. Furthermore, while Byzantion was dealing with them on one hand, it also had to deal with the Seljuks in the east, Normans in the west, and the Pechenek, Uz and Kuman communities in the north. During the last years of the Macedonian dynasty, Emperor Zoe seemingly marked Byzantine history. When Constantinos VIII died in 1028, he did not have a son to take over his position. Therefor e one of his three daughters was to ascend to the throne. His daughter Eudocia chose to become a nun. Zoe drove her other sister Theodora out of the competition and became the empress. She declared Romanos III Argyros the emperor, whom she had chosen as her husband. However, having grown tired of this marriage after a while, she had her husband suffocated. She had an affair with the son of a Paphlagonian farmer. After her husband died, she married her lover and ascended him to the throne as Michael IV. When he too died after six years, she shared the throne with her nephew, whom she had adopted-Michael V. However, before long, Michael was to dislodge Zoe from the throne and enclosed her into a monastery in Büyükada (Prinkipo Island). Having stayed in this monastery for a while, Zoe managed to escape and overthrew Michael V, punishing him for his actions by having him blinded. After sharing the throne with her sister Theodora for about a year, she married Constantinos IX Monomachos at the age of 64. When Emperor Monomachos died in 1055, Theodora ascended to the throne for the second time. Her reign lasted a year and afterwards, the regency of the Macedonian dynasty came to an end.

The emperors changing one after another in Byzantion were not able to prevent the loss of territory. When the Normandians subjugated the last Byzantine territories in Italy in 1071, the threat of the Seljuks emerged in the east. This is because the Great Seljuk State had adopted Islam and declared themselves the guardians of the Islamic Caliphate. Subjugation of Anatolia was required for the protection of the Caliph. To this end, the Seljuks subjugated Iran first and began to force the borders of Byzantion.

Alparslan, the young and venturesome sultan of the Seljuks took action with a large-scale army to subjugate Antolia. The Byzantine Emperor Romanos Diogenes moved to the east with an even larger-scale army to stop him. The two armies confronted each other in Malazgirt, near Lake Van. The Seljuk Sultan Alparslan shattered the Byzantine armies in this war and took the emperor hostage. Even though he had released the emperor after a while, the new emperor who occupied the Byzantine throne had his eyes blinded and enclosed him in a monastery in one of the Princes' Islands in Istanbul, where he died.

Now the gates of Anatolia were opened to Turks and they were establishing principalities (beyliks) in places which they had conquered. Turks founded the Anatolian Seljuk State, with the capital Konya, following the period of these principalities. The Kayı tribe which was led by Ertuğrul Bey was settled in Söğüt at the border with Byzantion. Thus Byzantion was stranded in a poky area, with only the capital and the neighboring territory left to it. The battles for the throne in Byzantion were continuing around this time. The Comnenos dynasty then took the leadership. The Byzantine Empire was to preserve its eminence and potency for one more century. Alexios I Comnenos (1081-1118) halted the Normandians and Pecheneks in the Balkans on one hand, and halted the progress of the Seljuks in Anatolia on the other hand. However, it neither had the power nor money in the treasury to drive them out of Anatolia. In the meantime, the Seljuks proceeded all the way down to the Arabian Peninsula and subjugated Jerusalem.

Latin Invasion of Byzantion

Alexios Comnenos planned to drive back the Seljuks by making an agreement with the Pope. Thus troops were gathered in 1096 and set out as the First Crusade, halting the Seljuks. They were to set out again in the same year after preparing a second army of Crusaders. This army reached as far as Antakya (Antioch) and Jerusalem taking command of these places. Around this time, Alexios Comnenos died, his son Joannes II Comnenos (1118-1143) took the leadership and this emperor married the daughter of the Hungarian King Ladislaus, named Eirene.

During the reign of the Macedonian dynasty in Byzantion, problems began to arise between the commanders of the Crusader army and the emperors. Pressure from the Crusaders over the local people had caused major discontent. Additionally, Jerusalem was taken by Selahattin Eyyubi in 1187, resulting in the launching of the Third Crusade. The Fourth Crusade was organized in 1203, while Alexios, demanded by the Crusaders was dethroned and killed in Byzantion. He was replaced by a latent emperor, Alexios V. Taking advantage of this, the Crusaders switched their route to Istanbul and arrived in the city in the spring of 1204. Alexios V had to escape. Latins were plundering the city, taking away whatever was of use. They even plundered the doors and windows, namely the 1000-year-old riches of Byzantion. Bronze tablets on the Stone Obelisk (Örme Sütun) in the Hippoddrome were being dismantled to be melted down and minted into coins. A group of sculptures in the Hippodrome, which was made up of four horses, was uprooted and moved to the St. Mark's Square in Venice. Constantinopolis was plundered from end to end. The Latins elected Count Baudouin of Flandres as the first Latin emperor. The new emperor allocated one fourth of the territories belonging to the state for himself, distributing the rest between the Venetians and the Crusader knights. Thus a Latin Empire was established in Constantinopolis.

Afterwards, the grandchildren of Andronicos I, one of the former emperors, founded a state known as the Greek Pontus State, while Theodoros Lascaris, who had escaped the city during the Latin invasion, established an exile administration in Nicaea. Thus, Constantinopolis turned into a colony of Venice in time. Having continued for about half a century, the Latin invasion ceased only in 1261. The emperor in Nicaea, Michael VIII Palaeologos, made an agreement with the Genovesians and conquered the city by attacking unexpectedly when the Latin soldiers were out of the city for a campaign. Thus the Latin invasion was ended. In Byzantion, Between 1261-1282, the dynasty of Palaelogos' established by Michael VIII Palaeologos came to power. This dynasty was to rule until the end of Byzantion. When the second emperor of the dynasty, Andronicos Palaeologos assumed the throne in 1282, the state was going through a depression, having become a toy for the Genovesians and the Venetians. The Genovesians secured themselves by surrounding Galata by walls. Galata Tower was situated as the major tower of those walls at the time. In the meantime, the Catalan leader Roger de Flor came to Constantinopolis to liberate the lands in Anatolia taken by Turks. Having lost the war he waged, he then took it out on the Byzantines and plundered the city in 1303.

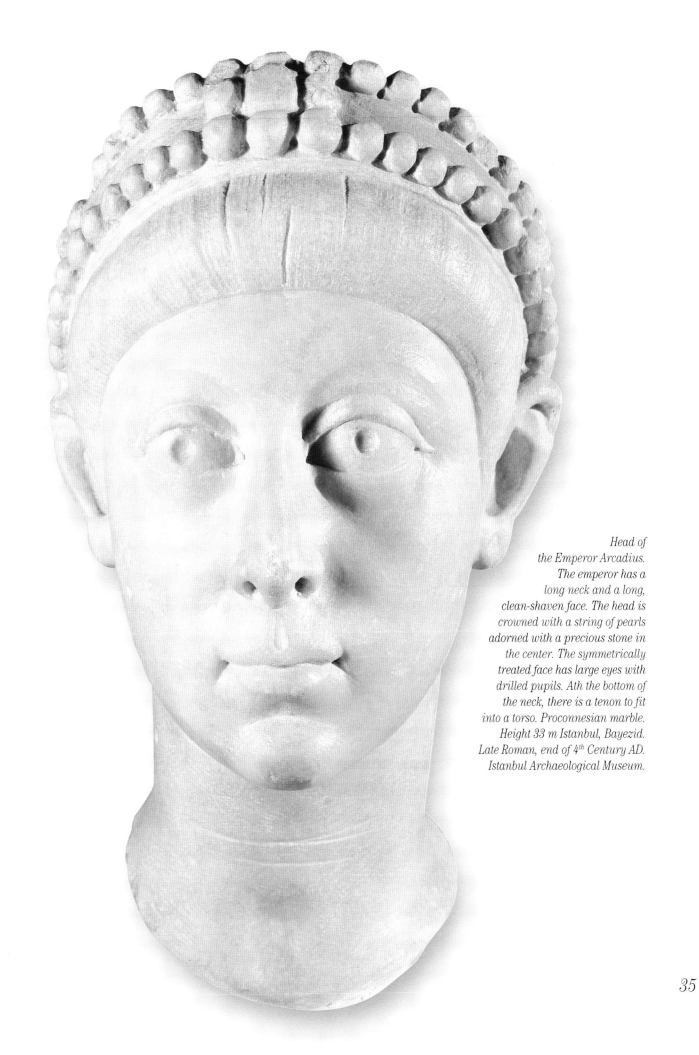

Head of the Emperor Arcadius. The emperor has a long neck and a long, clean-shaven face. The head is crowned with a string of pearls adorned with a precious stone in the center. The symmetrically treated face has large eyes with drilled pupils. Ath the bottom of the neck, there is a tenon to fit into a torso. Proconnesian marble. Height 33 m Istanbul, Bayezid. Late Roman, end of 4th Century AD. Istanbul Archaeological Museum.

Around this time, the Ottoman Principality (Osmanlı Beyliği) founded in Söğüt and led by Osman Bey, declared its independence in 1299, laying the first groundwork of a great empire. In 1308, the Anatolian Seljuk State fell and the Ottomans-now independent-began to conquer new territories and new castles in Byzantion. During the reign of Orhan Bey, an army was assembled with an increasing number chevaliers from 400 to 20,000. These dynamic forces began to defeat the Byzantine troops on every occasion. Additionally, Byzantine emperors who encountered trouble would resort to Orhan Bey for help. Emperor Andronicos III Palaeologos arranged his daughter Asporca to marry Orhan Bey, thus gaining his support. At this time, Constantinopolis was no different than ruins and its people were poor. The words of the Byzantine historian Nicephoros Gregoras from 1347, depicting the coronation ceremony of Joannes VI Cantacuzenos (1347-1354) perfectly reveals the state of poverty in Byzantion, "..... everybody knew that the jewelries on the crowns were made from glass, the clothes were not woven with real gold but with gilded yarns, pottery was from copper and everything which appeared as splendid "canfes" fabric (a fine type of taffeta) was nothing but painted leather." Emperor Joannes VI Cantacuzenos, who took the throne in this very state of poverty, wanted to secure his throne by having his daughter marry Orhan Bey, so that he could take a breath.

While the Ottomans were gaining strength, Byzantion, in contrast, was becoming weaker. The beginning of the end of Byzantion was now visible. By the 1440's, Byzantine soil in Europe and Anatolia were taken by the Ottomans, and Byzantion was stranded within the city walls. The Ottomans were also taking command of other states in Europe. Thus Byzantion stood as a snag in the middle of the vast territories of the Ottomans. Murad, who ascended to the throne after Orhan Bey, and his son Bayezid the Thunderbolt (Yıldırım Bayezid), both contemplated that it was time for Byzantion to be eliminated; therefore, a fortress was being built on the Anatolian side of the strait. However, the threat of Timur in the east enabled Byzantion to stay alive for some more time. While the defeat of Bayezid the Thunderbolt by Timur caused this desire to be postponed for a while, Çelebi Mehmed gathered the state together, and taking Byzantion was on the agenda again. Murad II, who replaced him, besieged Byzantion in June 1422 and when the siege prolonged, he lifted the siege and went on a campaign to Greece. Around this time, the Byzantine throne was occupied by Joannes VIII Palaeologos. In 1425, the emperor resorted to the Pope for another Crusade to be organized. The Crusader army organized in accordance with the wish of the Pope was made up of twenty five thousand people. When it crossed the Danube in 1444, it was defeated by the confronting Turkish army and dispersed. In the same year, Mehmed II, who was to be known as Mehmed the Conqueror later, replaced Murad II and he was determined to accomplish what his father left unfinished-to conquer Byzantion. Byzantion, which managed to survive with myriad of stratagems and tricks, would no longer stand as a problem in the vast Ottoman territories. The young Ottoman sultan took the conquering decision and initiated the preparations to this end. In 1449, sitting on the Byzantine throne was Constantinos XI Palaeologos as the last emperor. The destiny for the two emperors was to begin now.

Jesus healing the sick.
The arch panel on the western wall of the inner narthex of the Chora Museum features a scene of Jesus's miracles where he heals the sick. Jesus goes to a village together with his apostles and heals the sick in the village. There are three men sitting at the front, and seen at the back are a man holding a stick, women bringing their ailing children to Jesus and the rest of the village people.

City Walls of Istanbul

For many centuries, Istanbul was a city which aroused the admiration and envy of many states with its excellent position and dazzling riches. Keeping the possession of and protecting this city, which attracted attention like a precious jewel throughout its history, was possible through the walls of the city which are almost as famous as the city itself. With various repairs and additions throughout the history of Istanbul, these massive walls, which stopped the Arab and Bulgarian raids, protected the city for centuries. The city walls, having once surrounded Byzantion which was established on a small area when they were first erected, went through changes in time in parallel with the rapid development of the city; both by being demolished and rebuilt as well as with repairs and additions. When Roman Emperor Septimus Severius conquered the city, the walls surrounding it were extremely damaged; therefore, the emperor had the city surrounded with stronger walls covering a wider area. In the future, Constantinos engaged in comprehensive development activities; he had the old walls demolished and had new walls built which covered a larger area and better suited the expanded city.

Having become the capital of Eastern Rome with the separation of Rome into two, Constantinopolis continued to grow and the walls were no longer sufficient for the city. The city walls, which were built for the fourth time during the reign of Emperor Theodisios II, were damaged with the earthquake in 447. During the repair of the city walls, the threat of the Huns appeared, which required that various supplementary constructions be made outside the walls, in addition to the repairs and fortifications. A 2.5 m thick second wall with 96 towers, and a 20 m wide and 10 m deep dike, which was dug before this wall, secured the city with a three-partite defense line. These precautions took effect and Atilla redirected his armies from Istanbul to Rome. These massive walls defending Constantinopolis were made up of three sections, which were the Land Walls, Golden Horn Walls and Marmara Sea Walls. Each of them was remarkable with their own distinct features and functions. Let us explore the world-famous city walls of Constantinopolis starting with the land walls.

Land Walls: The Land Walls, which begin at the Marble Tower (Mermer Kule) near the Seven Towers Fortress (Yedikule Hisarı), measure 5632 m long and go all the way to the north and end at the Tekfur Palace. At these walls, which are products of military genius on their own, a hard-to-surmount system was created. Indeed, the walls guarded Byzantion against swords and rifles but they could not withstand the cannons brought by Mehmed the Conqueror in 1453, and the gaps opened by cannon balls prepared the end of Byzantion. The land walls had ten big gates in addition to its numerous service gates. Each of the big gates had two different ends opening into the interior and exterior walls. Strong towers were built at both sides of the main gates and thus the gates were supported by these towers. The first gate of the walls, the Golden Gate, is located 900 m from the Marble Tower. Having been

commissioned in 390 by the Roman Emperor Theodosios I, this gate was named 'Porta Aure' due to its golden plates. Later in 413, when Theodosios II was having the walls built, this gate was combined with the walls. Having once been built as a triumphal arch, the gate became a part of the city walls. The three-bay gate which measures totally 60 m has a tower at both sides, each measuring 17x18 m Formerly on the gate were the sculptures of Theodosios, Nike and a carriage pulled by an elephant. These sculptures fell from their places during the earthquakes in 740 and 866.

When Joannes V Palaiologos was having the gate repaired in 1389, he had it decorated with mythological embossments of Hercules's actions, Venus and Adonis, and the fall of Phaethon. These embossments were apparently still present after Mehmed the Conqueror took Istanbul. Indeed, the British envoy Sir Th. Roe is known to have wanted to take possession of them in 1620 without success, until when the 12-piece embossment was in situ. Afterwards, these embossments were somehow lost. Fatih Sultan Mehmed turned this place into an internal castle where the state treasury was kept, after adding new towers besides the towers here and surrounding it with walls. Later, when the state treasury was moved into the Topkapı Palace, the Seven Towers came to be used as a dungeon. After the Seven Towers, the Belgrade Gate is arrived at within the repaired walls. Having conquered Belgrade, Süleyman the Magnificent had the people he brought as company settle here; therefore, this gate was named as the Belgrade Gate. Just a little way within the rampart are the remnants of the Church of Panagia Belgradiu, which was built for the people who settled here.

Beyond that, the gate which was called 'Pege' during the Byzantines, in reference to the source of the Fountain of Zoodohos Pigi (Balıklı Ayazması), and as the Silivri Gate during the Ottomans. Located 100 meters inwards from the Silivri Gate is the İbrahim Pasha Mosque-one of the modest mosques of the Architect Sinan, and the Bâlâ Complex (Bâlâ Külliyesi) near it. The next gate was known as the Mevlevi Gate due to the Mevlevi convent located here. On this gate known as Region during the Byzantines is the epigraph of Constantinos, who built the walls. There is also the repair epigraph of Justinianos and his wife Sophia, and Narses, a Byzantine general. The gate known as Topkapı (Cannon Gate) today was the gate which Mehmed the Conqueror had beaten with his cannons and used to be known as the St. Komanos Gate. It survived to the present time in ruins but was re-erected with repairs and was given an impressive look again. The gate marking the beginning of the road going to Edirne was known as the Edirne Gate and is one of the gates through which Mehmed the Conqueror entered the city, and the epitaph on it relates to this. Rising right beside the gate is the Mihrimah Mosque, which was commissioned by the daughter of Süleyman the Magnificent, Sultan Mihrimah.

The City Walls extending northwards as seen from Yedikule, the beginning of the land walls.
The city walls of Istanbul, which are still erect, have three sections as land, sea and Golden Horn walls.

The surviving section of the Sea Walls by the coast of Samatya. The sea walls, which start at Sarayburnu and extend as far as the Marble Tower where the land walls begin, were built during the period of Emperor Theodosios. Emperor Theoplilos (829-842) had the demolished walls rebuilt.

Near the mosque is the Chora Monastery famous for its Greek-Orthodox Church. When proceeding north from here, the Tekfur Palace can be reached, which constitutes a part of the Blachernae Palace adjacent to the walls. This place is intriguing in that it was home to the last Byzantine emperors. The Theodosios walls end where the Tekfur Palace is located. Since the walls after this were weak, Emperor Manuel Comnenos had the walls rebuilt and supported them with several towers. In the middle of the walls is the Crooked Gate (Eğrikapı), the former name of which was Kaligari, and to the south of this is the Forty Fountains Cistern (Kırkçeşme Maksemi), where the water coming from the Belgrade Forests would accumulate. The walls commissioned by Comnenos ends with the Isaacios II Angelos Tower 400 m from the Crooked

Gate. Emperor Isaacios II Angelos had this tower built during his reign between 1185-1195, and when he was dethroned, he was blinded and sent to the Anemas Dungeon located in the neighborhood. Anemas, who the tower was named after, was an Arab-originated commander employed in the Byzantine army. The three-storey tower was later used as a dungeon. There are cells behind small gates inside the tower. Only the upper stories of the tower are visible today. The extraordinary panorama of the Golden Horn from here is worth seeing. Located right beside the Anemas Dungeon is the Ivaz Efendi Mosque with its graceful look, which was built by the Architect Sinan. When the Golden Horn is overlooked from here, the walls built by the Emperors Leon and Heraclios are seen.

These were built in the form of double rampart. On the inner walls, which were commissioned in 627 by the Emperor Heraclios against the Avar attacks, are three hexagonal towers. The walls on the exterior were commissioned in 813 to stop the attacks of King Krum of Bulgaria by the Emperor Leon V. The Land Walls take a turn here and merge with the walls of the Golden Horn. The construction of the St. Thekla Church within the walls was initiated by the Empress Pulcheria, and completed by the Emperor Leon I. The church became an important church after Hagia Sophia, since Mother Mary's shawl was kept here. This church, which was frequently visited by Byzantine emperors, was burnt in 1434 and was not rebuilt. Today there is the Tomb of Toklu Dede (Toklu Dede Türbesi) over it.

The Marmara Walls: These walls start at Sarayburnu and extend along the Marmara Sea for 8260 m and end at the Marble Tower near the Seven Towers Fortress. As mentioned before, the sea walls were built during the reign of Theodosios. However, large waves created by the south wind wore these walls out and partially demolished them. Over the groundwork of the demolished walls, the walls which can be seen today were commissioned to be built by the Emperor Theoplilos (829-842). The section at Sarayburnu, which was the beginning of the sea walls, were destroyed both because of the palace constructions as well as the construction activities of the railroads in 1871; therefore, it does not exist to this date. Formerly here was the gate of Hagia Barbara (Top). If the newly opened coastal road is followed, ahead from the sculpture of Piri

Shown here is the "Belgrade Gate" and section of its walls.
The city walls of Istanbul and several of the towers are still standing thanks to recent restoration.

41

Reis, an ancient Byzantine church named Hristos Filantropus is known to exist within the walls. Seen slightly ahead of this is an arch with its columns protruding from the walls, and these are the remnants of the İncili Kiosk, which was one of the exterior kiosks of the Topkapı Palace.

At this section was the Mangana Palace, which was once commissioned to be built by the Emperor Basileios I. There is the Stable Gate (Ahırkapı) about 500 m ahead from here. The reason why this gate is known with this name is that the palace stables were located here during the Byzantines and Ottomans. There is the Ahırkapı Lighthouse here, which was built during the reign of Osman III after a naval accident. As you watch the walls as the Kalyon Hotel and the restaurants are left behind, the three ornamented doors of a balcony on the walls can be seen and are remarkable. This is the balcony section of the Byzantine Bucoleon Palace. This palace was commissioned by Theodosios, and was also used by Constantinos VII Porphyrogennetos after being expanded. Later on, Nicephoros II Phocas (963-969) had a villa attached to the palace and resided here. Having been slandered and ruined during the Latin invasion, the palace then lost its esteem and was replaced by the Blachernai Palace in Ayvansaray.

Slightly further ahead, the port of Bucoleon Palace is reached, which was commissioned by Theodosios II. This port, which is in the form of a small indentation today, was decorated with marble quays and sculptures since it was the special port of the palace. The lion sculptures which used to be here are now at the Archaeological Museum. A gate was leading to this port, and is known as the Cracked Gate (Çatladı Kapı) today because it cracked during an earthquake during the Ottomans. There is the Little Hagia Sophia Church somewhere close to this section of the walls. This church will not be discussed here but later, together with the other churches. Slightly further ahead from here is Kadırga. Apparently this used to be a port too, and that is what it is named after. This port, which was used for military purposes, had a dockyard as well. The gate opening to the port was known as the Kadırga Port Gate or the Sophia Gate, referring to the name of the wife of Justinos II, who renovated the port. A little further ahead is the Sand Gate (Kumkapı) where there is a port which used to be known as Contoscalion. After Kumkapı, which is famous for its touristic restaurants, the New Gate (Yenikapı) can be seen. There are two churches here, which are not very old. As you proceed ahead, Samatya is reached. This is where the walls reappear. The railway bridge is helpful in that it signifies the location of the gate here. After this is the Gate of Roses (Narlı Kapı). Somewhere near this gate is the Studios Monastery and Hagios Joannes Basilica (İmrahor Mosque) from the Byzantine Period. Emperors would visit this church once a year to commemorate John the Baptist. The Marble Tower, which is seen slightly ahead, marks the end of the Marmara Walls.

The Golden Horn Walls When having the Marmara and land walls repaired and rebuilt, the Governor Constantinos had the Golden Horn Walls built as well, and merged these walls with the sea walls and ensured that the whole city was surrounded with them. Since there never was any threat anticipated from the Golden Horn, it was simply protected with a single wall. Moreover,

The Edirne Gate (Edirnekapı). This is where the most robust battles were fought during the conquest of Istanbul. Ottoman forces entered the city from here on May 25 1453.

The Belgrade Gate (Belgradkapı). On the land ramparts, which start at Yedikule, are important gates such as the Belgrade Gate, Silivri Gate, Mevlana Gate, Cannon Gate (Topkapı), Sulukule Gate, Edirne Gate and Crooked Gate (Eğrikapı).

the chain spread out across the Golden Horn made it highly secure. However, this chain had not worked for the Latins and they attempted to take command of the city twice through the waters at the Golden Horn, finally entering the city surmounting these walls. Even though some of the Golden Horn Walls, which had thus been severely damaged, were repaired by the Latins, the real repair took place in 1261 when the city was re-conquered. The walls, which extend for 5 km along the Golden Horn and measure 10 m in height, used to have 110 towers and 14 gates. From these walls, only a small section of which can be seen today, the section in the Eminönü-Sarayburnu direction has totally disappeared.

The Golden Horn Walls start at Ayvansaray. Here used to be the Ayvansaray Gate of the Blachernai Palace, where the emperors would come by sea, and take this gate reaching their palace on a horse. The Atik Mustafa Paşa Mosque located somewhere near the ramparts in Ayvansaray was transformed into a mosque from a church, the name of which is unknown. The church, which was constructed over the sacred fountaion (ayazma) of Blachernai in the Kuyu Street across the mosque, was one of the important churches of Byzantion and it burnt in 1430. The church which can be seen today is the Church of Mother Mary built in the 1900's. What comes after Ayvansaray is Balat. Bayezid II had the jews in Spain suffering from hardships brought here and allowed them to settle in Balat. Located here is the Balat Gate of the ramparts, which is also known as Joannes Prodromos Gate. This gate was named in reference to the Hagios Joannes Prodromos Monastery on the adjacent hill. Balat, which is a Jewish settlement as mentioned above, is home to many synagogues. Also located here are churches belonging to Greeks and Armenians as well as the Ferruh Kethüda Mosque built by the Architect Sinan, offering an intriguing setting. In the neighborhood of Fener, which comes after Balat, there is another gate known as the Porta Fenari (Lighthouse Gate), the reason is that there is a lighthouse nearby. The neighborhood of Fener is famous for the Greek Orthodox Patriarchate. Having changed location many times, the Patriarch has been here since 1601. Fener is predominantly resided in by Greeks. Therefore, the Greek High school, built from red bricks, is also here. Very close to the school is Hagia Maria Church from the Byzantine Period. This church, which is still in use, was built in the 13th Century in the name of Maria Muhliotissa-in other words Mary of the Mongolians.

Since more information will be given on this in the section for churches, let us continue our journey along the ramparts. Slightly further ahead, the gate known as Hagia Teodosia Gate is reached. This gate was named after the Hagia Teodosia Church, which is somewhat inside. This church was transformed into a mosque known as the Gül Mosque after the conquest. Opposite the church is the school which was sponsored by Adile Sultan, sister of Mahmud II, and across the apse wall of the church is the bath commissioned by Küçük Mustafa Pasha, a vizier (minister) of Bayezid II. This bath is one of the oldest in Istanbul. Afterwards, the neighborhood of Cibali is reached. The only surviving structure from the Golden Horn ramparts here is the Cibali Gate, which used to be known as 'Porta Pateas'. Moving onwards, the Golden Horn ramparts lead to the Yalı Kiosk in Sarayburnu. However, no trace is left from the ramparts in this section today.

A view from the Crooked Gate (Eğrikapı), which is the starting point of the Golden Horn Walls.

View of Anemas Dungeons. General Anemas, who commissioned these dungeons, was also immured in them. Many dethroned Byzantine emperors were too enclosed in these dungeons and suffocated.

Byzantine Palaces

The word palace in Byzantion was derived from the Latin word palation which comes from the Palatino Hill in Rome, where the palaces of Roman emperors would be located. After the center of the empire was moved to Byzantion, palaces resided in by the emperors were built in addition to the other buildings decorating the city and were known for their splendor and richness. From all of these palaces, we know about the Tekfur Palace based on its concrete form today, whereas our knowledge about the rest are derived from archaeological data and written sources.

The most important palace in Byzantion, which was initiated by Constantinos I and retained its importance until the 12th Century, is the 'Great Palace'. Established on a land between the Hippodrome and Hagia Sophia stretching all the way down to the sea, the palace came to span a large area with various palace units built by emperors over many years. The first addition to this palace was made for the two wives of Theodosios I. Theodosios II, who held the Byzantine throne from 400 to 450, expanded the palace towards the ramparts he commissioned to be built by the sea.

Having been enlarged with additions until the reign of Justinanos I, the palace was burnt during the Nika Revolt which broke out in 532, along with other buildings. After suppressing the revolt, the emperor had the Great Palace repaired, expanded and had its interior decorated with mosaics, while having such edifices as Hagia Sophia rebuilt. Located near the Sultanahmet Mosque's arasta, which is a row of shops of the same trade, the Museum of the Great Palace Mosaics is where these mosaics are exhibited, showcasing the prosperity of the palace.

The mosaics were skillfully crafted, depicting scenes from everyday life and nature. Their compositions include a cameleer, two hunters shooting a tiger with spear, pastoral life, peasants at work, children playing games, domestic and wild animals as well as mythological animals. The borders painted around the scenes add extra beauty to the composition. In his book 'Buildings', Prokopios mention the 6th Century city and the mosaics.

The entrance to the palace was from the direction of Hagia Sophia and would open into the Augusteion Square, which was located here. Since the entrance with rectangular walls was covered with bronze on top, it used to be called the 'Bronze House'. The ceiling of this spectacular entrance was also decorated with mosaics. Depicted on the mosaics were the

A detail of two hunters on a tiger hunt.
Great Palace (Büyük Saray) Museum of Mosaics.

victories won by Justinianos and his commander Belisarios in Italy and Africa, and the commander Belisarios was illustrated as presenting the spoils gained in war to the emperor. Another composition has the captivated Vandal and Goth kings saluting the Emperor Justinianos and Empress Theodora. Emperor Justinianos decorated the entry section of the palace known as Khalke, which was in the form of a two-storey tower, with sculptures as well.

This eminently ornamented entry section was already destroyed in the 8th Century, during the iconoclastic period. Located right behind this entrance were the guards' rooms. From here, Daphne Palace-the special section for the emperors-would be passed into. There were many chambers and halls in this section such as the throne chamber, feast hall and meeting halls. Direct passage was ensured from this special imperial section to the balcony of the emperor in the hippodrome, known as Katisma. After Justinianos renovated the palace, the emperors Justinos II, Justinianos II, Theoplilos, Basileios I, Constantinos VII and Porphyrogennetos VII repaired the palace and expanded it with numerous additions.

While Basileios I (867-886) was expanding the Great Palace, he had the Mangana Palace built at today's Stable Gate (Ahırkapı). This palace was made up of a large hall with an apse at its western end and side galleries. Furthermore, Basileos I also had a church added to the palace. The palace, which had early basilica plan and resembled a church including a hall decorated with holy imagery, was repaired by Heracleios, and was converted into a school for Byzantine secondary education during the reign of Michael III. The palace was used as an imperial court at the same time.

For example, in the 14th Century, the Patriarch Euthymios was tried here. Emperors would address the people from here, sitting on their throne within the apse, with lions at both sides. Before Manuel I Comnenos abdicated the great palace, he had a very colorful pavilion built from bricks, adorned with golden-gilded muqarnases. On the seaside, the Bucoleon Palace was commissioned by Theodosios II, as a section of the Great Palace. After the Emperor Constantions VII. Porphyrogennetos had this palace and the neighboring port expanded, it became a significant palace and made a name for itself. Nicephoros II Phocas resided in this palace, after having a villa attached to it.

Three ornate gates, which are seen on the ramparts today open into the balcony and are the only remnants from the Bucoleon Palace existing to the present time. Formerly at the entrance of the port, which was near the palace, was an antique sculpture representing a lion mangling a bull. There was a passage from this port to the palace, via a gate known as 'Porta Leonis', in front of which were two lion sculptures. This gate cracked during an earthquake in the Ottoman Period and thus has come to be referred to as the Cracked Gate (Çatladı Kapı).

The north western section of the Bucoleon Palace, which was located on the ramparts, formed the border of the Great Palace in this direction. The interior of the palace was decorated with golden-gilded mosaics. The palace, which was already devastated during the Latin invasion and was thus unable to be used, continued to be in ruins during the Ottoman Period. Therefore, a new settlement was established over it. In 1554, Mahmud Ağa, who was Kızlar Ağası (Master of

Border detail with the head of Oceanus.
Museum of Great Palace Mosaics

the Girls in the Harem), commissioned the Ağa Mosque over a cistern consisting of three sections. During the period of Osman III, the Stable Gate (Ahırkapı) Lighthouse was built by the sea. To the west of the Bucoleon Palace was the Hormisdas Palace. The Emperor Justinianos had spent his youth in this palace and later had the palace repaired and attached to the Great Palace. The Great Palace, which was plundered and damaged during the Latin Invasion, had become untenantable and the Byzantine emperors chose to reside in the Blachernai Palace located in the old Blachernai region to the west of the city, which is known today as Ayvansaray.

The palace complex, the first establishment of which dates to as far as the 5th Century, went through its actual development during the period of the Comnenoses. The first construction commissioned by Leon I (457-474) became the core of the Blachernai Palace, and soon afterwards, Anastasios I (491-518) had new additions built. In the following centuries, three pavilions were constructed over different terraces, among which the pavilion known as Okeanos became famous due to its embellishments. This set of buildings, which were made up of a large hall and various chambers, remained in use until the period of Comnenoses.

The palace, extending as far as the towers of Isaacios Angelos and Anemas, retains its excellent view even today. It has a gate on the Golden Horn shore, through which emperors could pass after arriving via the sea and reach their palaces uphill on horseback. The interior of the palace was adorned with mosaics and attained fame with its beauty in the Middle Ages, arousing admiration in its visitors. Many travelers also saw this palace and fell in love with it. One of them was the Rabbi Benjamin of Tudela. When Benjamin visited the city in 1161, he was received by the Emperor Manuel Comnenos at this palace and remarked on the splendor of the palace he saw as follows: "All the columns and walls were plated with gold. Battles of the emperor and his predecessors were pictured. The imperial throne in this palace was made from gold and adorned with precious stones. The imperial crown was ornamented with precious stones as well. These diamonds were so shiny that they spread enough light to illuminate the room without any other source of light."

Alexios I Comnenos received the nobles joining the first crusade here in 1095 and the European princes admired this richness. They took possession of this richness that they admired in 1204, when they invaded the city, during which all of the palaces burnt consecutively for two days and nights. The city became unrecognizable. When Michael VIII Palaiologos put an end to the Latin invasion; he came across palaces which were damaged in this way, without the riches that were once there. He had the Blachernai Palace repaired, in which emperors succeeding him began to reside. Meantime, the palace was decorated from 1281-1282 with mosaics depicting the emperor's Berat victory. During the last period of the Palaiologos dynasty, emperors were coronated here, consecration ceremonies were held here, and foreign ambassadors were received here.

In 1437, during his visit to the city, Spanish Pero Tafur revealed the pathetic condition of the palace by saying, "Emperor's palace must have been glorious in the past, but its current status, together with the outlook of the city, is pathetic enough to show how great the disasters that have been and are still being suffered". The only example of the Byzantine

A floor mosaic of the Great Palace depicts a tiger ripping apart a deer.
Museum of Great Palace Mosaics

Camel Jockey Mosaic.
Museum of Great Palace Mosaics.

palace architecture which exists to the present time is the Tekfur Palace, which was a part of the Blachernai Palace complex. Only some walls remain from the palace. The building, which is assumed to have been built by Manuel I Comnenos (1143-1180) and allocated for the crown princes, had a rectangular plan and two stories. Its exterior was made from red brick and had geometrical shapes of yellow-white marble. The lower floor, where there were five windows surrounded with marbles, opens into a courtyard via two double arches. On the upper floor of the eastern face were the remains of a balcony as well. The Tekfur Palace remained in solitude for a while, after which it was converted into a tile furnace in the 18th

Century by the Sadrazam (Prime Minister) Nevşehirli İbrahim Pasha. When Mehmed the Conqueror took Istanbul, the palaces were in ruins like the city itself, and thus he did not consider residing in these palaces. He first had a palace built for himself on the Bayezid Square, and had the Topkapı Palace built when this palace turned out to be too small. While the Great Palace was being developed on the south of the hippodrome, the palaces of Antiochos and Lausos were being built on the north of it. The Palace of Philoxenus was located over the Cistern of a Thousand and One Columns. Furthermore, numerous mansions belonging to the nobles were located on Mese Street. The main hall of the Antiochos Palace,

which has a hexagonal dome and six semicircle niches, was later transformed into the Church of Hagia Euphemia. Further above this was the palace belonging to Lausos-a noble who served important duties during the reign of Arcadios, and this palace was famous for its sculptures. Sculptures decorated the interior and exterior of the palace. The palace historian Pierre Gilles talks about the sculptures of the Lausos Palace in his book De 'Topographia Constantinopoleos' as follows: "The most remarkable among the sculptures is the 2 meter Athena Sculpture made from emerald green marble". A Byzantine palace historian, Georgios Kedrenos, reported that the sculpture Aphrodite of Knidos was in this palace and known as a famous sculpture everywhere, that this sculpture was made by Praxiteles, from white marble and appeared naked. Also located here were Lysippos's sculpture Hera of Samos and Phidias's sculpture of Zeus. The Lausos Palace was burnt during the fire which broke out in 476 in this region and the rare sculptures inside perished. Constantinos had also an imperial palace built in its capital, like the one in Rome. Many additions were later made to this first palace, which was situated to the south of the Hippoddrome and made up of many components, and it came to be named the Great Palace.

The Great Palace mosaics feature various subjects.
On this panel, leopards are seen devouring the deer which they hunted on top, while the bottom scene illustrates a mythological creature with a reptile it caught in its mouth.

Roads, Squares and Monuments

After preparations lasting five years (325-30), the city "Byzantion" underwent a change in name-becoming "Constantinople." At the same time, it was transformed into a city worthy of being the capital of the Roman Empire. Everything necessary was undertaken to make it even more attractive and more beautiful than Rome ever was. The new city found itself with new roads connected to newly constructed forums. Monuments and statues in the squares were brought in from as far away as Egypt, Greece and Rome as well as ancient Anatolian cities such as Pergamon, Ephesos and Antioch.

This mystifying new city carried on as the capital of the Eastern Roman Empire after 395. Byzantine emperors ascending to the throne added to the wealth of the city by embellishing it with new edifices. Like Rome, Constantinople was founded on seven hills. The first hill was the place of the previous city's acropolis over which Hagia Sophia and Hagia Eirene rose. The second hill, in Çemberlitaş, is where Constantine built a forum. The third hill is where Süleymaniye Mosque is today. The fourth and fifth hills are where Fatih and Sultan Selim Mosques stand, respectively. The sixth hill is closest to Edirnekapı, over which the Mihrimah Sultan Mosque rises. The final hill is that of Cerrahpaşa. Thus, the city of seven hills became decorated like a bride. However, the city was left in ruins during the Latin Invasion between the years 1204-1261, when all the bronze works were melted down and all of the beautiful statues were removed from their pedestals and carried away.

Let's now get acquainted with the roads, squares and monuments of Constantinople, the capital of yesteryear. The ceremonial and political life of the city during the Roman and Byzantine periods took place in the Hippodrome and the adjacent Augusteion Square. As we shall focus on the Hippodrome in a separate chapter, let's discuss the Augusteion. Constructed during the reign of Constantine, it was located in an enclosed field in front of the Hippodrome and the Great Palace. Constantine had a column erected in the center of the field and put a statue of his mother Helena at the top of it. This place derives its name from the word "Augusta," which means "Empress." Theodosios I erected a column next to this statue and topped it off with a silver statue of himself. In addition, there were several other statues here such as Eudoxia, the wife

Compared to today's relative calm, the Hippodrome once resonated with frenzied chariot races.

51

of Arcadius as well as one of Leo. These statues were situated on this square, which was essentially the front courtyard of the Great Palace. They were all damaged during the Nika Revolt of 532 but remained in their places until the Iconoclastic period of the 8th Century. While renovating the city, Justinian had the 35 meter high statue of Emperor Theodosios standing in the center of the square removed and replaced it with a silver statue of himself on a horse of bronze. Augusteion Square was surrounded by several structures, including the Great Palace, which was the largest church in the city, and the Patriarch and Senate buildings. Hagia Eirene was located the east of the Senate building in the area where the Byzantion acropolis was situated. There was also the Column of the Goths, located at a spot inside what is today Gülhane Park. The 15 meter high column made from blue-veined marble was topped with a Corinthian capital upon which there was a relief of an eagle. Set on top of a pedestal with steps, the column had an inscription from which it could be implied that it had been erected to commemorate the victory of Claudius over the Goths in the third Century. Representing the beginning of the roads extending west and out to all corners of the empire, the Million Stone was situated in the corner of this important square, next to the Basilica Cistern. It was once in the shape of a domed victory arch rising above a platform upon which the statues of Constantine and Helena with a cross in the center stood. Today, one can see the once-magnificent Million Stone in the shadow of the Ottoman "water scales" adjacent to the light rail line in the opposite corner of Hagia Sophia.

Comprising the backbone of the city is the Mese, which started from the Million Stone and extended to the Constantine Forum. The avenue was decorated on both sides with porticoes. Columns lining the avenue were topped with Corinthian or composite capitals. Its statue-lined outer edge, painted ceilings, and shops beneath the roofs all came together to create a picture of harmony. The shops here were all classified according to the merchandise sold. The Halkoprateius Church was situated behind the Basilica Cistern, which is directly behind the Million Stone at the start of the Mese. The Lausus Palace was positioned between the avenue and the Hippodrome while the Antiochus Palace and a church, the name of which is unknown, were also located between this palace and the Hippodrome. Further on down the Mese, one comes to the Forum of Constantine, which is in today's Çemberlitaş.

The oval-shaped Forum of Constantine, a symbolic place where the people would meet, was built over the previous city's necropolis. Ringed with two-storey porticoes, with arched entrances on the southeast and northwest sides, the Forum had statues of horses in the niches between its columns. Ancient sources mention that there was a nymphaeum to the west of the square. To the northeast was the Senate Building and in front of that were the porphyry porticoes, which featured two huge statues of

Constantine Column in Çemberlitaş.
One of Istanbul's oldest monuments, it was erected over the second hill,
Çemberlitaş. Damaged during a fire that struck during the Ottoman period,
it was reinforced with hoops to prevent its collapse.
Its name means "Hooped Stone" in Turkish.

Athena and Tetis. The square itself was decorated with numerous statues that Constantine had erected. The administration of Constantinople was conducted from this forum in particular; the city mayors and prefects would address the people from here. A column commemorating Constantine was erected in the center of this square. Known today as the "Çemberlitaş," the Constantine Column was formed by placing nine pieces of marble on top of each other. Marble laurel wreaths were placed on the column and some holy relics were buried underground during the positioning of this column, which was brought here in 328 from the Temple of Apollo in Rome. A statue of the emperor resembling that of Apollo was positioned at the very top of the 57 meter high monument. The head of this statue was adorned with seven rays with nails representing the suffering of Jesus hammered between them.

This statue was replaced by that of Emperor Julianus, then later on with a statue of Theodosios. The latter was toppled in a storm that hit the city in 1105. Emperor Manuel I Comnenos (1143-1180) replaced it with a Corinthian capital of marble, which was topped with a cross. This cross was brought down after the Turkish conquest in 1453. Cracks developed in the column as a result of a fire in the 17th Century. They were repaired by Sultan Mustafa II, who reinforced its pedestal, wrapping the pillar with copper hoops. It is because of these hoops that the Constantine Column was subsequently named "Çemberlitaş," which means "Hooped Stone" in Turkish.

Continuing down the Mese from the Forum of Constantine, one reaches the Forum of Theodosios in Beyazıt Square. Constructed by Emperor Theodosios, it is identical to the Forum of Traianus in Rome, but on a slightly smaller scale. It was called "Forum Tauri" after Prefect Tauri. There was also a huge statue of a bronze bull in the center of this square. In 386, the Column of Theodosios I was erected in the northern part of this forum. Reliefs symbolizing the victories of the emperor were placed close to the top. At the very top of this column was a statue of the emperor sitting on a silver horse. Though this statue came down in an earthquake that struck in 480, the column remained standing for many years. Angiolello recorded that he had seen the column during his visit to the city in 1477, which implies that the column had remained erect until at least this date.

To the north of the Mese was the Capitol, which was one of the ancient pagan temples. Theodosios II converted this building into a university where courses such as Greek, Latin, philosophy and law were taught.

The Philadephieum was not so much a square as a junction decorated with many statues. Although its location is not precisely known, it is thought to have been in the place where Laleli Mosque stands today. There were once statues here of the three sons of Constantine, embracing each other. These statues were carried off by the Latins, who subsequently erected them in front of the Church of St. Marco in Venice. Today, this group of statues is known as the Tetrarchia Group. A second road that broke off from the Philadephieum passed next to the Church of the Apostoleion,

The "Kıztaşı" (Maiden's Monument) was constructed by Prefect Tatian on behalf of Emperor Marcian in the year 452.

traversed the Aetius open-air cistern, and then over to Edirnekapı. As for the Mese, it passed on to the Forum of Bovis to reach Amastrianun Square, which was situated between Beyazıt and Aksaray. Embellished with statues of Zeus, Heracles and Hermes, this square had a sports arena as well as an area of heavy commercial activity. There was also a theater located in the immediate vicinity. Famous as a place where death sentences were carried out as well as a center of soothsaying activities, this square, as well as the nearby theater, was destroyed during the latter part of the 8th Century. It was replaced with a palace known as Eleuterius, built for Empress Irene. From here, the Mese reached the Forum of Bovis, which was known to have been situated in today's Aksaray on the plain where the Mese and Lycus Stream converged. The name of the forum was derived from a huge bronze kettle wrought in the shape of an ox.

This kettle, which was brought here from Pergamon, was used as an oven during votive ceremonies. Like the city's other squares, this one was decorated with porticoes and statues. In the middle of the square once stood statues depicting Constantine and Helena holding silver crosses. All these statues disappeared in a fire that struck in 562. From here, Mese turned up to the seventh hill at Cerrahpaşa. Dating back to 403, the Forum of Emperor Arcadius was the last forum to have been built in Constantinople. Emperor Arcadius erected a column, decorated with reliefs symbolizing victories won over the Goths, in the center of the forum. His son, Theodosios II had a statue placed atop the column of Arcadius riding a horse.

This statue was toppled in an earthquake in 740, while the column itself was brought down intentionally in 1715 as it posed a threat to the surrounding area. However, before it was torn down, the reliefs decorating it were all drawn, and published in Paris in 1702. The pedestal, 8-9 meters of which still survives, can been seen in a garden of a home found on Haseki Kadın Street in Cerrahpaşa. Another monument is that of "Kıztaşı" (Maiden's Monument), which is situated in Sarıgüzel, Fatih. It was erected by Prefect Tatian in 452 to commemorate Emperor Marcian. Measuring 17 meters in height, the granite column was positioned on top of a marble pedestal.

The statue of Marcian that once topped it was brought down by the Latins. Its name was derived from the reliefs of a pair of angels on its pedestal. The Mese continues west from the Forum of Arcadius to reach the city gate in the walls of Constantine. From here, the avenue makes a sharp turn and heads south to reach Porto Aurea, also known as "Altın Kapı" in the walls of Theodosios II. Byzantine emperors returning from their victorious campaigns would enter the city through this gate and retreat to their palaces, saluting their people who lined the length of the Mese. Now, let's take the time to mention something about Leander's Tower and Galata Tower, two landmarks that have graced the city skyline since the Byzantine period.

The Hippodrome

As a place where yesterday's chariot races were held, the cries of victory resounded, and endless exuberance was experienced. Today, the Hippodrome stretches through Sultanahmet Square in comparatively deep silence, in the shadows of obelisks of the past. Nevertheless, it was once a place for social gatherings, where political conflicts occurred, and where thousands of voices rose in unison during both the Roman and Byzantine eras. The grounds where excited shouts cheered on chariots jockeying for position echoed, later becoming the place where the people would express their dissatisfaction. Contests in which the "Blues," representing the sky, the "Greens," representing the earth, the "Whites," representing water and the "Reds," representing fire, were previously held here. Later the "Whites" and "Reds" diminished and ultimately disappeared, leaving only the "Blues" and "Greens," groups representing two separate political ideologies.

The silk awning of the imperial loggia was the harbinger of contests to take place the following day. The "Blues," who represented Orthodoxy and the large land barons would cheer on their chariot jockeys competing against those of the "Greens," who represented merchants, artisans and Monophysites. Over time, the fervor of these races became transformed into a rebellion against the emperor; the Greens and Blues, with their differing ideologies, staged a joint riot against the emperor. What was to be called the Nika Revolt led to the burning to the ground of the Hippodrome, Hagia Sophia and the Augusteion in 532.

The construction of the rectangular-shaped Hippodrome, which stretched in an east-west direction, was started by Septimius Severus and completed by Constantine around 330. The Hippodrome measured 440 meters x 117 meters. Its entrance, where a statue by Lysippus of a chariot drawn by four horses was situated, was from Hagia Sophia Square. In a semi-circular shape facing East-West, the section across the entrance was known as "Sphendone." It rose up via galleries, as the ground here was inclined. Wild beasts used to be kept in the galleries, which were later used as a cistern. When Petrus Gyllius passed through here in 1544, he acknowledged that the gallery, surrounded by 17 columns, was still intact. This section remains as the back end of Marmara University. The gallery walls can be seen to the right of the road sloping down to the shore. There is also a cistern located across these walls. As the Great Palace was once situated on the site where the Sultanahmet Mosque is today, the imperial loggia, called the "Kathisma Palace," faced this direction as well. The loggia was reached from the palace via a winding staircase. Placed over a platform supported by four marble columns, the loggia had a marble throne for the emperor to sit on as well as armchairs for his entourage. There were undoubtedly other chambers found adjacent to the loggia. For instance, the guards' chamber was beneath the loggia. The grandstands of the Hippodrome were at first made of wood, but because they all burned down during the Nika Revolt, Justinian had them made of marble.

The section for women at the Hippodrome consisted of a gallery with bars posited over 37 columns that were connected with vaults. The center of the Hippodrome where chariots raced was called the Spina and was decorated with a number of monuments. These included the Serpent Column, which Constantine had brought from Delphi, the Obelisk of Egyptian Pharoah Thutmosis III, which was shipped here from Egypt but erected many years later, as well as the Column of Constantine VII Porphyrogenitus, which was erected here by the emperor of the same name in the Late Byzantine period and which once had bronze placards attached to it. Ancient sources tell us that there

The relief carvings on the base of the Egyptian obelisk that the Emperor Theodosios had erected in the hippodrome at Constantinople show the great importance that was attached to the events that took place there. The hippodrome was the natural focus of most of the secular life of the city, and the presence of the Emperor would have been obligatory. A special 'royal box' was built for him and the Empress, which could be entered directly from the Great Palace. It was erected over a period of 32 days during the year 390.

were seven other columns besides these obelisks, with a statue of dolphins at one end of the Spina and egg-shaped emblems of the gods Neptune, Castor and Pollux at the other end. In addition, there were statues-one of which had been sculpted by Diocletian-that had been brought here from the previous capital, Nicomedia, positioned in front of the imperial loggia. There were up to 60 statues on top of the walls of the Hippodrome, which reflected the splendor of this structure.

Among the most popular forms of entertainment held in this place, where the emperor and his subjects carried on with their daily activities, were the chariot races. Commencing at the gate, seven laps would be run around the Spina. Chariot jockeys who won these races would gain the great admiration of the people and become famous. There were statues of several jockeys in the Hippodrome. These include the one of Porphyrius, a famous rider during the reign of Anastasius I.

During the Ottoman period, the Hippodrome was the scene of javelin throwing on horseback, which is why it is called "At Meydanı (Horse Square)" in Turkish. In addition to other sporting events, this is where the weddings of Ottoman crown princes were held. Cut blocks of stone where removed from the foundation of the Hippodrome to build the İbrahim Pasha Palace, known today as the Museum of Turkish and Islamic Arts. The construction of this palace spelled the end of Süleyman the Magnificent Hippodrome of the Byzantines. However, the statues here had disappeared well before the Ottomans came into the picture. The work of Athena with a lance was destroyed by the Christians, and the Latin Duke Henricus Dandolo carted off the statue of Lysippus' chariot pulled by four horses and had it erected it at the entrance of the Church of St. Marco in Venice.

In the northern part of the Hippodrome is the German Fountain, which was presented by Kaiser Wilhelm II as a gift to Ottoman Sultan Abdülhamid II. Cast in 1898 by the German architect M. Spitta, it was placed in this site in 1901 and given the name "Alman Çeşmesi." Supported by columns, the dome of the fountain is decorated with golden mosaics on its interior and tiles on its exterior.

Now, let's try to imagine the old days in the splendid Hippodrome as we get acquainted with the monuments remaining today.

The Egyptian Obelisk

Two monuments can be seen right next to each other in Sultanahmet Square today. The one containing Egyptian hieroglyphics was brought from the Temple of Karnak in Egypt by Constantine, but it was not immediately put up due to technical reasons. It was erected by Theodosios I in 390, when it was commemorated with his name. Including its pedestal, it stands 24.87 meters high. It sits on a pink granite pedestal weighing 200 tons and has reliefs that depict the life of Emperor Theodosios. On its northern face are the Byzantine Arcadius and his wife Eudoxia sitting in their

Views of both the Serpent Column and Egyptian Obelisk.
The hieroglyphics inscribed on the latter tells of the victories of Pharaoh Thutmosis III, whereas the former was presented as a votive at the Temple at Delphi by the Greek cities for their victory over the Persians in 479 BC.

Hippodrome loggia. Its western face shows Emperor Theodosios on his throne with his wife and children sitting with Arcadius and Honorius, with defeated enemies in front of them. On its eastern face is a depiction of Emperor Theodosios watching a chariot race with his two sons on one side and Valentinian II on the other. Brought from Egypt, this obelisk was transported here from the shore over a specially made road. From the inscription of the pedestal, it took Prefect Proclus 32 days, putting up scaffolding all around it. The hieroglyphics on this single-piece obelisk, which was erected at the Temple of Karnak in Lower Egypt by Pharoah Thutmosis III in 1547 BC., describes his victories. The east face of the obelisk, from which a section of the lower part has broken off, displays the words, "Thutmosis III of the 18th dynasty, master of Upper and Lower Egypt, on the 30th anniversary of his reign, as conqueror of the seas and rivers, has set up this obelisk for the countless anniversaries to come." The inscription on its southern side, states, "Thutmosis, the all-powerful and all-just son of the Sun, ruler of Upper and Lower Egypt, has penetrated as far as Mesopotamia, at the head of his armies, has shown his might on the Mediterranean, and has fought great battles."

The western face reads, "Thutmosis, son of the Sun, who bears the crowns of Upper and Lower Egypt on his brow through the strength, might and wealth of Horos, after paying tribute to the god Amona, built this work for his father, the god Amon-Ra, that it may spread light like the rays of the sun to Mankind." The northern side is inscribed with the pictorial symbols, "Thutmosis paid tribute to the god Amon-Ra, and then, with the might and power of Horus he determined to take the borders of his country as far as Mesopotamia."

Column of Constantine Porphyrogenitus

Situated at the back of Sultanahmet Square, the Serpent Column was most likely made towards the end of the 4th Century, during the reign of Arcadius. It was repaired later on by Constantine VII Porphyrogenitus (913-59), who also had it bronze-plated. This is why it is commonly referred to by his name. This ancient monument is a roughly built pillar of stone 32 meters high. The bronze plates depicted the victories of Constantine VII Porphyrogenitus and his grandfather Basil I (867-86). It is unfortunate that the Latins removed these plates to mint coinage during their occupation of Constantinople.

The Serpent Column

Situated in a gap between two monuments, the Serpent Column was placed here by Constantine the Great, who had it brought from the Temple of Apollo at Delphi. Dating from the Hellenistic period, this trophy was dedicated to Apollo as a token of gratitude by the 31 Greek cities that had defeated the Persians in the battle of Plataea (479 BC.). According to tradition, the bronze serpents were cast from the shields of the fallen Persian warriors and a gold kettle was positioned on top. The Latins removed this kettle from its place during the occupation of Constantinople and melted it down as well.

Column of Constantinople VII Porphyrogenitus.
It has lost its brilliance as the plates covering it were removed during
the Latin Invasion.

Galata Tower

An important site that continues to attract much attention in Istanbul today is the Galata Tower. Situated between Karaköy and Tünel, the tower offers a magnificent panoramic view of Karaköy. It was constructed as the principle tower of the surrounding protective walls in 1348 by the Genovesians, who had a colony in the Galata District. First named the "Tower of Jesus," it remained within the newly constructed walls; both the tower and walls were raised a bit higher in 1448. All but 13 meters of the tower collapsed in an earthquake that struck in 1509. It was reconstructed by the Ottomans, who used it as a dungeon in the 16th Century to keep prisoners of war who worked in the Kasımpaşa Shipyard. The tower was rebuilt once again in 1794, after a devastating fire that engulfed the district, with an additional storey with windows extending on four sides and topped with a conical roof. It was subsequently used as a fire tower, only to be repaired in 1875 after it was once more gutted by fire. The 68 meter high tower, which had 12 stories including the basement floor, was completely renovated and opened as a tourist attraction in 1967. The tower is famous as the site where, during the reign of Sultan Murad IV in 1632, Hezarfen Ahmed Çelebi leapt from the top of the tower in a pair of homemade wings. Çelebi is known to have landed in Doğancılar Square in Üsküdar, on the Asian side of the Bosphorus.

Leander's Tower

Situated on a group of submerged rocks just off the shore from Üsküdar and regarded as the symbol of Istanbul, Leander's Tower (or Maiden's Tower) was first erected in 410 BC. by the Athenian Commander Alcibiades to observe maritime vessels sailing in from the Black Sea.

It was used as an observation tower throughout the Byzantine period. Emperor Manuel I Comnenos (1143-1180) converted the tower into a fortress. Ancient sources mention that he wanted to prevent enemy ships from getting through the Bosphorus by tying one end of an immense chain from the nearby Damalis Hill and stretching the other end over to the Marble Tower in the Mangana district of Sarayburnu. After conquering the city, Sultan Mehmed II converted the tower into an observation tower. It was destroyed in an earthquake that struck in 1509 and was subsequently rebuilt using timber planks. The wooden tower was to be repaired several times, but it was in 1725-26 that the Grand Vizier Damat Ibrahim Pasha had it replaced with a stone block tower after being destroyed in a fire. Sultan Mahmud II ordered it to be completely renovated in 1832. Turned over to the Lighthouse Administration in 1857, it was recently restored and given a totally new appearance. It is currently operated as a tourist attraction. The Leander's Tower is the source of a number of legends, one of the most enduring of which surrounds the tale of a young maiden named Hero and her lover Leander.

For some reason, Hero is locked up in this tower and, guided by a torch held in her hands, Leander would swim across the Bosphorus every night to be at her side. However, as fate would have it, the torch was blown out by the wind, and poor Leander lost his way, perishing in the stormy waters of the Bosphorus. It is because of this tale that western sources refer to the Leander's Tower as the Maiden's Tower. However, this story is actually in reference to Leander of Abidos and Hero of Sestos who lived along the shores of the Dardanelles Strait. Over time, this story became erroneously identified with Leander's Tower.

Another legend concerning the tower dates back to the Byzantine Empire. According to the legend, soothsayers prophesied that the daughter of a Byzantine emperor was to die from a snakebite. The emperor had his daughter kept in this tower to protect her from any such dangerous snakes. However, the girl's lover sends her a basket of figs and alas, a serpent slithers out of the basket to bite her with his poisonous fangs. Fate has coupled this everlasting tale as the one most suitable for the Leander's Tower.

Byzantine Cisterns

The Eastern Roman Empire, which ruled over Istanbul for a long thousand years and which came to be known as Byzantion later on, was exposed to sieges many times. During these sieges, adversary powers that surrounded the ramparts cut off the water of the city in an effort to leave the city without water so that it would fall. As a precaution against this threat, the Byzantines built large cisterns which eliminated the water problem. Since the Ottomans did not value backwater, they did not use these cisterns but repaired and used the Mazlum and Valens aqueducts, which remained from the Byzantines, and built the aqueducts of Mağlova, Uzun Kemer and Güzelcekemer, solving the water problem of the city.

As we take a look at all the examples since the time they first began to be built, we see two distinct groups of construction as open and closed cisterns. In today's Istanbul, in the neighborhood of Çukurbostan, water coming from sources outside the city was accumulated in cisterns, the interior of which was daubed with a special mixture to eliminate water leakage and where it was left to rest and was cleaned through deposition.

The best preserved open cistern is Fildamı, which is near the hippodrome of Veliefendi in Bakırköy. This cistern, which is surrounded with 4 meter thick and 11 meter high walls, measures 127 x 76 m This cistern was constructed to meet the water demand of the army and to provide water for the newly established Byzantine neighborhood named Hebdemon. During the Latin invasion in 1204, the neighborhood was plundered and transformed into a small fishing village, with the cistern losing its importance. After Istanbul was conquered and found to be in ruins, the Turks brought elephants here, therefore, it came to be known as Fildamı (Elaphants' Stable). The open cistern that is located below today's Karagümrük Stadium, was commissioned in 421 by the governor Aetius, during the reign of Emperor Valentianus.

Another open cistern, which was constructed in Cerrahpaşa during the reign of Emperor Anastasios (491-518), is the cistern of Hagios Makios measuring 170 x140 m This cistern, which was named after the neighboring Hagios Makios Church, is also known as the Altı Mermer Cistern today. The cistern which is below the Sultan Selim Complex was commissioned towards 460, by the Gothic commander Aspar, who came in the aid of Byzantion, and measures 152 x152 m Currently, it is home to the service buildings of the Fatih Municipality.

The closed cisterns known in Istanbul today, which numbered around 70, have rectangular and square plans. They are covered on top by brick arches and vaults resting on stone columns. In

The second largest after Basilica Cistern was Cistern of a Thousand and One Columns (Binbirdirek Sarnıcı), which has 224 columns measuring 64x54 m (below).

The Theodosios Cistern.
The cistern, which is located in Eminönü
Municipality, was built between
428-443 as commissioned by Theodosios
(401-450), who became emperor after
Arcadius, following the split of Rome in
two. The cistern is open to visit today.

Three different scenes of the
Basilica Cistern.
It has recently been cleaned and
opened for visits. Reflections on
the water emanating from the forest
of pillars are quite striking.
These Medusa column heads were
placed under the short pillars of
the Basilica Cistern as support.

addition to meeting the water demand, they also constituted the terraces of buildings such as palaces, churches, monasteries and private properties. For instance, the cisterns of the Mangana Palace located on the sea-facing slope of the Topkapı Palace and the Great Palace have been built in this way. With fear that he would be drowned, the Emperor Heracleios (610-641) had some of these cisterns filled; however, Basileios-who held the throne from 867 to 886-had them reinstated, ensuring that they would be functional. Since these cisterns were used as gardens, they were called Çukurbostan, meaning hollow garden.

The largest and the highest in architectural value among the closed cisterns is the Basilica Cistern (Yerebatan Sarnıcı) located in the vicinity of Hagia Sophia. The cistern is known as the Basilica Cistern because there used to be a commercial basilica over it and was built by Justinianos in the 6th Century primarily to meet the demands of the palace. Inside this cistern, which spans an area measuring 140x70 m, there are a total of 336 columns made up of twelve rows with twenty eight columns each. The columns measure 8 to 10 m and it has been

calculated that, with these measurements, the cistern can take up to 75,000 m³ of water. Supporting the ceiling over the Corinthian-capped columns are brick vaults. Some columns have Medusa-head bases placed in a reversed position, suggesting that these were brought here from a spectacular monument from the Roman Era.

Located here before the cistern was a basilica, which served as a cultural center during the period of Constantinos. Within the basilica there was a courtyard containing many sculptures. The basilica is also known to have included a library of hundred and twenty thousand books. The library was built in 476 by a person known as Illos, during the period of Emperor Zenon (476-491). The basilica is not mentioned after the 10th Century. During the Nika Revolt, this basilica was burnt along with other buildings. While Justinianos I ordered the demolished buildings to be

reconstructed, he also had the basilica repaired in 542. Additionally the current cistern was built after having the basilica undercut.

After Istanbul was taken, the water of the cistern was used for the irrigation of the gardens of the Topkapı Palace, which was later discontinued leading to the oblivion of the cistern. However, it was rediscovered by Frenchman Pierre Gilles, who visited the city around 1544-1547. This cistern, which remained inoperable for many years, was revealed to French Pierre Gilles when he saw the residents of the neighborhood dangling their buckets down to pull up water. The cistern was forgotten again after this, but from 1986 to 1988, fifty thousand tons of mud has been removed from it and it was opened to tourism after arrangements were made.

Another intriguing closed cistern is the Cistern of a Thousand and One Columns, which is thought to have been the palace cistern of Philoxenus-a senator who had immigrated from Rome to this newly-established city. The cistern measuring 64 x 56 m includes a total of 224 columns with a series of 14x16. All of the columns and column capitals which support the vaults and arches are plain, and the capitals are in the form of a truncated pyramid. The cistern measures 20 m in height and thus two columns were placed one on top of the other to reach the ceiling, as the height of one column was not enough. All of the columns and capitals here were especially made for this place and are not recovered materials. On the column bodies are protruding rings. The cistern receives light from the windows which are at the same level as the road.

Close to this cistern, beneath the building of the Eminönü Municipality in the Pierre Loti Street, is the Theodosios Cistern. The cistern, which is located in the vicinity of the Sultan Selim Mosque, has a rectangular plan and 28 columns placed at regular intervals, seven of which are made from granite, while twenty one are from white marble. Column bodies and capitals are from recovered material. The cover on top is in the form of small-sized cross vaults. This cistern, which is an important work of Byzantine Period, remained empty for centuries, being filled with rubble and earth. Known as the Sultan Cistern today, it was brought into cultural life to host special organizations after restoration in 2000.

Apart from these cisterns, many other cisterns are also known to exist in various parts of Istanbul. While the annex building to the Archaeological Museum was being constructed in the yard of Topkapı Palace, a large cistern was uncovered. Byzantine cisterns are known to exist in Soğukçeşme Street behind Hagia Sophia, beneath the Complex of Merzifonlu Kara Mustafa Pasha in Çemberlitaş, and beneath Istanbul Erkek Lisesi (Istanbul Boys' High School). There are also many other closed cisterns in Istanbul, such as the cistern in Fatih, beneath the At Pazarı (Horse Market) Square, over which there used to be a church, the cistern discovered in Bayezid during the construction of the university parking lot, the great cistern before the Sultanahmet Mosque (Blue Mosque), and the cistern to the east of the hippodrome, which remains beneath the houses today.

Sultan's Cistern.
The cistern is located in the Sultan Selim district and has been serving tourism after being repaired in recent years.

The Cistern of a Thousand and One Columns (Binbirdirek Sarnıcı).
The cistern has been restored.

Byzantine Churches and Monasteries

As Istanbul evolved into the new capital of the Great Roman Empire, Christianity became a free religion, after which it became the official religion of the Roman Empire. Hence, alongside the ancient pagan temples, churches and monasteries of this new religion began to emerge. Istanbul is home to numerous churches and monasteries from the Byzantine Period. The oldest is the church of Hagia Eirene, which was burnt in 532 during the Nika Revolt together with Hagia Sophia and which was reconstructed during the reign of Emperor Justinianos. Around 50 churches and monasteries built during the last periods of Byzantion are known to exist. Among them, 40 churches were transformed into mosques from the period of Mehmed the Conqueror to Murad IV, and around 25 of them exist to the present day with their new names.

Serving as the Chora Museum (Kariye Müzesi) today, the Chora Monastery holds world-renowned mosaics. The Pammakaristos Monastery in the neighborhood of Çarşamba, which is located on a hill overlooking the Golden Horn, was dedicated to Mary. It was also transformed into a mosque by Murad III, and was named the Fethiye (Victory) Mosque in reference to the victory of Azerbaycan and Georgia. Representing all the characteristics of late Byzantine architecture, the building has a Greek-cross plan and is covered with a dome in the middle resting on four thick piers. It is still partially used as a mosque. There are mosaic depictions of Jesus together with 12 Torah prophets on the dome at the center, as well as Jesus, Mary, John the Baptist, saints and patriarchs in the interior of the church.

The church which is located by the Marmara Sea and is known as the Little Hagia Sophia due to its plan resembling that of Hagia Sophia was built by the Emperor Justinianos and his wife Theodora from 527 to 536, and was transformed into a mosque during the time of Bayezid II, by the Chief Harem Eunuch Hüseyin Ağa, after adding a five-dome place of last congregation-a mosque porch where latecomers would pray-and a minaret with a single balcony. The church, which was one of the leading central-plan structures of the Byzantine Era, was dedicated to Sergios and Bacchos. Before Justinianos's ascension to the throne, a rumor arose that he plotted an assassination against the Emperor Anastasios. The two saints-Sergios and Bacchos-whom the emperor dreamt of saying that Justinianos was innocent, and Justinianos was saved. When he eventually took the throne, he had this church built to pay his tribute of gratitude to the saints. The interior of the church is circular and the prolate dome covering it rests over eight piers. The walls, which represent dainty masonry, are surrounded with an epitaph having the names of the Emperor Justinianos and his wife Theodora. Furthermore, the column capitals, which were crafted

Mosaic on the dome of the Chora Monastery Church portrays the figure of Christ (Chora Museum).

like lacework, have the monograms of the emperor. The Bodrum Mosque, which is located on Sait Efendi Street in Laleli, used to be the church of the Myrelaion Monastery and was transformed into a mosque by Mesih Pasha-a descendent of the Palaiologos dynasty who became sadrazam (prime minister) in 1500. It was built by Romanos I Lakapenos (920-944), who jointly became the emperor with Constantinos VII, near his private palace. While the cross-plan church was being built, the 30 m circular building near it was transformed into a cistern to meet the water demand of the monastery. When Romanos I Lakapenos died, he was buried in this church, just as his wife and children Christophoros and Constantinos VII.

Another church which currently exists is the Kalenderhane Mosque located near the Bozdoğan (Valens) Aqueduct in Şehzadebaşı. Even though its old name has not been discovered, it is thought to be the church of the Akaleptos Monastery, which was built in the 11th Century during the period of the Comnenoses. The cross-plan church is covered by a dome. The colorful marble pieces remaining on the side of the shrine reveal that the interior had opulent decorations. It was converted into a mosque by Mehmed the Conqueror after the conquest, and was named the Kalenderhane Mosque, since it was allocated for the dervishes in the army called 'kalender'. During a recent research by an American group in the mosque, an epigraph having the name of St. Fransiscus has been found, showing that the church was used as a Catholic church during the Latin invasion from 1204-1261. The Joannes Prodromos Church, which is located in the Imrahor neighborhood now and which was constructed in 461, was transformed into a church and dervish lodge by Imrahor Ilyas Bey at the time of Bayezid II. Representing a fine example of early-Christianity basilicas, the church is separated into three naves by two rows of columns and is remarkable with its floor mosaics.

Atik Mustafa Mosque by the Golden Horn in Ayvansaray is also a cross-plan church built in the name of St. Thekla in the 9th-10th Century. The church was transformed into a mosque during the reign of Sultan Bayezid II, its dome was repaired, and the chamber to the right of the shrine was arranged as the tomb of an authority figure. The baptism pool before the building is at the Istanbul Archaeological Museum. The Byzantine church by the Golden Horn, which is thought to have a connection with a monastery in Cibali, was transformed into a mosque in 1499 and named the Rose Mosque (Gül Camii). It was a church built in the name of Hagia Euphemia in the 9th Century, whereas, its name is thought to have been changed later as Hagia Theodosia. The cross-plan building appears very tall. The dome and the upper sections evolved into their current appearance during the Turkish Period.

The Monastery of Lips Church at the corner of the Vatan Street was transformed into a dervish lodge and mosque by Fenarizade Alaeddin Ali Efendi at the time of Bayezıd II, and Sheik Isa at the time of Murad IV turned this place into a dervish lodge and named it the Fenari Isa Mosque. During the reign of Leon VI, it was built by the admiral of the fleet Costantinos Lips in 907, in the name of Mother Mary, and was enlarged with later additions. Michael VIII Palaiologos's wife Queen Theodora had a second holy sepulcher church attached to the south of the current temple,

St. Mary Pammakaristos Church. Built in the 11th Century, this church was converted into the Fethiye Mosque by Murad III in 1591. Now open as a museum, visitors can view the numerous mosaics of Jesus Christ covering the walls.

A close-up view of the inner Parecclesion Dome of the St. Mary Pammakaristos Church (Fethiye Museum).

devoted to Hagios Joannes Prodromos, and these churches became the familial sepulcher church of the queen, with many from the dynasty of Palaiologoses also buried here. The Women's Monastery of Lips as well as a hospital affiliated with the monastery is also known to exist in the neighborhood of the church. The building which is made up of two adjacent churches and two wings attached to the west and south of them was repaired after the fire of l633 in 1636 by the sadrazam Bayram Pasha, during which it went through great change, with two large arches built inside the two churches. It was devastated in 1918 by a fire, and was repaired in 1960 and reopened to visitation. On Şemseddin Gürani Street of Vefa, the Vefa Church Mosque is located, which used to be a small but charming Byzantine church. The church was transformed into a mosque in 1488, in the name of Molla Gürani-a renowned scientist during the period of Mehmed the Conqueror. It must have been given the name of Vefa Mosque due to the respect for Sheik Vefa, a much-loved figure who came and settled in this neighborhood after the conquest. Even though the church is said to have been the Hagios Theodoros Church, it is not known for sure which Theodoros Church it is. The building, which apparently was built around the 11th or 12th Centuries, has a Greek-cross plan with four columns and a protruding apse. The vivacity created by brick embellishments, which are the major characteristic of the Byzantine architecture, is remarkable. Here, rows of blind niches, intertwined walls built from rock and bricks and elegant long windows are typical examples of the art of the Paleologs. During this period, an exterior narthex was built on the western side. During the studies in 1936, on the southern dome of the narthex, which is decorated with mosaics, images of Mary and the child Jesus, and on the segments of the interior surface, mosaics depicting the Torah prophets have been found. In today's

Views of the "Small" Hagia Sophia Church built under the orders of Emperor Justinian and Empress Theodora between 527-36.

neighborhood of Kocamustafapaşa, the church which was transformed into a mosque by Koca Mustafa Pasha-a sadrazam during the period of Sultan Bayezid II-must have been the church of Apostolos Andreas Monastery which was established in the 13th Century after the Latin invasion. During the Turkish Period, the exterior of the mosque was completely changed, with traces of Byzantine architecture left only at the interior. The Ahmed Paşa Masjid in the Çarşamba neighborhood of Fatih is the Hagios Joannes Prodromos Church, which was also transformed into a mosque during the reign of Murad III. The Zeyrek Church Mosque, which is located in Zeyrek at a location overlooking the Atatürk Boulevard, was the church of the Pantokrator Monastery-one of the largest and most important monasteries of Byzantion. It was commissioned by Emperor Joannes II and his wife Eirene to be built by the architect Nicephoros. This complex, which comprised a monastery, hospital, old people's home and a church, was plundered during the Latin invasion and only three churches remained standing. The southernmost church is the Pantokrator Church, which apparently had floors decorated with mosaics. In this church are graves belonging to the descendents of Mother Mary in the north, and the descendents of the Comnenoses in the middle. After the conquest, it was transformed into a madrasah (Islamic college) by Mehmed the Conqueror. Later it became a mosque and was named after the first teacher of the sultan as the Zeyrek Mosque. Today, the Pantokrator Church is being used as a mosque. In Fatih, on a slope overlooking the Golden Horn, the Pantepoptes (all-seeing) Monastery was commissioned by Alexios I Comnenos's mother Anna Dalassena in 1087. This church belongs to the monastery and has a Greek-cross plan. A 12-corner drum with a window on all aspects bears the dome. The church and the monastery were transformed into a mosque and a dervish

Two views of the churches of the Pantocrator Monastery in Zeyrek. Comprised of three separate chapels that were ordered by Emperor John II and his wife Irene. The center structure was constructed as a "grave chapel."

The Bulgarian Church.
This church is made of iron. It was cast in
Vienna in 1898 and was assembled in its
current location by the coast of
the Golden Horn. The interior of
the Neo-Gothic church is
also made of iron.

lodge by Mehmed the Conqueror. Because it was later used as an almshouse (imaret), it came to be known as the Old Imaret Mosque. Another church that was transformed into a mosque in Istanbul is the Arab Mosque. When Karaköy was under the rule of the Genovesians, it was built over a former church as the St. Dominic Church in Gothic style, by the members of the Dominican order. It was transformed into a mosque after the conquest of Istanbul, and it was named the Arab Mosque after the Muslim Arabs expelled from Andalucia and Spain were settled in here. The mosque was restored from 1910 to 1912, and was opened to use. In addition to many churches which were transformed into mosques, small churches were also used as masjids. Masjids such as the Monastery Masjid in Topkapı, the İbrahim Pasha Masjid, which remains within the Cerrahpaşa Hospital, Sheik Süleyman Masjid in Zeyrek, and the Balabanağa Masjid in Laleli as

well as the Sheik Murad Masjid by the Golden Horn can be given as examples. Some churches in Istanbul were not transformed into mosques but continued to function. Among these is the Panagia Moukhliotissa Church in the neighborhood of Fener, which exists to the present time. The church, which was constructed over a Late Roman grave structure, is also known as the Maria Palalogia Church. Maria was the illegitimate daughter of Michael VIII Palaiologos. Around the beginning of the 13th Century, when Maria was on her way to the Mongolian Palace to become the bride of Hulagu Khan, the Khan died and was replaced by his son Abaka Khan. Maria had to marry him. When Abaka Khan was killed by his brother Ahmed after a few years, Maria returned to Byzantion and chose to become a nun and had this church built. On the walls of this building are the copies of Mehmed the Conqueror's commandment that it shall remain as a church. In Fener,

the Greek Orthodox Patriarch too has a historical building. After the conquest of Istanbul, the Patriarchate, which was near Hagia Sophia, was relocated to the Church of the Holy Apostles (Havariyyun) in Fatih. While Gennadios, who was appointed as patriarch by Mehmed the Conqueror, continued his service here, the desolate church was demolished. When it was decided that the Fatih (Conqueror) Mosque was to be built in its place, the Patriarchate was moved to the Pammakaristos Church first, and then to the Hagios Demetrios Kanabu Church in Fener in 1597, and later to its current location. The building, which was constructed around 1720, was repaired in 1830 and has recently been repaired again and opened. Located inside the Patriarchate is the Church of Hagios Georgios and many religious items are kept in the church. The Patriarch's throne-a masterpiece of wood carving, and the mosaic Mother Mary icon beside the bible tables,

which was brought from the Pammakaristos Church, are among the spectacular works. Furthermore, there are also coffins of three female saints in the church. Since the Bulgarians did not want to remain committed to the patriarchate, they had a neo-Gothic style church built in 1898, which is visible today in the Golden Horn. The church, which was cast from iron by the firm Wagner in Vienna, was brought here and assembled here. The Church of the Peripleptos Monastery located in Samatya was connected to the Armenian congregation after the conquest, and the Church of Sulumanastır Surp Kevork was built in place of this church in 1870. In Istanbul, Catholic and Orthodox Armenian churches are open for worship today in many places. Furthermore, Orthodox and Catholic churches as well as Jewish synagogues also exist besides them. The fact that mosques are side by side with churches is a demonstration of the Turkish tolerance for various beliefs.

A ceremony attended by the Russian Orthodox Patriarch at the Russian Church. There are numerous churches and synagogues in Istanbul, belonging to Greeks, Armenians and Jews. These are open to worship side by side with the mosques. Istanbul is one of those rare places in the world where different religions meet with tolerance.

Hagia Eirene

Situated in the outer courtyard of Topkapı Palace, the Church of Hagia Eirene, the oldest church in Istanbul, was constructed during the reign of Constantine the Great (307-337). Together with several other structures, this church was burned to the ground during the Nika Revolt of 532. It was reconstructed in 548 only to be heavily damaged as a result of earthquakes that struck in the 8th Century. Emperor Constantine V had the church completely renovated and its interior decorated with mosaics and frescoes. It is known that the church was expanded during the 11th-12th Centuries. After the conquest of Constantinople in 1453, it was drawn into the Sultan's Walls and subsequently used as an armory and a warehouse where war booty was kept. For this reason, the church bore the name "Cebehane" and converted into a sort of weapons museum during the reign of Sultan Ahmed III (1703-30). It was repaired in 1846 by Topkapı Field Marshall Ahmed Fethi Pasha, who turned it into the first Turkish museum, called "Müze-i Hümayun," in 1869. The structure was used as the Military Museum starting in 1908, and finally it was turned over to the Ministry of Culture in 1978.

After Hagia Sophia, Hagia Eirene is the largest church in Istanbul. Measuring 100x32 m, it consists of three naves and has a basilica-like appearance. It is comprised of a naos, a narthex, upper and lower galleries and an atrium. The naos is divided into three naves with columns and pillars and is covered with domes and vaults. The main dome, which has 20 windows, is 15 meters wide and 35 meters high. There is a depiction of a cross in the apse. Moreover, one can see an inscription of two lines taken from the Pentateuch there. One passes from the naos into the narthex through one of five doors and from the narthex into the atrium through one of another five doors. This is the only Byzantine church in Istanbul to have survived with its atrium intact. Ringed with porticoes and vaulted arches, it was made narrower during the Ottoman period with the addition of another row of porticoes. Constructed during the reign of Justinian I, it is believed that the interior decoration of the church was quite ornate. However, the mosaic and frescoes have long since disappeared as a result of damage caused by earthquakes and other disasters. Currently open to the public as a monument/museum, Hagia Eirene is also a venue where various fine arts and cultural events are held.

Church of St. Irene.
Adjacent to the Hagia Sophia Museum and within the outer court of
Topkapı Palace, this church was built by the order of Emperor Justinianus (518-527).
Covered by a central dome flanked by two semi-domes, it is the second largest
Byzantine church in Istanbul.

Hagia Sophia

After Constantinos the Great declared once-forbidden Christianity as a legal religion, churches began to rise in the city beside the Pagan temples. Due to the will of his father Constantinos the Great, Consantnios II had the first building constructed in basilica fashion, with a wooden roof. An inauguration ceremony was held in Fenruary 360 for this building, which remained standing for 44 years and afterwards was was burnt in June 20, 404 during a revolt. However, it was repaired at the time of Theodosios II and opened for the second time in 415. This new building remained standing for about one hundred years, after which it was burnt and completely devastated during the Nika Revolt which broke out in 532.

When Hagia Sophia-one of the leading monuments in world art history-was first built, it was named 'Megale Ecclesia' meaning the great church, and since it was devoted to Holy Wisdom, it was named 'Hagia Sophia' starting from the 5th Century through the entire Byzantine Period.

Emperor Justinianos decided to have the burnt church rebuilt with extraordinary size. He assigned the two architects; Isidoros of Miletos and Anthemios of Tralles to this task. Construction materials from all regions of the empire and marble from major marble quarries were brought, and the construction was initiated with 7000 workers lasting for about 5 years 10 months, ending on December 27, 537. During the inauguration, the emperor disclosed his admiration by saying, "I thank God for providing me the opportunity to build a place of worship as such".

The building was inaugurated only after the completion of the rough construction; the building was not fully complete and the dome had not fully settled in static terms. The mosaic decorations of its interior continued until the period of Justinos II (565-578). When the earthquake in 558 led to fractures in the main dome, and the half dome to the east, the ruling Emperor Justinianos assigned Isidoros's nephew Young Isidoros to its repair. Isidoros built a more durable dome by raising the dome 7 m higher and using a more light-weight material. After the repair job was finished, the church was re-opened with a ceremony on December 23 in 562.

During the Iconoclasm, which was an important movement in Byzantine history lasting from 726 through 842, figure pictures in Hagia Sophia were removed and replaced by crosses. With the conclusion of the Iconoclastic period in 843, ruling Michael III began with the decoration of the church with mosaics. However, the fire in 859 interrupted this decoration work. Still, the greatest damage was done by the earthquake after ten years and one of the half domes to the west was demolished. The Emperor Basileios I issued that the necessary repairs be carried out; even the damages caused by the earthquake in 869 were recovered. When the western section of the dome collapsed one more time with the earthquake in 989, Basileios II had the church repaired by an architect named Trdat, during which time the 16 ribs of the dome were changed.

Following the five-year repair, the church was opened for worship again on May 13th 994. Romanos III (1028- 1034), who ascended to the throne afterwards, had the interior decorations of the church completed.

During the Fourth Crusade in 1204, the Western Christians invading Byzantion damaged Hagia Sophia as much as they damaged the city. They took the silver plaques on the Emperor's Gate as well as golden and silver crosses, and plundered the religious items along with them.

After the Latin invasion, which ended in 1261, during the period of the Paleologoses, the Emperor Mihael VIII commissioned the architect Ruchas to repair the church, and Andronikos II (1317) had the support abutments built on the east and northern section. However, the earthquakes in 1343 and 1346 caused additional damage here, and a part of the dome was demolished together with the eastern arch and certain sections. When another place to the east of the dome was also demolished in 1354, repair was carried out with the money collected from the people.

Mehmed the Conqueror had noticed the desolate condition of the church during the conquest of Istanbul. He performed the first Friday salat here, thus transforming Hagia Sophia to a mosque. Ottoman sultans who succeeded him also carried out repairs and additions, which helped this edifice reach to the present time. After the minaret was attached to Hagia Sophia in 1481, a second minaret was added during the reign of Bayezid. Selim II had the worn building repaired by the Architect Sinan and reinforced it with support abutments. During the reign of Murad III, who ascended to the throne afterwards, repair work continued and two more minarets were added to Hagia Sophia.

Tombs were also built for the deceased Ottoman sultans in the yard of Hagia Sophia; its baptistery was transformed into a tomb as well. Hagia Sophia, which went through repairs during all periods of the Ottoman Empire, was subjected to substantial repair work by the Swiss architect Fossati during the reign of Sultan Abdülmecid. While the building was being repaired, the mosaics inside were also cleaned and brought to light.

During the Republic Period, on November 24, 1934, it was decided that Hagia Sophia should be turned into a museum and it has been open to visits as a museum since 1935.

The fountain which is seen in the yard belongs to the Ottoman period. Located right in front of it is the primary school which was built during the reign of Mahmud I. The remnants beside Hagia Sophia entrance are from the church built during the reign of the Emperor Theodosios.

Three gates lead to the exterior narthex of Hagia Sophia, which is made up of nine sections, and five different gates, which are made from oak and covered by bronze, lead to the interior

Aerial view of Hagia Sophia. As one of the world's largest churches, it has remained intact for almost 1500 years. After Fatih the Conqueror took Istanbul and transformed Hagia Sophia into a mosque, a brick minaret was built in its southeast corner. The two minarets in front of Hagia Sophia were built by Sinan the Architect (Mimar Sinan) during the reign of Murad III (1574-1595). Seen in front of Hagia Sophia are the tombs of the Ottoman Sultans. Built by Architect Sinan, they belong to Selim II, Murad III (1546-1595) and Mehmed III (1595-1603). The Baptistery was transformed into a tomb for Sultans Mustafa I and Ibrahim. The building seen in the very front is the Haseki Hürrem Sultan Bath.

Next page: The interior of Hagia Sophia. The domed basilica-type building consists of a large central nave, flanking naves on the northern and southern sides, and two nartexes on the western side. The 100 m long building measures 79.30 meters from the Imperial Gate to the apse alone.

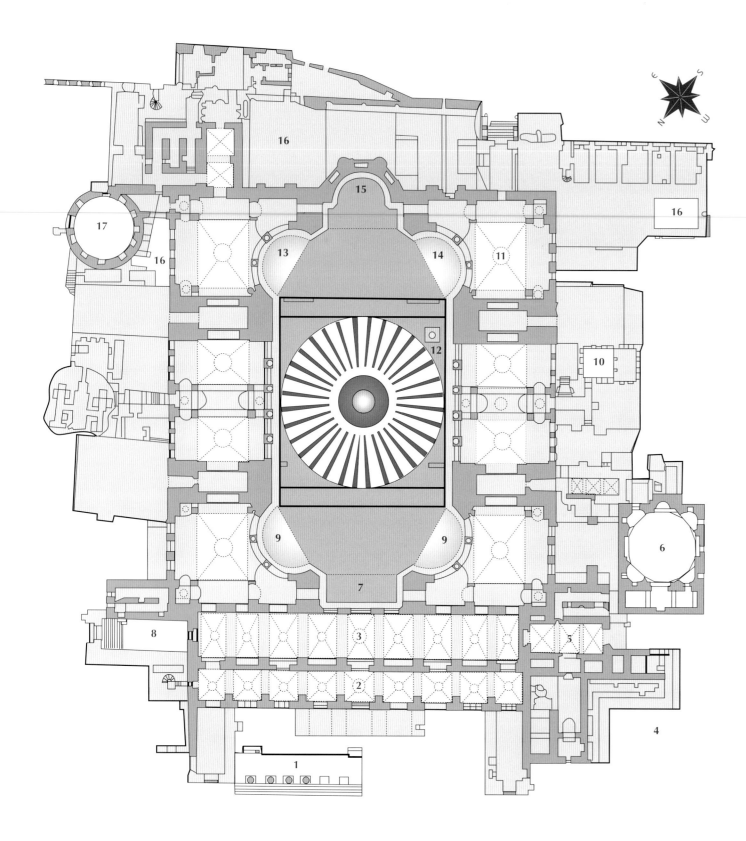

narthex from here. The gate which is to the south of the interior narthex and which serves as the exit of the museum today was brought from a temple in Tarsus in 838 and attached. In this section, on a three-figure mosaic panel on the southern gate of the interior narthex, Mary is depicted in her navy blue dress holding the child Jesus in her lap, against a golden-gilded mosaic background, with monograms stating that she is the mother of God, on both sides of her head. The Emperor Constantinos, who is to the left of Mary, is illustrated as presenting Mary the model of Constantinopolis, which he established. The script beside it says "the great emperor Constantinos among the Saints". Constantinos was depicted with clothing of the 10th Century, when the mosaic was created, rather than his own time. The Emperor Justinianos (527-565), who is to the right of Mary, is illustrated as presenting Mary the model of Hagia Sophia, which he had built. This mosaic was built from 986-994 as commissioned by Basileios II, during the repair of Hagia Sophia.

Hagia Sophia is important for its mosaics as well as in terms of architecture. The upper sections of the marble coatings, the interior of the arches, vaults and domes are decorated with mosaics made from either naturally colored stones or stained glass, as well as mosaics made by applying thin glass on gold leaf. After the building was transformed into a mosque, these mosaics were untouched, and they were covered with daub at the time of Süleyman I.

The main venue of Hagia Sophia is entered through the nine gates from the interior narthex. The bronze-plated gate in the middle of these gates was allocated for emperors, and the mosaic on the gate illustrates the Emperor Leon VI (826-912) as prostrating before Jesus. In the scene on the mosaic, Jesus is sitting on a throne, against golden-gilded mosaic background, and is illustrated as the Pantokrator, the sovereign of the cosmos. He is holding the holy book in one hand, and making a sanctification sign wih the other hand. Seen on his either side are Mary and the chief angel Gabriel within medallions.

Through the gate, the main venue; in other words the Naos-which is covered with a 55 m dome-is reached. The dome, which evolved into its elliptic form after various repairs, measures about 31 m, and is known to have had a cross in the past as well as the mosaic of Jesus since 842. The mosaic of Jesus was distorted in 989, and completely came off in 1346, after which Joannes Palaiologos had the 11 m diameter mosaic of Pantokrator Jesus made within a medallion in 1355.

Four large piers support the dome, and the pendentives formed by the large arches which interconnect the piers provide a transition to the dome. The four large green one-piece columns at each of the northern and southern ends of the central area support the gallery floors, and the 6 green columns in the galleries of the upper floor bear the large arches that bear the dome. Among the 107 columns inside the church, 40 of them are on the lower floor, 67 are in the upper galleries. The capitals of these columns, which had been carried from antique temples, have the monograms of the Emperor Justinianos and his wife Theodora.

Plan of Hagia Sophia.

1.The remains of the previous Hagia Sophia; 2.Exonarthex; 3.Narthex; 4.Fountain; 5.South Gate; 6.Baptistery; 7.Imperial Gate; 8.Gallery Ramps; 9.Marble Urns brought from Pergamon; 10.Library of Mahmud I; 11.Mutatorion; 12.Omphalos; 13.Sultan's Loge; 14.Mimber; 15.Apse-Mihrap (Shrine); 16.Ottoman-era Structures; 17.Treasury

The Imperial Gate.
There is a mosaic of Leon VI on the gate. In the center of this mosaic, which dates to the 920s, Jesus is sitting on a throne and Emperor Leon VI is bowing down in front of him. On the left-hand-side of the medallion that is on the mosaic is the Virgin Mother while on the right is the Archangel Michael. Jesus is making the sign of blessing with his right hand; on his left hand is an inscription that says, "Peace be upon you, I am the light of the world."

From the two angel figures on the bema vault of Hagia Sophia, Gabriel, which is to the right, is in good condition, whereas only the tips of the wings and the feet of Michael, which is to the left, can be seen. On the pendentives which ensure transition to the main dome are four angel figures. Those in the east are original, whereas there is no certain information regarding the ones in the west. There are pathriarch figures on the naves in the northern tympanon, which were created in the 10th Century. The 9th Century mosaic of Mother Mary on the half dome of the apse, which was created after the Iconoclastic period in place of the cross here, is the oldest mosaic of Hagia Sophia and depicts Mary as sitting on a throne and holding the child Jesus.

The path which is to the north of the interior narthex leads to the upper galleries of Hagia Sophia, which are covered with barrel vaults. There is a passage into the southern gallery via a marble gate, beside the priest chambers, which are at the south of the gallery. After passing this gate, which is a replica of a bronze gate, there appears the trio mosaic of Deisis on the right side, illustrating Jesus in the middle, with Mary to his right and John the Baptist to his left. The lower sections of this mosaic have not survived to the present time. In this mosaic, Mary and John the Baptist are interceding with Jesus for people. On this panel, Jesus is illustrated against a golden-gilded background, having a halo with a cross sign around his head. Jesus, who is seen in half body, is making a sanctification sign with his right hand, while holding the holy book in his left hand. A blue cloak is seen on the left shoulder of Jesus. Only the head and the right shoulder of Mary, who is to the right of Jesus, remain. John the Baptist, who is on the left, is illustrated as slightly bending for interceding. At the head level of the figures are the monogram letters of the shortened forms of their names.

On the Comnenos mosaic, which appears slightly ahead of the Deisis mosaic from the 12th Century, Mary is shown as holding the child Jesus in her lap, at the center, with the Emperor Joannes II Comnenos (1118-1143) on one side and the Empress Eirene on the other side. The Emperor was depicted with a dignified expression, in a frontal view. The pouch at the hand of the emperor probably symbolizes the 1000 gold pieces he had given in aid to Hagia Sophia. The empress in her ceremonial outfit is holding a roll. Besides these, the panel where there is also a portrait of their son Alexios Comnenos was created in 1122 and is a realistic example of portrait art. Another well-known mosaic in the upper gallery is the mosaic of Zoe. At the center of the panel is the pantokrator in his navy blue outfit, depicted as sitting on a throne and making a sanctification sign with his right hand while holding the holy book in his left hand. To the left of Jesus is the Empress Zoe standing, and to his right is Constantinos IX Monomachos (1042-1055)-the last husband of the empress. These mosaics belonging to the 9th Century inform us well on Byzantine palace outfits and realistic portrait art.

Located in the northern gallery of Hagia Sophia, on the eastern facade of the two piers is the mosaic commissioned by Alexandros during his one-year reign, who became emperor in 912. On the marble railing plaques by the side of this pier is a carved depiction of a galleon, and on the other marble railing plaques are some carved depictions as well. This world-renowned edifice, which survived since 1500 with its architecture and mosaics, continues to be important today.

The bottom parts of the 12th Century Deesis Mosaic have deteriorated over time.
In the middle of the mosaic, Jesus is depicted, while on the left and right, respectively,
are depictions of Mary and John the Baptist. The facial expressions of all three figures
are immaculate. The face of Jesus, who is holding the Bible in one hand and making
a sign of blessing with the other, is filled with compassion. The expression of
the others, on the other hand, is clearly that of beseeching.

Chora Monastery

The Chora Monastery, which is situated in the Edirnekapı district of Istanbul, holds a very important place in the world of art history, with its past dating back as far as the 6th Century and its mosaics and frescoes which are as precious as jewels.

The structure, which was built as a monastery over a ruined chapel in 536 by the Byzantine Emperor Justinianos I, was seriously damaged by the 'iconoclasts' –the icon opponents– in the 8th Century and today's building was commissioned by Maria Doukaina-Alexios I Comnenos's mother-in-law-over the old remains, with a different architectural style between 1077-1081 and the church of the monastery was dedicated to Jesus. Today the only remnant from the monastery complex is the church section. During the 57 year Latin invasion of Istanbul, which lasted from 1204 to 1261, the monastery suffered damage again and was repaired and given its current appearance from 1315-1321 by Theodoros Metochites, who was the advisor and treasury minister of the Emperor Andronicos II, at the same time being a historian, poet and philosopher. Metochites had some additions made to the building such as an annex building to the north, an exterior narthex to the west and a sepulcher chapel to the south (parecclesion), and had the building decorated with mosaics and frescoes.

In 1328, Andronicos's grandchild, who overthrew him from the throne, sent Metochites –the favorite person of the former emperor– to exile and seized all of his belongings. Having spent two years in exile, Metochites returned to this church, which he had repaired, as a poor monk and was buried in the sepulcher chapel which he himself had built beside the church when he died in 1332. Chora continued to serves as a church for 58 years after the conquest of Istanbul, and was transformed into a mosque by Hadım Atik Ali Pasha –Bayezid II's grandvizier– in 1511. Its mosaics and frescoes were then covered by wood shutters and whitewash, and a minaret was added outside of the building. After the mosque was transformed into a museum, it was restored from 1948-1958 by the American Byzantine Institute, the grout and whitewash covering the mosaics and frescoes were removed and necessary repair work was carried out, thus giving the church its current look.

The building functions as a museum today and comprises an interior and exterior narthex to the west, a chapel to the south as well as a gallery to the north. The floors of the main building and the walls of the interior narthex are covered with marble. The main venue of the building is covered by a large dome at the center and 5 other smaller domes around it.

This section is wholly covered by mosaics and the chapel to the south is ornate with frescoes. The naos, which functions as the main worshiping area in the main building is located at the center of the structure. The eastern extension of the naos is known as the bema or the holy area where the altar table is located. Pastoforium is located on the two sides of the bema. The northern chapel, where the liturgy of gratitude was prepared, is known as the 'prothesis', while the southern chapel, which was used as a changing room was known as the 'diaconicon'. From the 14th Century onwards, the diaconicon functioned as a special chapel. Its two-storey northern annex merges with the naos. The lower floor of this section must likely have been used as a changing room.

The mosaics on the interior and exterior narthexes of Chora entail subjects which can be characterized as following or complementing one another. While the 18 events telling the life cycle of Mary are depicted on the northern wing of the interior narthex with all their beauty, important events of the holy family, Jesus's birth and baptism are depicted on the north of the exterior narthex. Jesus's miracles and his deeds while disclosing the word of God are displayed on the southern wings of both of the narthexes. On top of the mosaics are short scripts and symbols describing that mosaic.

In our plan, the exterior narthex is studied under sections A-B-C-D-E-F. In section A, on the mosaic 1 in the left most, the Journey to Bethlehem is depicted in three scenes. The left of the scene is devoted to Joseph's dream. In his dream, he is annunciated by an angel as to the actual reason of Mary's conception, and in the back are Mary and Zachariah's wife Elizabeth talking, with the actual scene showing Joseph while he was taking Mary from Nazareth to Bethlehem where Jesus was born. The mosaic 2 illustrates the holy family's journey to Jerusalem, and the mosaic 3 has medallions of saints.

On mosaic 4, which is on the dome-like vault and which was greatly damaged, stairs are seen in the north as well as the lower section of Jesus's golden robe which is remarkable. On the second dome-like vault, on the mosaic 5, which depicts John the Baptist bearing witness of Jesus, John the Baptist points at Jesus on one hand, while a heron attacks a snake on the other hand.

On the first arch panel of the eastern wall, mosaic 6 illustrates the scene of census count which was held for tax purposes. What is really intriguing here is the fact that the census collector was depicted in an outfit worn by Byzantine palace officers as sitting on a throne before the Syrian Governor Quirinus. On the arch of this section,

Aerial view of Chora Monastery.

Next page:
Theodore Metochites presents Jesus with a small model of the Chora Monastery Church that he built.

Plan of Chora

A
1. Journey to Bethlehem
2. Holy family's journey to Jerusalem
3. Medallions of the saints
4. Christ among the doctors
5. John the Baptist bearing witness of Christ
6. The census count
7. Medallions of the saints

A-B
8. Anne and Mary
9. St. Andronicus
10. Other saints
11. Tarachus
12. St. Joachim

Tomb G (15th Century)

B
13. Return of the Holy Family from Egypt to Nazareth
14. Medallions of the saints (St. Laurus, St. Flarus, St. Menas of Phrygia, St. Victor, St. Vincentus)
15. Jesus' baptism by John the Baptist
16. Temptation of Christ
17. Birth of Christ
18. Medallions of the saints (St. Philemon, St. Leucius, St. Agathanicus, St. Thyrsus, St. Appollonius)

B-C 19. Mary and Christ Child
20. St. George
21. An unidentified saint

C 22. The Virgin Blachernitissa above the entrance door
23. Christ Pantocrator above the entrance to the inner narthex
24. The Cana miracle (water being turned to wine)
25. Multiplication of the loaves

C-D 26. John the Baptist
27. St. Demetrius
28. An unidentified saint

Tomb F (dated 1330, tomb of a member of a Palaiologos family)

D 29. Flight of Elizabeth and John the Baptist
30. St. Eugraphus, Menas of Alexandria, Hermogenes
31. An unidentified scene
32. Christ healing a leper
33. St. Abius, St. Gurias, St. Samonas
34. The Magi before Herod

D-E 35. An unidentified saint
36. An unidentified saint
37. An unidentified soldier saint

Tomb E Tomb of Irene Raulaina Palaiologos 1325

E 38. St. Sergios or St. Bacchos
39. Mothers' mourning
40. Interrogation of King Herod

41. An unidentified saint

F 42. The Samaritan woman at the well
43. Massacre of the innocent
44. Command for killing of the innocent

45. Christ healing a blind man
46. Healing of a paralytic in Bethseida Pool
47. Healing of a paralytic in Capernaum

F-K 48. St. Euthymius

K 49. Holy Family's flight to Egypt
50. Magi returning to the East
51. An unidentified scene

J 52. An unidentified scene
53. Christ healing a man with the withered hand
54. Christ healing a leper
55. Christ Pantocrator and the ancestors
56. Christ's genealogy 1st Line
57. Christ's genealogy 2nd Line
58. Christ healing a blind and dumb man
59. Christ healing the multitude
60-62-64-67. Medallions of angels
61. Christ healing two blind men
63. Christ healing Peter's mother-in-law
65. Christ Chalkites and Virgin Mary
66. Christ healing the woman with the issue of blood

J-I 68. St. Paul
69. The Virgin fed by an angel
70. Education of the Virgin in the temple

I 71. The Virgin receiving the skein of wool for the temple
72. Presentation of the Virgin to the temple
73. Metochites presenting the model of the church to Jesus

I-H 74. St. Peter
75. First seven steps of Mary
76. Zachariah praying for the rods of the suitors

H 77. Mary's engagement with Joseph
78. Mary's blessing by the priests
79. Mary caressed by her parents
80. Birth of the Virgin

H-G 81. Joachim and Anne meeting at the Golden Gate
82. Joseph taking the Virgin to his House

G 83. Genealogy of Mary
84. Medallions of angels
85. Joseph taking leave of Mary

Tomb H The tomb of despot Demetrius Palaiologos who died in 1340
86. Joachim's offering rejected
87. Annunciation to St. Anne
88. Joachim in wilderness
89. A medallion of an angel
90. Annunciation to Mary at the well
91. Death of the Virgin
92. Christ
93. The Virgin Hodegetria

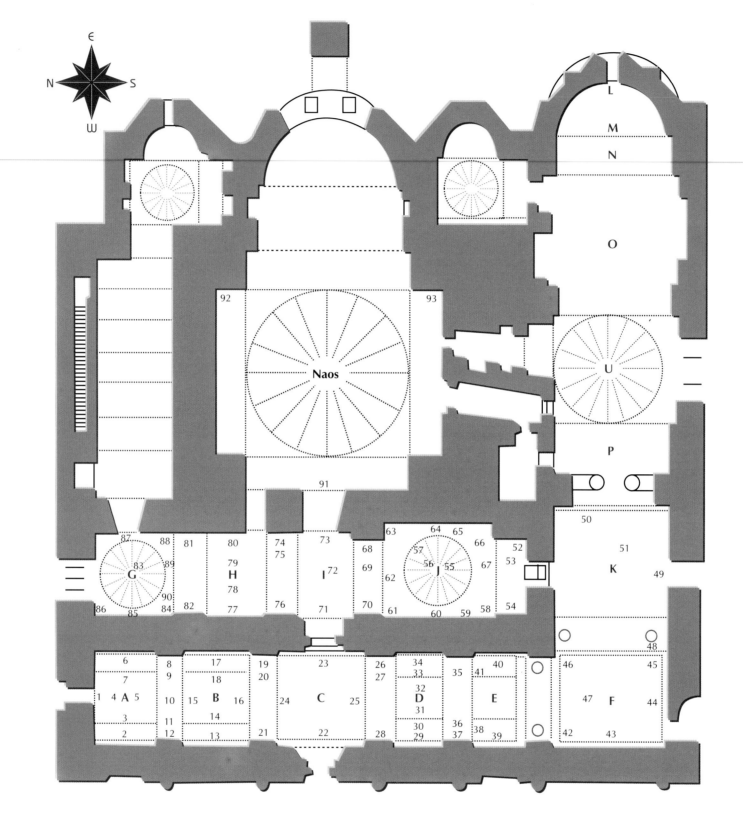

saints are seen in medallions. On the part which connects section A to section B, mosaics 8-12 illustrate Anne and Mary together with saints. In the composition of return to Nazareth in mosaic 13, which is located on the first arch panel, there are two interrelated scenes. In the first one, Joseph is warned by an angel in his dream. In the second one, Joseph is illustrated as carrying the child Jesus on his back. On mosaics 14 and 18, there are depictions of saints in medallions. On the vault of the section B, mosaic 15 has the scene in which John baptizes Jesus. On the southern half of the same vault, mosaic 16 depicts the temptation of Christ with scenes made up of four parts around a medallion. Satan is depicted with wings and a dark face attempting to tempt Jesus. On the second arch panel of this section, the mosaic 17 illustrates Jesus's birth, with Mary lying on the bed and Jesus washed by the midwives to the left. Joseph is shown as contemplating on the other side, with angels described above while informing the shepherds of the birth. On the section BC, mosaic 19 has depictions of Mary and the child Jesus while mosaics 20-21 have saints.

When section C is arrived at, there is mosaic 22 over the entrance gate to the museum depicting Virgin Blachernitissa, with angels worshipping on both sides. Mary is illustrated as praying in the middle, with Jesus in her womb, and a depiction of an angel on each of her two sides. The epitaph on the panel reads "the mother of God, the place of the one who does not fit anywhere". Opposite this panel, above the entrance gate into the interior narthex, the mosaic showing Christ Pantocrator is marked as 23. On this panel, Jesus is holding the Bible, which is adorned with precious stones, in his left hand, while making a sanctification sign with his right hand. Around his head are the letters IC-XC, which are his Christogram.

Above the mosaic of Mary, at a corner of the vault, there is the scene of water turning into wine, which is one of Jesus's miracles. Jesus, Mary and Peter are shown on this mosaic 24 at the wedding at Cana, during which the wine ran out and Jesus transformed water into wine. This mosaic on the vault depicts the workers as filling a large jug with water, and the host as extending the wineglass to Jesus without knowing about the miracle. The mosaic 25, which is on the southern half of the same vault, illustrates the scene of multiplication of the holy bread. Here, Jesus consecrates five loaves of bread and gives them to two of his disciples after splitting them into pieces, to be distributed to the crowd. The pieces remaining from the feast fill 12 baskets.

The mosaics 26 and 27 on the arch between the sections C and D show John the Baptist and St. Demetrios. Mosaic 28, which is again at the same place, indicates the grave of an unidentified saint. In the section D, the mosaic 41 which is to the right at the entrance, Elizabeth and John are illustrated as escaping from the soldier chasing them with a sword in hand. The Mosaic 30 has saints, and 31 has an unidentified scene. The mosaic 32 illustrates Jesus while healing a leper, with only the lower parts of Jesus's body being visible as standing across the leper with spotted legs. The mosaic 33 has saints, and the

'Christ Pantocrator' mosaic above the door leading to the inner narthex .
A view from the inner narthex.

mosaic 34 has three magi before the King Herod. This mosaic shows the magi from the east as reporting the birth of Jesus to the king and that he would dethrone him. In return, the king says, "Go and find that child, so that I can prostrate before him". However, he was not sincere.

Section DE, 35-36 shows unidentified saints and 37 shows the grave of an unidentified soldier who was at the same time a saint. In section E, to the right on the arch, mosaic 38 has either St. Sergios or Bacchos. In the scene of 'mothers' mourning for their children' on the mosaic 39, which is located on the wall side of the arch, the agony of the women embracing their murdered children are read from their faces. From the scene of the 'King Herod's interrogation' on the mosaic 40, only himself and one of his guards remain. Here, Herod is interrogating in order to find out about the new-born king of the Jews. The mosaic 41 depicts an unknown saint.

The dome-like vault located at the south west corner of the building is marked as F; the arch panels have Jesus's childhood, and the vaults have scenes from Jesus's sermons and saints are illustrated on the arches. The scene of 'Jesus at the well and the Samaritan women', which is to the right of the entrance in this section, is shown as 42; however, Jesus's depiction has been deformed. On the scene 44, the three oracles dispatched to Bethlehem by the king to find Jesus are shown as finding Jesus but they are being told in their dream to return where the king is. Accordingly, the oracles return to their country without informing the king. The King orders that all of the children up to two years of age in Bethlehem and the neighborhood be murdered. The complementary scenes signified as 43 'massacre of the innocent' show soldiers taking little children from their mothers and putting them to the sword. Located on the south western pendentive is the scene where Jesus is healing a blind man, which is marked as 45.

At the south western corner of the vault, the scene showing Jesus healing the paralytic in Capernaum is marked as 47. Jesus is seen here addressing the paralytic, who is lying in a rich bed with his four bearers. Not many mosaics remain in section K. Mosaic 48 at the passage has a saint, mosaic 49 on the southern wall, in a distorted form, has the holy family's flight to Egypt, mosaic 50 has the return of the magi to the east and 51 has an unidentified scene. A door leads from this section into the interior narthex.

The inner narthex, which is best preserved with its paving, wall and vault coatings, provide scenes from the life of Mary and Jesus in a sequential order. The three sections here tell the stories of Mary. On both sides of the entry into the naos are depictions of St. Peter and St. Paul within frames. St. Paul, which is to the right, is illustrated wearing a blue tunic, and St. Peter, which is to the left, is illustrated as holding in his right hand the roll of letters he

The Anastasis (Harrowing of Hell) Fresco is found on the apse of the Chora Monastery Church parecclesion. It shows Jesus descending into Hell to save the sinners. An impressive look of the Anastasis fresco. Here Jesus is shown descended to Hell to raise Adam and Eve from their sarcophagi

wrote and in his left hand the key of the heaven. Seen above the gate which ensures a passage into the main venue is Jesus on a throne and a person who is making a donation. Here, Theodore Metochites is kneeling down and presenting the model of the church to Jesus depicted in a seated position. On the dome of the first section in the inner narthex, the mosaic 83 has Mary at the center as holding the child Jesus in her lap, surrounded by her lineage described in 16 parts. Also in this section are the scenes such as the good news to St. Anne, Joseph taking leave of Mary, the goods news of the angel to Mary at the well. In the second and third sections are scenes depicting the birth of Mary, her first seven steps, her presentation to the temple, and her engagement with Joseph.

On mosaics 55, 56, 57, which are inside the dome within the narthex, Jesus is depicted at the center, with 24 of his first line of ancestors from Adam to Jacob shown around him, and 15 children of Jacob illustrated below that as the second line. On the pendentive of the dome, which is marked as 61, is the scene of Jesus healing the two blind men, and on 58 is the scene of him healing a blind and mute person. Jesus is shown pointing at the two blind men, together with the two of his apostles. Also in here are such miracles as the healing of the woman with the issue of blood and Jesus healing the mother in law of the apostle Peter.

The scene of Deisis (Christ Chalkites), which is inside an arch located towards the naos side of the dome depicting Jesus and his lineage, Mary is shown in profile and Jesus with a frontal view; however their lower sections were lost. Under Mary, who is engaged in prayer, Isaacios Comnenos is seen as kneeled down. Isaacios-the youngest son of Alexios Comnenos-had the eastern part of the church repaired, which is probably why he was depicted here. Beside Jesus is Melane. Maria, who was the daughter of Michael Palaiologos, was sent as bride to the Mongolians and returned later on and became a nun taking the name Melane. She must have been placed in this panel due to her services.

In the naos, where only few mosaics could be preserved, the scene of Mary's death located right above the entrance, Mary is laid on the coffin, surrounded by the apostles and the other mourners and with the figure of Jesus behind, who is coming down from the sky with a halo of light to carry her soul to the heaven. This mosaic is marked as 91. On the southern pier of the apse, on the panel shown as 92, Jesus is standing and holding an open bible in his left hand. Mosaic 93 depicts Mary and the child Jesus. Both are within a frame and highly damaged.

The paracclesion, which is one of the most successful works of the architecture of the Palaiologoses, is divided into two square sections, limited with an apse on the east and covered by a high dome with windows and a lower vault. As in the narthexes, the subjects in the paracclesion too belong to Mary and Jesus.

The walls of the chapel are full of figures of saints in a standing position, and arched tombs or niches were placed in between. The domed western section was devoted to Mary, and the eastern section to the Last Judgment. From the main venue, to reach this section, which extends alongside the church, one would need to pass through a narrow passage between two columns. In this section, which was built as a sepulcher chapel, there are a

total of 4 tombs with the Meochites's tomb located at the left end. The other two tombs are inside a niche on the southern wall of the paracclesion and they belong to Michael Tornikes, a rich Byzantine notable, and his wife Eugene. In the paracclesion, subjects related to the doomsday are illustrated in the form of frescoes.

The most remarkable fresco of this section is the magnificent fresco of Anastasis (resurrection) located on the half dome of the apse. At the center of the panel is Jesus in his white clothes, releasing people from the hell who lived before his time and were not baptized. He is holding Adam with his right hand, and Eve with his left hand, and taking them out of their tombs and resurrecting them.

Beneath the feet of Jesus is Satan tied from his arms and hell is seen with its gates wide open. There are apostles to the right and left of Jesus. John the Baptist, who is to the left above Adam, is pointing at Jesus with his hand. Near him are Solomon, David and the others engaged in prayer. To the right is Abel, Adam and Eve's son, holding a shepherd's crook standing over the sarcophagus of Eve. There are five other men behind him. Below the fresco of Anastasis are the illustrations of 6 church fathers.

Two of Jesus's miracles are given in the bema section on the side wall of the apse. On the southern wall of the apse is a fresco of Mary affectionately holding the child Jesus. Behind that is the depiction of St. George. The scene of Last Judgment, which decorates the vault just above Anastasis, is one of the most crowded scenes of Byzantine art after Anastasis. Right at the center of the panel is Jesus seen as sitting on a throne. Mary, to the left, and John the Baptist to the right, are asking Jesus for intercession for humanity. On both sides are the twelve apostles sitting on the benches. Above them is the snail carried by an angel, symbolizing the universe. At the bottom are Adam and Eve seen as kneeled down on both sides of the throne.

To the right of the vault are the sinners burning in the hell. In the other sections are groups of depictions such as the Chorus of the Chosen, the rich man burning in the hell and other figures. To the left are the figure of St. Peter accompanying the chosen on their way to the heaven, and then the angel depiction, and the depiction of the good thief as half naked, with a cross in his hand, and the figure of Mary sitting among the trees and angels in the heaven. Furthermore, on the pendentive are the figure of the rich man and the fresco of the beggar Lazarus opposite it. To the west of the vault are two flying angels, blowing into a pipe, as well as angle and child figures.

On the dome of the paracclesion is Mary within a medallion, holding the child Jesus in his gilded clothing, 12 angel figures with shiny clothing on the dome segments, and four Bible writers in sitting position on the pendentives. Beneath the dome, on the walls and arches are the staircase of Jacob, Jacob dreaming underneath, Mary and the child Jesus at the top. The scene of Moses among the burning bushes and just beyond that, the continuation of the carriage of the Ark of the Covenant. To the left of the window with three openings, the Prophet Solomon and the Israeli people are seen, whereas to the right are scenes such as the conflict of an angel and the Assyrians near Jerusalem. Frescoes of the combatants are also seen here.

Ottoman Period in
Istanbul

Ottoman Period in Istanbul

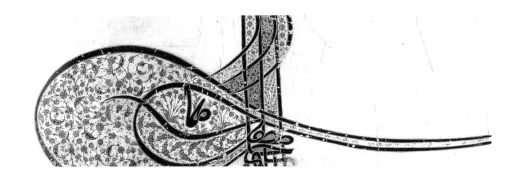

Following the Malazgirt War on August 26, 1071, which opened the gates of Anatolia to the Turks, the Seljuks directed their conquests towards the west and established the Anatolian Seljuk State in 1075 making Iznik (Nicaea) the capital. The Kayi tribe of the Oguz Turks, which was led by Ertuğrul Bey, was forced to migrate from their homeland due to oppression from the Mongolians and settled in the Karacadağ neighborhood to the west of Ankara. Around the mid 13th Century, they were sent to Söğüt, which was located near the border with Byzantion, and the Seljuk sultan assigned the leader of Kayi the task of protecting and expanding the border against Byzantion. Thus Ertuğrul Bey, the marcher lord of the Anatolian Seljuk State, made Söğüt the tribe's home. After his death, his son Osman Bey took on the leadership, expanding his territories taking advantage of the riots, chaos and battles for the throne in the Byzantine Empire. Convinced that he had gained enough power, he declared his sovereignty and established the Ottoman Principality in 1299, which is accepted as the establishment date of the Ottoman Empire. After Osman Bey, his son Orhan Bey took Bursa and made it the capital of the Ottomans. Orhan Bey extended the borders of the principality as far as Rumeli (European territories of the Ottomans) and when he died, Murad I assumed leadership and began to make his presence exhaustively felt in the European territories.

Around the end of the 1300's, the Ottomans passed the Dardanelles (Çanakkale) and made Edirne the capital, and thus the Turks became the inhabitants of Europe. Yıldırım Bayezid, who took over the Ottoman throne after Murad I, was defeated by Timur. Later, Çelebi Mehmed had to re-establish the state. Afterward, his talented and brave son Murad II took on the leadership in succession of his father. During his term, the Ottomans began to ride their horses over European soil again for 30 years. Byzantion still continued to exist in Istanbul in this period. In 1432, Mehmed, the fourth son of Murad II, was born. This child, who was to be awarded the title of Mehmed the Conqueror in the future, had barely completed ten years of age when he was appointed the governor of Manisa. Shehzade (Crown Prince) Mehmed was lectured by decent teachers, while at the same time growing up to be molded as part of the governmental affairs. When he definitively mounted the Ottoman throne after his father's death, he was only 19. However, when his father was still alive, he had temporarily ascended to the throne twice and had a first-hand experience with the problems of the state, which matured him and provided him with enough background knowledge to help solve many issues including Byzantion.

Sultan Mehmed ended the problems in Anatolia which had been caused by the principality of Karamanoğulları for many years, and afterwards, began the preparations in Edirne for taking Byzantion. Around this time, religious discrimination and poverty prevailed in Byzantion. Byzantion was engaged in the controversies concerning the merger of the eastern and western churches; the public were opposed to such a merger. Among the opponents of this idea were Lucas Notaras, who was the highest ranking person after the emperor, and Gennadios Scholarios, whom Sultan Mehmed later appointed as the patriarche. Notaras said "I would rather see the Muslim turban in the midst of the city than the Latin miter." While Byzantion was immersed in its internal problems, the Ottoman ruler first had the Rumelian Fortress (Rumeli Hisarı) built to control the straits, across the Anatolian Fortress (Anadolu Hisarı) which was commissioned by Yıldırım Bayezid. This would ensure the control of the straits and serve as a precaution against the likely aid which could arrive via the sea. Urban –a Hungarian cannon maker who had escaped Byzantion and taken refuge in the Ottomans– was assigned to the task of casting cannons that could demolish the Byzantine Walls which proved to be insurmountable over the 1000 years. In addition to these cannons, which were known as Sahi, the production of wheeled towers and mortars were among the other preparations. These massive cannons played an important role in the conquest of Istanbul.

After the preparations were completed, Sultan Mehmed sent an envoy to the Byzantine Emperor Constantine and demanded that the city be submitted without any blood shed. However, upon the message from the emperor that they were ready to make war, the Ottoman army came before the land walls of Istanbul and commenced the besiege on April 6, 1453. The Ottoman army made up of 150-200 thousand people and the artilleries were placed against the land walls, which streched from Ayvansaray on the Golden Horn coast all the way to the Golden Gate on the Marmara Sea coast. Sultan Mehmed sent envoys to the emperor one last time, calling him to submit the city. When this was rejected, the artilleries began to hit the walls with sounds unheard of until then. Very tough battles were being fought and the Byzantines were immediately repairing the damaged parts of the walls which protected the city. Venetians and Genovesians too were helping Byzantion with their fleets. The Sultan had the opinion that the Ottoman navy was not sufficiently used during the besiege and that this was the reason why the siege prolonged, so he made that important decision to facilitate the conquest of Istanbul. Some of the vessels in the Ottoman navy would be tugged via the land and

Previous page:
General view of the Süleymaniye Mosque, which Architect Sinan referred to as a work from his Assistant-Master period.

A portrait of Sultan Mehmed the Conqueror.
Painted by Gentile Bellini in 1480.
The National Gallery-London.

would be launched into the Golden Horn waters where the walls were weak. Slipways were installed over a route starting at the shore before Tophane (cannon foundry) and leading all the way to Kasımpaşa. In order for the vessels to be slided over the slipways, olive oil, clarified butter and lard oil were bought from the Genovesians in Galata, and the slipways were greased. On the night of April 21-22, the vessels were launched into the Golden Horn via the adapted road. The artilleries belonging to the Turkish navy in the Golden Horn began to shoot the walls. Serious combat continued in the following days as well. Finally, after a besiege of 53 days and four big assaults, Constantinopolis-the capital of the Eastern Roman Empire for 1125 years-was conquered on Tuesday May 29,1453.

The first thing Sultan Mehmed the Conqueror did after taking Istanbul and thus terminating one of the most important states of the history –the Eastern Roman Empire– was to go to Hagia Sophia. The people who had gathered there and the Patriarche bowed to greet him, Sultan Mehmed said to the Patriarche, "Incline not, for I tell you and your friends and the rest of the people that from this day onwards, you shall have no fear from me the Sultan Mehmed, concerning neither your lives nor your freedom". Later, Sultan Mehmed turned Hagia Sophia into a mosque and performed the first Friday salat (prayer) there. The restructuring of the city began; masters brought from all corners of the country-which had then become an empire. Mehmed the Conqueror brought families from Anatolia and Rumeli (European territories of the Ottomans) in an effort to increase the population of Istanbul. Meanwhile, he had a palace constructed in the Bayezid (also spelled Beyazıt) Square. When this palace proved to be too small, he initiated the construction of today's Topkapı Palace in 1465. At the same time, he was having the Fatih Mosque Complex (Fatih Külliyesi) built over the Church of the Holy Apostles (Havariyun Church) in the district of Fatih. Grand viziers and pashas were also working alongside the sultan in the reconstruction of Istanbul. The Grandvizier Mahmud Pasha was having a mosque complex (külliye) built in the marketplace made up of buildings such as a mosque, bath and tomb in 1462, Murad Pasha was having a complex built in Aksaray, and Rum (Greek) Mehmed Pasha was having a complex built in Üsküdar. This new capital of the Ottomans was being rearranged in accordance with the Islamic customs and traditions; religious buildings were being constructed on one hand and marketplaces were being established for the development of trade in the city on the other hand. Within a short time following the conquest, buildings such as mosques, madrasahs (theological schools), baths and tombs left Turkish mark on Istanbul.

After taking the whole of Anatolia and Crimea, Mehmed the Conqueror fell sick during the preparations of his campaign to Italy and passed away at the age of 49 in 1481. He was buried in his tomb located in the Fatih Complex, which he had built himself. Upon his death, his son Bayezid II ascended to the Ottoman throne. Having a calm nature unlike his father, Bayezid II was a poet and was devoutly religious. During his reign, the practice of Ottoman sultans marrying the daughters of the principalities or kings was stopped; instead, a harem was established for the education of concubines, who were to

A detail of Shehzade (Crown Prince) Mustafa's caftan.

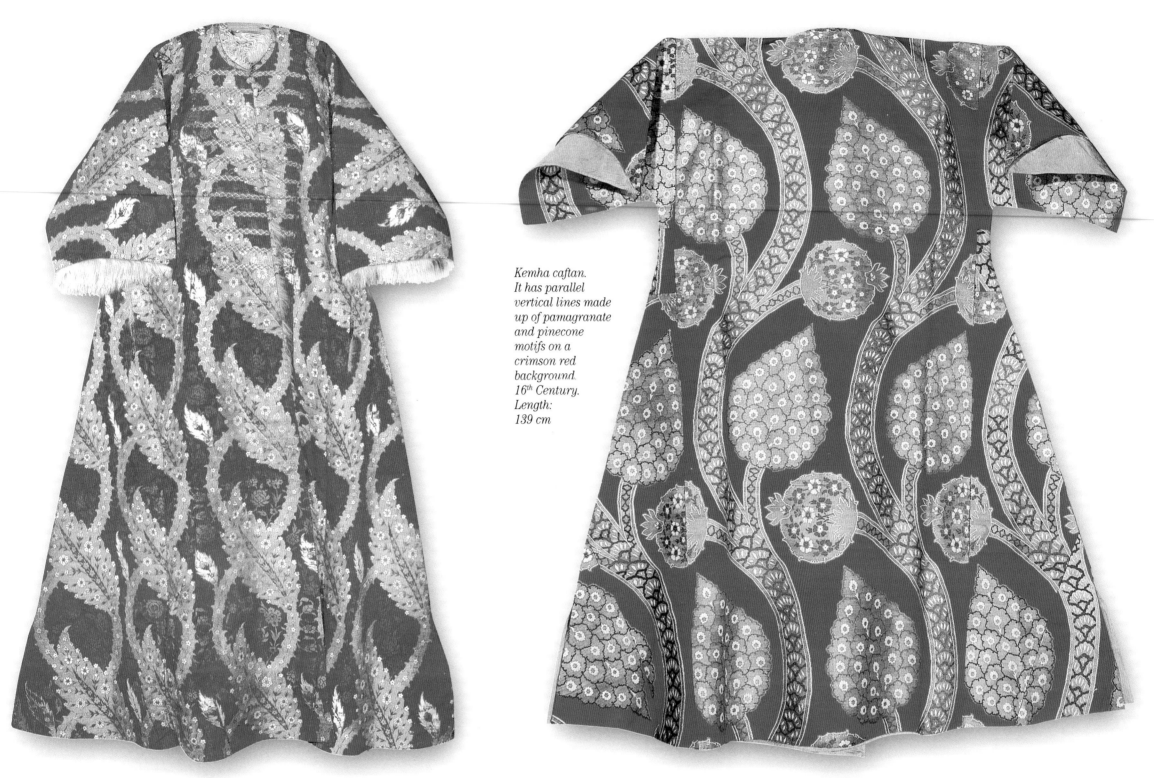

Kemha caftan. It has parallel vertical lines made up of pamagranate and pinecone motifs on a crimson red background. 16th Century. Length: 139 cm

A fur-lined brocade caftan belonging to Bayezid II (second half of the 16th Century). The collarless caftan, which was made with high-quality brocade, has pockets and slit on both sides. The design on the fabric consists of vertical, curling branches that intersect one another, against a ruby background.

become sultan's wife. The most important act of humanity during Bayezid II's reign was that he saved the Muslims and Jews in Andalucia from Spanish oppression. In 1492, Muslims as well as around 150,000 Jews were settled in the Ottoman territories. During the reign of Bayezid II, Istanbul suffered the most severe earthquake in Ottoman history on September 14, 1509. During this earthquake, which was known as the Little Doomsday (Kıyamet-i Suğra), 109 mosques and masjids as well as 1070 homes in Istanbul became unusable, while approximately 5000 people lost their lives. The old water dikes were also demolished. For the reconstruction of Istanbul, a person from every twenty household and twenty two coins per household were collected. Thus, 37,000 paid workers from Anatolia and 29,000 from the European territories were gathered, around 3,000 architects and carpenters were brought, and the reconstruction activities were completed in 65 days. This construction and repair work also covered the city walls of Istanbul as well as some important places such as the dungeons in Galata, the Galata Tower (Galata Kulesi), the Maiden's Tower (Kız Kulesi), the Rumelian and Anatolian Fortresses and Lighthouses, Çekmece bridges and the Silivri Castle (Silivri Kalesi). Through the efforst of Sultan Bayezid II, Istanbul was nearly reconstructed as a whole

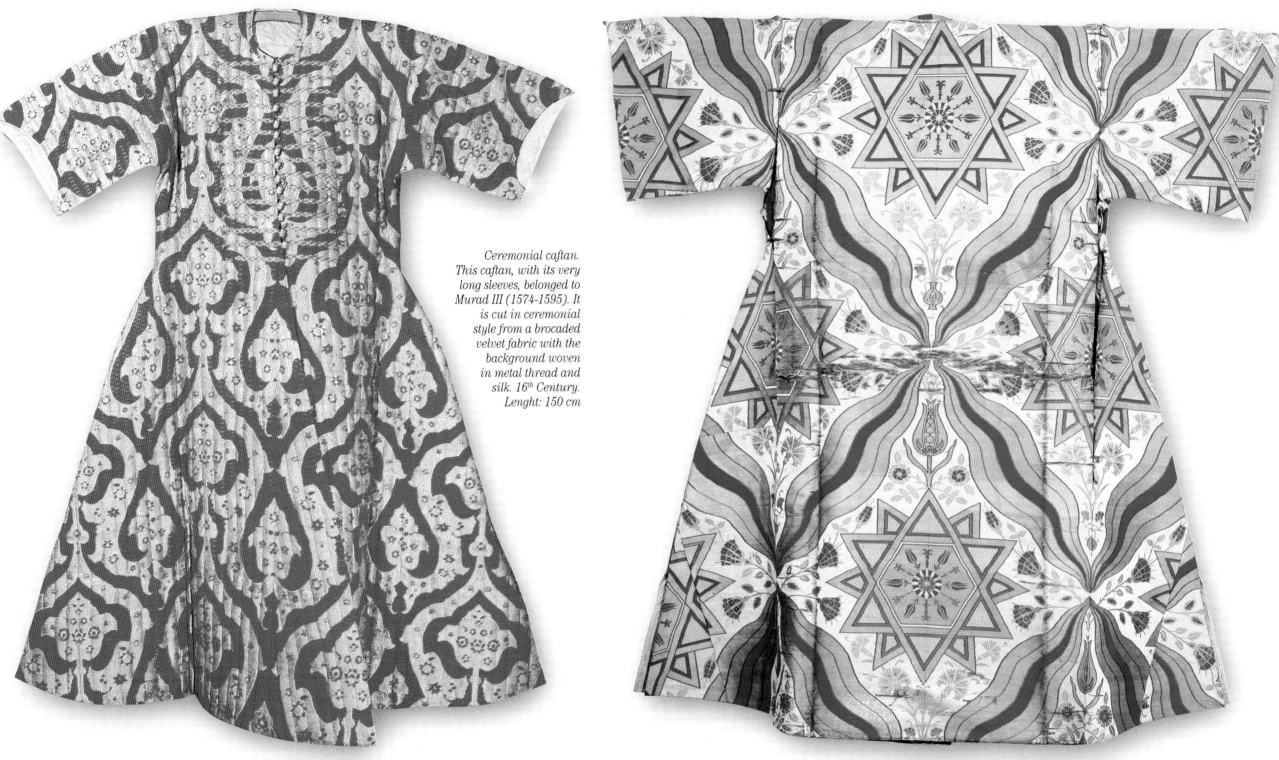

Ceremonial caftan. This caftan, with its very long sleeves, belonged to Murad III (1574-1595). It is cut in ceremonial style from a brocaded velvet fabric with the background woven in metal thread and silk. 16th Century. Lenght: 150 cm

Caftan with star pattern; blue, cream, and red silk and gold; compound satin with supplemental twill (kemha); dark red silk lining bordered with yellow silk. Mid 16th Century. Lenght: 141 cm

within a short time. The construction was wholly supervised by the Architect Hayreddin. After the completion of the construction, food was distributed to the poor for three days and nights upon the command of the sultan.

As Sultan Bayezid II was leaving the throne to his youngest son Selim due to the battles for the throne among the princes and the pressure from the the Janissaries (derived from the Turkish word yeniçeri, meaning "new soldier"), he counseled his son "Do not depart from justice, be merciful to the weak and helpless. Show affection to the destitute, and if you want everyone to submit to you, then you should utterly respect the ulema

(theologians), and be not harsh to anyone unless necessary." He passed away on his way to Didymoteicho and his corpse was buried in his tomb located at the Bayezid Mosque. Selim I (also known as Sultan Yavuz Selim or Selim the Grim) ascended to the Ottoman throne in 1512 at the age of 42 and fit great accomplishments in his short-lived regency. At the end of Selim's Campaign to Egypt, the Muslim holy lands were passed to the control of the Ottomans. The items known as the Holy Relics, which are located in the Topkapı Palace today and which include the cardigan, tooth, flag and sword of the Prophet Muhammed, were sent to Sultan Yavuz Selim on July 6, 1517 from Hedjaz. Thus

on August 29, 1516, the caliphate passed from the Abbasid dynasty to the Ottoman dynasty. During his eight-year short regency, Sultan Yavuz Selim was constantly on horse back and enlarged the territories of the empire by 2.5. He also filled the empty treasury he took over from his dad to full capacity. He sealed the gate of the treasury and said this in his will: "Whoever among my grandchildren can fill up the treasury with gold, as I did, shall seal it with his own seal, otherwise the Imperial Treasury (Hazine-i Hümayun) shall be sealed with my seal. This will was respected and after that date, none of the sultans managed to fill up the treasury and thus the gate of the treasury was sealed with the seal of Sultan Yavuz until the bankruptcy of the Ottomans after 400 years. Sultan Yavuz Selim increased the capacity of the Golden Horn Shipyard, which was used during the time of his grandfather Mehmed the Conqueror. He laid the groundwork of the Sultan Selim Mosque (Sultan Selim Camii) but did not live long enough to finish it. This building was completed by his son Süleyman I. Sultan Yavuz Selim died in 1520 and his tomb is located in the Sultan Selim Mosque. Sultan Süleyman, who is known among the Turks as Süleyman the Lawmaker whereas among the foreigners as Süleyman the Magnificent, was the only son of Yavuz and received an excellent education. Even though he ascended to the throne at the age of 25, he led the state affairs with a great success. It is accepted that the Ottoman Empire led its brightest period during the 46-year regency of Sultan Süleyman. Süleyman was inspired by the vision of Alexander the Great to establish a world-wide empire, and this led him to launch campaigns to Asia and Africa as well as Europe. Sultan Süleyman, who was very strict about justice and fairness, would not tolerate the slightest action that would threaten the state. He prepared a new code book taking the code book of Mehmed the Conqueror as the basis, and thus came to be known as Süleyman the Lawmaker. It was during his time that Ottomans established close relations with the western states. Especially, the trade agreements known as the capitulations were signed with France, which were to lead to the devastation of the Ottoman economy in the following years.

Süleyman the Magnificent left his mark on the era by launching campaigns to the east as well. It was during his time that the territories stretched as far as Asia, Africa and Europe and the size of the empire reached 17 Million km². During this time, works created by the scientists and artist educated in law, mathematics, architecture and miniatures took their places as the masterpieces of the Turkish cultural history. Süleyman the Magnificent's much beloved wife Hürrem had a poetic heart like himself. During his campaigns when the two would be apart, Hürrem's poems would console him and re-enliven him. Later on, Sultan Süleyman was totally devastated by the loss of his sons Mehmed, Mustafa and Cihangir and died on September 6, 1566 during his campaigns to Zigetvar (Szigetvár) at the age of 72, in an exhausted condition. The corpse of the Ottoman sultan was brought to Istanbul and was buried at the Süleymaniye Mosque, which he had commissioned by the Architect Sinan. His wife Hürrem Sultan is

Presentation of gifts to Süleyman the Magnificent on the occasion of the circumcision of his sons Bayazid and Cihangir in 1530. Arifi. Süleymanname. Dated 1558 Topkapı Palace Museum Library.

A miniature showing the accession to the throne of Sultan Selim II held in the ceremonial tent in Belgrad in 1568. Nakkaş Osman, Nüzhet el Esrar el Ehbar der Sefer-i Zigetvar.

buried beside him. In his lifetime, Sultan Süleyman had the Shehzade Mosque (Şehzade Camii) built for his son Mehmed and had him buried in a tomb located within the mosque complex. Thus the era of Süleyman the Magnificent came to an end and the only remaining heir Selim II ascended to the throne. During his eight-year tenure, the state was administered by the Grand Vizier Sokullu Mehmed Pasha. Selim II had a calmer nature compared to his father Süleyman; he held a peaceful administration, without launching any campaign. Sultan Selim II wrote poetry with the pen name Selimi. When he died in 1574, he was buried in his tomb, which was built by the Architect Sinan in the yard of Hagia Sophia. He was succeeded by his son Murad III, after whom the Ottoman throne was ascended by his son Mehmed III in 1595. During the period of Mehmed III, who remained on the throne until 1603, the Celali Revolts broke out in Anatolia, continuing for 17 years with intervals and weakening the social order and economy of the state to a great extent. It was the end of the magnificent period of the Ottomans and thus the stagnation years began in the 16ᵗʰ Century. There were diverse reasons why the course of events deteriorated in the Ottoman Empire. After the period of Süleyman the Magnificent, the sultans began to send their grand viziers to expeditions in place of themselves and they were appointing the top government positions not to those who had merits but those who managed to win favor through various methods. The sultan's mother as well as the eunuchs in the sultan's harem became involved in these appointments. The weakened state authority brought about internal revolts and these revolts resulted in big loses as well as social collapse. The princes were no longer being sent to provinces as governors; instead, they lived in the harem. As a result, without much knowledge about the state administration and the public, the sultans ascending to the throne proved to be incapable in administering the state. In addition to the

administrative insufficiency, the shrinking revenues of the Ottoman state too were one of the important reasons of the downfall. Since the geographical discoveries decreased the importance of the trade routes passing through the Ottoman territories, the customs duties were no longer pouring in. Because no new conquests were made, there were no longer booty revenues either. Furthermore, the capitulations which were awarded to France during Süleyman the Magnificent for aid, now became exploitative and began to serve as the greatest factor weakening the Ottoman economy. As the economy thus weakened, the military became inclined to deteriorate. There was lack of training and discipline in the army, the Janissaries began to rise in insurrection constantly on grounds of subsistence hardships. Given all this, winning another victory was becoming only a dream.

In Europe, on the other hand, great scientific and technical developments were taking place. As a natural outcome of this, the Ottomans began to lag behind Europe. This lag, which was not very important at the beginning, was growing more and more, causing the gap to widen. This period had started with Mehmed III. When he died in 1603, he was replaced his son Ahmed I, during whose term the Sultanahmet Mosque (Blue Mosque)-one of the spectacular works of art in Istanbul-was built. Sultan Ahmed I died at a very young age and was succeeded by Mustafa I, whose health was not in good condition. Due to his poor health, he was replaced by Ahmed I's son Young Osman (Genç Osman in Turkish). The reason why he was called Young Osman was that he was only 14. This sultan wanted to bring the corrupt ways to an end, but the intrigues of those whose interests were harmed as well as of Kösem Sultan-a famous one among the mothers of the sultans-caused him to be executed. He was replaced by Murad IV (the 11-year old son of Kösem Sultan) in 1623. Now the administration of the state was Kösem Sultan's area of expertise, which continued until Murad IV reached 20 years of age. Because Murad IV died early, Kösem Sultan retained the state administration also during the period of İbrahim (her other son). Due to the inconsistent behavior of the new sultan, Mehmed IV, who was six years old, was given the throne. Kösem Sultan wanted to continue administrating the state during this child-aged sultan as well, which brought her into a big conflict with the mother of the sultan, Hatice Turhan Sultan. Eventually Kösem Sultan was asphyxiated to death. A very intelligent woman, Hatice Turhan Sultan appointed Köprülü Mehmed Pasha as grand vizier and ended the regency of the women in the state administration. Mehmed IV, who died in Edirne while hunting in 1687, was succeeded on the throne respectively by Süleyman II, Ahmed II and Mustafa II. When the third campaign in the Ottoman history to Austria during the period of Mustafa II ended in a fiasco; the Ottomans lost a large part of their territories in Europe with the Treaty of Karlofça (Karlowitz) signed in 1699. This treaty became the end of the Period of Stagnation and the beginning of the Period of Decline in the Ottomans. During the Period of

Decline, which lasted about 150 years, Europe gradually made progress widening the gap with the Ottomans, while the latter became weaker and weaker in contrast to the development of Europe. In the Tulip Era (Lale Devri), which was during the reign of Ahmed III from 1718-1730, the Ottomans experienced peaceful years. With the reigning Ahmed III and his grand vizier Nevşehirli Damat İbrahim Pasha, Istanbul began to lead a tranquil and comfortable life. This enlivened the entertainment and art life in the city. While this new life style led to discontent in some segments of society, efforts by the French military experts to apply their new military training methods in the army were also met with great enmity from the Janissaries. This is because the Janissaries had completely moved away from military spirit and engaged in trade. The defeat on the Iranian front was taken as a pretext by the opportunists and the rebellions began before long. Patrona Halil-a bath masseur-raised a rebellion together with the flosam and jetsam people he gathered around himself. He then opened up the jails, winning the inmates over to his side. The rebellion became widespread within a short time and some of the Janissaries joined with this band of looters as well. The outcome was many beheaded statesmen and the dethronement of Ahmed III, who was replaced by his nephew Mahmud I. Now the rebels were at every level of the state. The fact that civil service jobs were now being sold in return for bribes, and the despots took whichever decision they wanted during the Imperial Council (Divan-ı Hümayun) meetings raised public abhorrence against them.

Mahmud I, who was a far-sighted and intelligent ruler, took hold of the state administration in time. He managed to win the favor of public because he suppressed the rebels and skillfully ruled the state. He was raised with a decent education and was at the same time a poet and composer. During Mahmud I, Austria was defeated, Belgrade was taken back, and Serbia and Walachia (historical region in Romania known as Eflak in Turkish) was liberated from invaders. A treaty was signed with Iran to ward off the aspirations of Nadir Shah over the Ottoman territories. Mahmud I had many libraries established, the main one being the Hagia Sophia Library. He assigned an Armenian architect named Simon Kalfa to the construction of a European-style mosque, which later came to be known as the Nuruosmaniye Mosque; however this assignment aroused reactions and thus the project was dispensed with. Among his edifices are the Arap İskelesi Mosque in Beşiktaş, the Iskele Mosque in the neighborhood of Rumeli Hisarı (Rumelian Fortress) and Yıldıztepe Masjids. His period represents the last glorious days of the Ottomans. Suceeding to the throne after Mahmud I respectively were Osman III, Mustafa III and later Abdülhamid I. During these sultans too, the Russo-Turkish war as well as the war with Austria continued. Following the defeat inflicted by the Russians, Sultan Abdülhamid I had a stroke in1789 and died after a while. Selim III, who took the throne after Abdülhamid I, was sensitive towards art by his nature. Selim, who ascended to the throne at a time when the French Revolution

broke out and when the Ottoman State was at war with both Austria and Russia, was a well-educated ruler who believed that that drastic changes needed to be made in the country. For the first time in 1797, during the period of Selim III, a group from Europe performed an opera in Istanbul. Antoine Ignace Melling, French architect and artist, constructed many buildings in Istanbul. The palace built by Melling for Selim III's sister Hatice Sultan in the district of Ortaköy became quite famous among the people of Istanbul and the Europeans. The innovations initiated by Selim soon caused disturbance among certain circles, mainly the Janissaries. The Janissary troops were hostile towards the military organization established under the name New Order (Nizam-ı Cedid) and eventually they rose in insurrection led by Kabakçı Mustafa. Not to shed blood, Selim III avoided resorting to the New Order troops but this resulted him being overthrown. He was thus replaced by Mustafa IV in 1807. Following these developments, Alemdar Mustafa Pasha, the ayan (provincial notable) of Rusçuk (Rousse, or Phyce as in Bulgarian), came to Istanbul to reinstate the throne to Selim; however Selim was asphyxiated by the command of the Sultan Mustafa IV. His assassins had barely started pursuing the prince Mahmud when Alemdar Mustafa Pasha arrived at the palace. Alemdar Mustafa Pasha punished all of the rebels, dethroned Mustafa IV and ascended the prince Mahmud to the throne, who was the son of Nakşidil Sultan. Mahmud II was pro-western and he had received a decent education thanks to his uncle Selim III. He was at the same time a poet and calligrapher. He undertook the necessary innovations in the government. He wished to modernize the state and integrate it with the western civilization. He preferred to stay at the timber coastal palaces by the

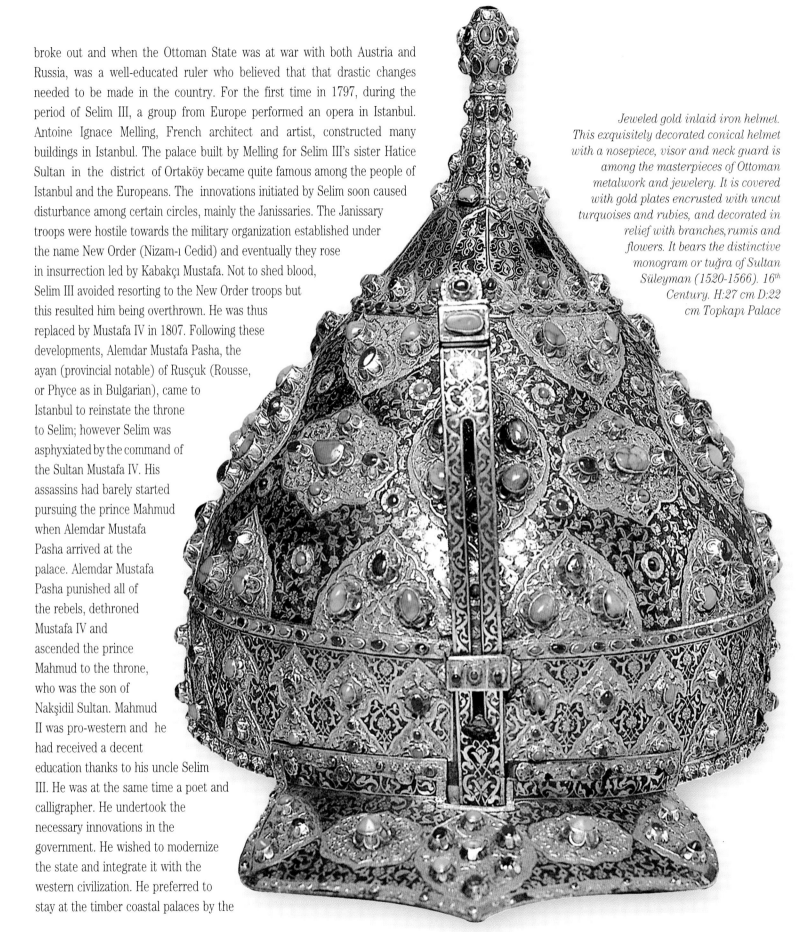

Jeweled gold inlaid iron helmet. This exquisitely decorated conical helmet with a nosepiece, visor and neck guard is among the masterpieces of Ottoman metalwork and jewelery. It is covered with gold plates encrusted with uncut turquoises and rubies, and decorated in relief with branches, rumis and flowers. It bears the distinctive monogram or tuğra of Sultan Süleyman (1520-1566). 16th Century. H:27 cm D:22 cm Topkapı Palace

Bosphorus rather than Topkapı Palace and thus had them renovated. When he died in 1839, he was succeeded on the throne by his oldest son Abdülmecid. Like his father, Abdülmecid was pro-western too. With some of the debts he incurred from abroad, he had palaces and kiosks built. Major edifices of this period are the Dolmabahçe Palace, Beykoz Summer Palace (Beykoz Kasrı), Küçüksu Summer Palace (Küçüksu Kasrı), Mecidiye Mosque, Teşvikiye Mosque. Upon Abdülmecid's death in 1861, his brother Abdülaziz ascended to the Ottoman throne. This sultan, who was fond of wrestling, javelin and hunting, predominantly worked on the modernization of the Ottoman Navy during his tenure. This is why most of the loans borrowed from the European states were spent to this end in this period. It was during Abdülaziz when sufficient state-of-art artilleries and rifles were provided for the ever-increasing number of soldiers in the Ottoman Army. The Beylerbeyi Palace and afterwards, the Çırağan Palace were also constructed during his time with loans. After he was dethroned in 1876, he was replaced by his nephew Murad V. Due to his poor health condition, this sultan remained on the throne for 93 days. When he was dethroned, he was allowed to reside in the Çırağan Palace and was replaced by Abdülhamid II. Abdülhamid, who began his regency in the Yıldız Palace instead of the Dolmabahçe Palace, curtailed many liberties due to his strict discipline. Abdülhamid II, who ruled for 33 years, attached importance to public works and education. The 1st Constitution and the 2nd Constitution of the Ottoman history were proclaimed during the 33-year reign of this sultan. Upheavals arising in the country following the Constitutional period was terminated by the Operational Army (Hareket Ordusu) brought from Macedonia. Commander of this army was Mustafa Kemal, who was later to be known as the founder of the Republic of Turkey. After the March 31 Incident, Abdülhamid II was dethroned in 1909 and was replaced by Mehmed V Reşad. Sultan Mehmed Reşad ascended to the throne at a very senior age. He remained on the throne for nine years, died in 1918 and was replaced by Mehmed Vahideddin. During this time, the Ottoman State had entered into the World War I by the side of Germany. When Germany was defeated at the end of this war, the Ottomans were deemed defeated as well, and their territories were shared by the Allied Powers. Under the leadership of Mustafa Kemal Pasha, Turks engaged in a battle of freedom and became victorious. Invading troops were fought off from Anatolia and the new state of Republic of Turkey was thus established. The center of the new state was no longer Istanbul but Ankara.

A ceremony in Topkapı Palace during
the reign of Selim III, Oil on canvas.
The painting shows the sultan enthroned before the Bab-üs Saade
during the traditional holiday ceremonies at the Ottoman Court.
The figure of the sultan is flanked on the left by his Grand Viziers,
the Sheyh ül Islam, Kaptan Pasha and the Chief Eunuch-Kızlar ağası.
To the right are the silahdars and the crown princes, with the crested
halberdiers alligned along the portico, along with the eunuchs of
the Privy Quarters-(Enderun Ağaları). Other ranks, including
the peyks and solaks and leading statesmen are arranged around
the court in their appropriate order, 152x206 cm.

Ottoman Mosques in Istanbul

Perhaps the most charming buildings in Istanbul today are the mosques which invoke admiration with their minarets rising up to the heavens as if reaching for God. During the first years of the Ottomans, mosques were covered with a dome, which constituted the main architectural scheme. However, mosques went through constant development in terms of the plan scheme, which continued until the last stage of the Ottoman Period. Among them, the selatin mosques, which were commissioned by the sultans, hold a distinct place both with their appearance, their inner decorations and the comparatively higher number of minarets. Besides the sultans, the sultan mothers as well as pashas commissioned mosque complexes (külliyes), which quickly changed the appearance of Istanbul. Mosque complexes, which were functionally important buildings, formed a unity with social structures built around the mosque of the complex such as a madrasah (Islamic theology school), school, almshouse, hospital, and caravanserai. The buildings here were for providing shelter and food for the public as well as to serve as education institutions.

Changes seem to have occurred in the Ottoman architecture after the conquest of Istanbul in 1453. Depending on their time, the mosques were built in the Classical, Baroque, Rococo and Empire styles. Mosques built from the period of Mehmed the Conqueror to Süleyman the Magnificent served as the initiators of the Classical Period. Leaving their mark on the Classical Period, works of the Architect Sinan, who was the chief architect during Süleyman the Magnificent, reach the highest rank of the monumental Ottoman architecture. Eyyüb-el Ensari, who was the standard bearer of the Prophet Mohammed, lost his life during the siege of Istanbul by the Arab troops during the 7th Century and was buried here. Shortly after Mehmed the Conqueror sieged the city, he had a mosque complex built at the location where Ebu Eyyüb-el-Ensari lost his life. The mosque of the complex, which was built in 1458 in the district of Eyüp, was demolished in the 18th Century and was rebuilt in 1798 during Selim III. The main venue of the mosque is covered with a central dome in the middle and eight smaller domes at the peripheries. The internal courtyard is surrounded by a porch with 13 domes resting on 12 columns. Beside the mosque courtyard is the madrasah chambers, whereas the almshouse is to the south east of the complex. Opposite the mosque is the Eyüp Tomb, which is overflowing with visitors everyday.

Mehmed the Conqueror encouraged his viziers (ministers) and pashas for the development of Istanbul as well. Led by the sultan's example, the grand vizier (prime minister) Mahmud Pasha became the first statesman to establish a large complex made up of a great mosque, a great bath, an inn (today known as the Kürkçü Han), a tomb, madrasah, almshouse and school built near the Grand Bazaar (Kapalıçarşı) in 1462. The main structures of the complex are the mosque and the madrasah which form a religious core, whereas the bath and the inn were built over a separate plot.

One of the most notable deeds of Mehmed the Conqueror was the establishment of his own mosque complex. This set of buildings, which came to be known as the Fatih Mosque Complex (Fatih Külliyesi), were constructed over the Byzantine Church of Holy Apostles (Havariyyun Church), by the architect Sinan-i Atik from 1463-1470. The complex was made up of a mosque at the center, the Mediterranean and Black Sea madrasahs on either sides, as well as buildings such as the hospital, homeless shelter, almshouse, caravanserai, children's school, bath and library.

In 1472, while one of Mehmed the Conqueror's viziers Rum Mehmed Pasha was having his mosque complex built, which was made up of a mosque, tomb, madrasah and a bath, Murad Pasha was having another complex built in Aksaray. The Sheik Vefa Complex (Şeyh Vefa Külliyesi) was constructed in 1476, where a tomb was added after the death of the sheik in 1480. Mehmed the Conqueror's successor Bayezid II had his own mosque complex built on an important square of Istanbul. This masterpiece mosque complex, which was built by the Architect Yakup Bin Sultan Şah from 1501-1506, is one of the first examples of Classical Period architecture. It is composed of a mosque, madrasah, bath, almshouse and a tomb. Davut Pasha, who became grand vizier during Bayezid II, had a mosque complex built in the Cerrahpaşa neighborhood in 1485. This complex was made up of a madrasah, almshouse, school and a fountain, whereas nothing remains from the almshouse today. The epitaph of the square-planned and single-domed mosque, was written by Sheik Hamdullah. Again during the period of Bayezid II, Atik Ali Pasha, who once was a white eunuch and then rose as high as grand vizier, had a mosque complex built in 1496 in Çemberlitaş. The mosque of this complex is made up of a main venue covered with a large dome and a half dome as well as a place of last congregation (the place where latecomers would pray) with five domes. The middle dome with a diameter of 12.5 m has peculiar ornamental engravings. It is also known that Atik Ali Pasha had another complex built at Karagümrük in Fatih.

Having ascended to the throne after Bayezid II, Sultan Yavuz Selim ran from campaign to campaign during his 8-year regency. His son Süleyman the Magnificent had the Sultan Selim Mosque (Sultan Selim Camii) built on the fifth hill of Istanbul in 1522. The architect of his mosque, which is the third selatin (sultans') mosque in Istanbul, was Acem Ali. The mosque has a dome with a diameter of 24 m and height of 33 m The interior is plain without any columns and there are tile decorations above the windows. In the courtyard, which is surrounded by porches that are covered with 20 domes, there are tile decorations above the windows and engravings on the interior of the domes. The mosque complex included a homeless shelter adjacent to the mosque, as well as a children's school, bath, tomb, and an almshouse which is nonexistent today. Together they created a distinctive outlook over the Golden Horn, changing the appearance of Istanbul.

Towards mid-16th Century, the Ottoman Empire reached the peak of its political, military and economic power, becoming one of the greatest empires of that age. It proved its entire might and power, while at the same time leaving its mark on the era by building magnificent architectural monuments. It was very fortunate that Architect Sinan was cultivated during this period. As a devshirme (child collected to be trained by the

government), Sinan was brought to the palace during the period of Sultan Yavuz Selim, from the Ağırnas village of Kayseri. With his intelligence and observations, he ascended the rank of chief architect. His works, which opened a new page in the Ottoman monumental architecture, were a product of his life-time studies on the works before his time, melted in his own pot. Sinan's first work in Istanbul was the Haseki Mosque Complex (Haseki Külliyesi), which was commissioned by Süleyman the Magnificent in 1539 for Hürrem Sultan, who had lately become devoutly religious. This complex was made up of a mosque, madrasah, children's school, almshouse, hospital and a fountain, and it bore all the architectural characteristics of the first half of the 16th Century. The single-dome mosque, which was built separately from the complex, has a shrine (mihrab) with Baroque ornamentations, a pulpit (mimber) from marble, and its podium is decorated with wood tessellations. This classical Ottoman-style madrasah was decorated with colored underglaze tiles and one of these tile panels is at the Tiled Kiosk (Çinili Köşk) today. Another monumental masterpiece of Sinan was the Shehzade (Crown Prince) Mosque Complex (Şehzade Külliyesi) which Süleyman the Magnificent commissioned for Prince Mehmed. It is made up of a mosque, tomb, madrasah, almshouse, shelter, soup kitchen, school, caravanserai and a muvakkithane (time keeping house). The architect Sinan created an ideal building system with four half domes within the mosque of the complex, which was completed in 1548. Sinan began the construction of a mosque complex for Süleyman the Magnificent's daughter Mihrimah Sultan in Üsküder, in 1547, which was completed in the same year. Surviving from this complex today are the mosque, tomb, madrasah, fountain and bath, whereas the caravanserai and the almshouse do not exist to the present time. Sinan seems to have experimented something new in this mosque by using three half domes. The second large-scale endeavor of Sinan was the Süleymaniye Mosque Complex (Süleymaniye Külliyesi) on a hill overlooking the Golden Horn, which was completed from 1550-1557.

The mosque complex built by Architect Sinan in Silivrikapı, in 1551, for the Grand Vizier Hadım İbrahim Pasha, had a plain mosque with its squinched dome and the place of last congregation with five domes. Still, the wooden geometric tessellations and ivory inlays on the gate of the mosque reflect a decent example of wood workmanship. The mosque that was built in 1555 in dedication to the Fleet Admiral (Kaptan-ı Derya) Sinan Pasha was also a work by Sinan. Here, the plan scheme of the mosque in Edirne with a three-balcony minaret was repeated. With this mosque, the great master also experimented with the first six-columned mosque. Grand Vizier Kara Ahmed Pasha intended to commission a mosque complex as well, but it remained unfinished due to his death. Sinan completed this mosque complex made up of a mosque, madrasah, children's school and a tomb in 1558. The dome of the rectangular-planned mosque rests on 6 columns and is supported by 4 half domes. The pediments of the windows and cabinets on the shrine wall of the mosque are decorated with 16th-Century Iznik tiles and its dome is decorated with engravings. The Rüstem Pasha Mosque Complex (Rüstem Pasha Külliyesi) built by Sinan in Eminönü in 1560 has a mosque adorned with 16th-Century Iznik tiles. The system used here rests on 8 elephantine pillars, four of which are attached to the wall while the other four are detached.

In the mosque complex built for Süleyman the Magnificent's daughter Mihrimah Sultan in 1562-65 in Edirnekapı, the main venue of the mosque is covered by a single dome with a

diameter of 19 m and height of 27 m It was expanded with three-domed spaces on two sides. The marble shrine in the mosque is adorned with muqarnas and gilt and the marble pulpit has a lattice-work with rumi, palmetto and geometric tessellations. In this mosque, which is located right beside the walls, the interior of the dome and the walls are decorated with engravings. The Sokullu Mehmed Pasha Mosque Complex (Sokullu Mehmed Pasha Külliyesi) built on a sloping land in Kadırga, around 1577, is an edifice showing the mastership of Sinan. On the windows of the mosque, which has the richest examples of 16th-Century Iznik tiles are Qur'anic verses on a dark blue background. The shrine and the pulpit inside are beautiful examples of masonry. From 1569-1578, Sinan built the Selimiye Mosque in Edirne, creating a monumental masterpiece for the reigning Sultan Selim II. After his Shehzade (prince) and Süleymaniye mosques, the architect finally considered this mosque the work of his 'mastership' period. Another work of Sinan is the Piyale Pasha Mosque which was built in dedication to the Fleet Admiral (Kaptan-ı Derya) Piyale Pasha in 1573 in Kasımpaşa. The rectangular-planned mosque measuring 30x19.5 m has a shrine, which has double niches and measures 3 m in width and 7.5 m in length. Here, 13 different 16th-Century tiles, which are very high quality, are remarkable. The tile verses located on the window pediments are the works of Çerkez (Circassian) Hasan, who was the student of Ahmed Karahisari. Painted and gilt motifs are seen on the sides of the cages of the women's loge.

Selim II died in 1574 and was succeeded by his son Murad III. Thus, Sinan, who served during three different Ottoman sultans, continued to produce new works for 14 more years during this new sultan. The mosque built for Sokullu Mehmed Pasha by Sinan in 1577, in Azap Kapı, is covered by a 12 m. diameter dome. A small sample of the Selimiye Mosque in Edirne was applied here. Sinan built the Atik Valide Mosque Complex for Murad III's mother Nurbanu Valide Sultan in Toptaşı in Üsküdar, from 1577-1583. He also added a caravanserai here for caravans from Anatolia to reside in. High quality 16th-Century Iznik tiles were used on the shrine of the mosque and the band of script. The Zal Mahmud Pasha Mosque Complex (Zal Mahmud Paşa Külliyesi) in the Defterdar Street in Eyüp was constructed in 1580 by Sinan and is made up of two madrasahs, a tomb, fountain and a mosque. Around the marble shrine inside the mosque, high quality 16th-Century Iznik tiles were used in the form of a border. On the pediments of the windows on the shrine wall are panels with verses written on them, against a dark blue background, in sülüs style (or thuluth as in Arabic). After this, Sinan created his smallest mosque complex by the sea in Üsküdar, in 1580, for Vizier Şemsi Ahmed Pasha from the Isfendiyar dynasty. The 8x8 m sided mosque of the complex with a square plan is located by the sea and looks splendid.

The mosque complex for the Fleet Admiral (Kaptan-ı Derya) Kılıç Ali Pasha dated 1580-81 is the work of Sinan as well and is located in the neighborhood of Tophane. Inside the mosque of the complex and at the place of last congregation, high quality 16th-Century Iznik tiles were used. At the place of last congregation, written on the two sides of the portal is Basmala (the opening verse in the Qur'an meaning "In the name of God, most Gracious" and another verse. Inside the mosque too, on the rectangular pediments of the windows, Basmala and a verse are inscripted in sülüs (thuluth) style, against a dark blue background. They are surrounded by a border with an arabesque (intertwined) design with palmettos. On the shrine, there are white sülüs inscriptions against a dark blue background

on the tile facing extending as far as below the upper windows. Besides these, engravings also seem to have been used in the mosque. The Military Judge İvaz Efendi Mosque Complex (Kazasker İvaz Efendi Külliyesi) was built by Architect Sinan in 1585. Only the mosque and the fountain remain from the mosque complex today. The single-domed mosque is surrounded by five half domes and its shrine is ornamented with excellent tiles.

The Head Eunuch Mehmed Ağa Mosque (Darüssaade Ağası Mehmed Ağa Camisi) located in Çarşamba in Fatih, which was constructed also in 1585 by Davut Ağa trained by Sinan, bears the style of Sinan. Another mosque built by Davut Ağa is the Grand Vizier Mesih Pasha Mosque (Sadrazam Mesih Paşa Camisi) in Fatih dated 1586. The mosque has multiple windows and thus it is very well enlightened. Tile ornamentations were used around the marble shrine and window pediments. The shrine, which is finely crafted with geometric lattice, brings extra richness to the mosque. In 1538, Sinan was very old and unable to work. Architect Davut Ağa built the Vizier Nişancı Mehmed Pasha Mosque Complex (Vezir Nişancı Mehmed Paşa Külliyesi) and the mosque, doing his best to fill Sinan's shoes. Sinan shut his eyes to life after the age of 90, in 1588, leaving behind hundreds of mosque complexes, bridges, mosques, baths and tombs. He was buried in his tomb at the Süleymaniye Mosque. Thus, the Classical Ottoman Period ended with him and a less productive period in architecture began.

Mosques in the Post-classical Ottoman Period

Following the death of Sinan, construction activities seem to have diminished a little in the 17th Century. During this period, which we may also refer to as the Late Classical Era, new trends did not emerge, but the 16th Century influence continued to dominate; still, some remarkable buildings were constructed.

The mosque which was commissioned by Takkeci İbrahim Ağa in 1591, outside of the Topkapı area, is unknown. This mosque, which is square planned and has a timber roof, also has a charitable fountain (sebil) and an ablution fountain. In this mosque, which is embellished with 16th-Century Iznik tiles, tile panels between the shrine and windows are remarkable, illustrating grape brunches among grapevine branches. What add more beauty to the mosque are the tiles with compositions featuring vases full of carnations and flower bouquets, and cypress trees, underneath all of the windows. This mosque, which is famous for its tiles, underwent repair in 1831 during the period of Mahmud II. Davut Ağa, who became Chief Architect in place of Sinan, built the Cerrah Mehmed Pasha Mosque Complex in 1593. The mosque of this complex, which is located on the Cerrahpaşa Street today, was established over a slope and the dome resting on six piers was expanded towards the sides with two exedras.

Murad III's mother, Safiye Sultan, of Venetian origin, wanted to commission a mosque complex. The New Mosque (Yeni Camii), which she had initiated in 1597, in Eminönü, remained unfinished for a long time due to deaths and political incidents. In the first years of the regency of Sultan Ahmed I, during which Chief Architect Dalgıç Ahmed Ağa served until 1605, a recession was observed in architecture. The Celali Revolts, which continued throughout the 17th Century, consumed the economic power of the state. The Ottoman State devoted its strength to suppressing these revolts and thus was unable to allocate resources to large-scale constructions. Despite all these, however, the Sultanahmet Mosque

The Rüstem Pasha Mosque, built in 1560 by Architect Sinan. In spite of being built on a narrow piece of land, it is remarkable for the beauty the tiles that embellish its interior. They extend all the way up to the upper galleries, the interior of the dome and up to the tops of the columns.

(Blue Mosque) which Ahmed I commissioned to Sedefkar Mehmed Ağa at the beginning of the 17th Century, stands out as a building reflecting the glory of the empire. Sultan Ahmed I died at a very young age and the remaining sections of his mosque complex as well as the tomb were only completed during Mustafa I, his succeeding brother, and Osman II. After Osman II, Murad IV ascended to the throne as a child and his mother Kösem Sultan (Mahpeyker) took all the government operations under her control as the mother of the sultan. Murad IV died after the campaign to Baghdad. During the last period of Murad IV, Kösem Sultan commissioned a mosque complex to the Architect Kasım Ağa in 1640, in Üsküdar. This complex was made up of a madrasah, children's school, ablution fountain, charitable fountain and two baths. The mosque complex is located in Toptaşı in Üsküdar and the interior of its mosque is embellished with 17th-Century tiles. This is why the mosque is also known as the Tiled Mosque (Çinili Camii). The timber-made place of last congregation, which surrounds the building on three sides, is a different application in mosque architecture. Inscribed on the tiles of the window pediments of the mosque is Ayat-al Kursi (the throne verse of the Qur'an). A thin band of script above the window is the Surah al Fath (the Chapter of Victory). Kösem Sultan continued her influence during the reign of her other son Sultan İbrahim, who ascended to the throne after Murad IV. However, İbrahim was dethroned due to his insufficiency and his son Mehmed IV ascended to the throne in 1648 at the age of 7.

Kösem Sultan wanted to continue her influence like a mother of sultan during the reign of her grandson as well, and entered into a cut-throat struggle with the sultan's mother Hatice Turhan Sultan. This struggle finally resulted in the assassination of Kösem Sultan in 1650 and thus Hatice Turhan Sultan collected all the power at her hand and appointed Köprülü Mehmed Pasha as grand vizier. Hatice Turhan Sultan dedicated herself to prayer afterwards and wanted to commission a mosque. Grand Vizier Köprülü Mehmed Pasha proposed that, rather than building a new mosque, she should complete the New Mosque Complex (Yeni Camii Külliyesi) which had been initiated by Safiye Sultan and remained unfinished until that day. Turhan Sultan took to this idea and decided to have this mosque completed, which had remained unfinished for 65 years. Meanwhile, the chief architect Koca Kasım Ağa died in 1660 and was replaced by Mustafa Ağa. With fast-paced work, Mustafa Ağa completed the mosque complex from 1661-1663 and thus the New Mosque became the last great edifice of the Sinan style enlivened by the architects he had raised.

The Köprülü dynasty, which had the control of the Ottoman politics in the 17th Century, engaged in development work as well as politics. Köprülü Mehmed Pasha commissioned the Köprülü Mosque Complex (Köprülü Külliyesi) on the Imperial Road (Divan Yolu) in 1661, which was completed by his son Ali Bey in 1683. Another mosque complex on the Imperial Road was seemingly commissioned in 1683 by Merzifonlu Kara Mustafa Pasha. At the beginning of the 18th Century, around the 1700's, a mosque complex spanning a wide area and made up of a masjid, madrasah, library, shops, charitable fountain and an ablution fountain, was commissioned in Saraçhane by the Grand Vizier Amcazade Hüseyin

An interior view of the Sokullu Mehmed Pasha Mosque
and the tile decorations above its mihrab.
The mosque was built by Architect Sinan in 1571.

Pasha from the Köprülü dynasty. Both the Köprülü Mosque Complex and the octagonal-body masjid within the Amcazade Hüseyin Pasha Mosque Complex are covered with a dome. These were built separately from the madrasah and were given a different identity due to functioning also as classroom. With Ahmed III, who reigned from 1703-1730, a new period began. This period which is known as the Tulip Era (Lale Devri) saw the emergence of different styles in architecture besides a cultural change. However, the mosque complex commissioned by the mother of the sultan Gülnuş Emetullah Sultan in Üsküdar in 1708 was built maintaining the old style rather than following the change. The mosque complex, which was made up of a children's school, almshouse, time keeping house, tomb and a charitable fountain, also had a lavishly ornamented, octagonal ablution fountain made from marble, at the center of its porched courtyard. The tomb was built in the external courtyard, representing an open-top architecture. Located near the tomb is the charitable fountain of the mosque complex. In this complex, step-by-step changes deviating from the Classical Period are observed in the decorative elements, reflecting a transition to the Baroque style. The Abdülhalim Madrasah located behind today's Town Hall (Belediye Sarayı) was built in 1707. In 1708, Ahmed II's grand vizier Çorlulu Ali Pasha had a small mosque complex built on the Imperial Road, in conformity with the tradition of the previous mosque complexes.

Innovations in art life began to be seen with Ahmed III's grand vizier Damat Nevşehirli İbrahim Pasha. Due to expansive cultural exchange with France, the French culture held a significant place with the Ottomans. Famous grand vizier Damat Nevşehirli İbrahim Pasha -the hallmark figure of the Tulip Era-had his mosque complex built in 1720 on the Dede Efendi Street, beside the Shehzade Mosque. The stone-and brick-made mosque of the complex has a square plan and is covered with a dome rising on an octagonal drum. Its courtyard measures 31x22 m and it is a full-fledged mosque complex with an ablution fountain at its center and clerics' school (darülhadis) chambers, a madrasah, a charitable fountain, library and a marketplace at the peripheries. These buildings have engraving ornamentation representing the characteristics of the Tulip Era. Grand vizier İbrahim Pasha established a tile factory at the Tekfur Palace in Eğrikapı, in 1725 in order to carry on the art of tile with the tiles to be produced. Tiles produced at the Tekfur Palace began to be used in many buildings constructed from this date onwards. Meanwhile, from 1722-1730, Shipyard Chamberlain Eminzade Hacı Ahmed Ağa commissioned the Ahmediye Mosque Complex (Ahmediye Külliyesi) in Üsküdar. This complex was made up of a mosque, madrasah, library, charitable fountain, ablution fountain and a tomb.

With the Patrona Halil Rebellion, the Tulip Era came to an end, Ahmed III was dethroned, and Sultan Mahmud I (1730-1754) ascended to the throne. During this period, a mosque complex was commissioned by Grand Vizier Hekimoğlu Ali Pasha in 1734 in Cerrahpaşa. This complex was made up of a mosque, library, tomb and a charitable fountain. Ali Pasha and his family are buried in the tomb of the complex. Tiles from the Tekfur Palace were used inside the mosque. The architects of the mosque complex which is the latest work of the Classical Turkish architecture were Çuhadar Ömer and Hacı Mustafa. The mosque complex commissioned by the Grand Vizier Seyyid Hasan Pasha in Beyazıt entails a group of buildings such as an inn and a shop; and a madrasah, school, charitable fountain and an ablution fountain across the street. Hacı Beşir Ağa, who was a eunuch during Ahmed III

and Mahmud I, had a mosque complex built in Cağaloğlu, across today's police office, in 1745. There is an epitaph above the gate of entry of the mosque inscribed by Yesarizade Mustafa İzzet.

Now, religious works began to be built in the Baroque and Rococo styles which intensely became visible in embellishments. The leading among the edifices representing the importance of new architectural elements and bearing Baroque impact is the Nuruosmaniye Mosque. The reigning sultan Mahmud I wished to commission a mosque for himself and the mosque complex planned by Simon Kalfa began in 1748 in front of the gate of the Grand Bazaar, where originally a masjid was located. However, Mahmud I died before the mosque was finished and was replaced by his brother Osman III, who completed the mosque in 1755. This is why the mosque was known as Nuruosmaniye. The mosque is surrounded by a broad external courtyard with two gates and is made up of its auxiliary buildings such as a madrasah, almshouse, library, time keeping house, charitable fountain and an ablution fountain as well as the surrounding 142 shops. There are 14 domes in this wholly marble-covered mosque and they sit on 12 columns. The square-planned mosque has a 26 m diameter dome and its interior is enlightened by 174 windows. There is the Surah al Fath (the Cahpter of Victory) in the form of a band on the wall. Over the main entry is the loge of the muezzin (caller of the daily prayer), while the sultan's loge is ascended via a ramp to the left of the shrine. Osman III's mother Şehsuvar Sultan and some princes are buried in the tomb of the mosque, not the sultan who had the mosque built.

Mustafa III, who ascended to the throne in 1757, valued development activities during his 17-year regency. He had the Fatih Mosque and the mosque with a three-balcony minaret in Edirne (Üç Şerefeli Cami) rebuilt. During this period, new works were created and many of them were mosque complexes. Sultan Mustafa III had the Ayazma Mosque built in Üsküdar for his mother Mihrişah Sultan, from 1757-1760. This mosque is in the Baroque style. Sultan Mustafa III's own mosque complex, which he had built in Laleli from 1759-63, includes a mosque, charitable fountain, almshouse, inn, bath, marketplace and a tomb. The architect of the mosque complex is Tahir Ağa. After its construction, the mosque was demolished by the earthquake in 1765 and it was repaired in 1782 during the period of his brother Abdülhamid I, by Seyid Mustafa Ağa. In front of the square-planned mosque is its courtyard with 18 domes sitting on 18 columns. At the center of the courtyard is an ablution fountain with a dome carried by 8 columns. Lying in the decagonal tomb are Sultan Mustafa III and his son Selim III.

Zeynep Sultan, who was the sister of Sultan Mustafa III, commissioned a mosque complex to be built by Architect Tahir Ağa in 1769 on Alemdar Street. Only the Baroque mosque and the children's school have survived to the present time from this complex. Abdülhamid I (1774-1789), who succeeded Mustafa III on the throne, continued the development activities, and in 1774, he began to have his mosque complex built in Bahçekapı by Tahir Ağa. The mosque complex was made up of a madrasah, almshouse, children's school, charitable fountain, ablution fountain, marketplace, library and a tomb, all surrounding a small masjid. This mosque complex was completed after 5 years, in 1780. Most of its buildings are demolished today. While the Fourth Foundation Inn (Dördüncü Vakıf Hanı) was being constructed, its charitable fountain and ablution fountain were carried to the corner of the Zeynep Sultan Mosque across the Gülhane Park. The madrasah is an

The Ortaköy Mosque, which Sultan Abdülmecid had Architect Nikagos Balyan build in 1853. Situated on the coastline, it has a beautiful silhouette against the Bosphorus Bridge in the background. It was constructed using the Empire style. The mosque is covered by a single dome that is supported by four beams and a tower in each corner. Gorgeous stones were used to decorate the building. The two-storey private gallery of the sultan at the front of the mosque stretches across its western facade. Together with its two minarets, seen from the sea, the mosque is a wonderful sight to behold.

important building with its two-storey cubicles. A basement was added beneath the cubicles. There is a marble tomb to the southern end of the madrasah. Sultan Abdülhamid I commissioned a mosque complex to be built in Beylerbeyi for his mother Rabia Sultan by Architect Tahir Ağa in 1777. The mosque complex is made up of a madrasah, almshouse, charitable fountain, bath, children's school, time keeping house, tomb for the princes and two ablution fountains. The most important building of the complex is its seaside mosque, which looks spectacular from the sea with its 15 m diameter dome. The last work commissioned by Abdülhamid I was the Emirgan Mosque built in 1780. During the reign of Abdülhamid, an ablution fountain and an open-air prayer place (namazgah) were commissioned by Esma Sultan in 1779. The flat space over the cistern was used for praying. Fatma Şebisefa Kadın, one of the wives of Abdülhamid I, commissioned a mosque complex on the Unkapanı Street in 1787. This complex was partially demolished during the road construction; however, its single-domed Baroque mosque can still be seen.

Sultan Selim III took on the leadership after the death of Abdülhamid I from 1789-1807. He had a keen sense of art and history has recorded him as an accomplished composer. The sultan was very fond of his mother and he commissioned a mosque complex to be built in Eyüp for his mother Mihrişah Sultan in 1792 by Architect Arif Ağa. This mosque complex is the first characteristic work of the period of Selim III. This building was completed in 1795 and it is made up of the tomb of the sultan's mother, almshouse, charitable fountain and a school. The tomb, which is made from white marble, has two stories and 12 segments. It departs from the previous examples due to the evolvement of Turkish Baroque towards

The Shehzade Mosque, described by Architect Sinan as a work from his apprenticeship period. It was built in 1544 for Crown Prince Mehmed, the deceased son of Sultan Süleyman the Magnificent.

The Mihrimah Sultan Mosque in Edirnekapı, Istanbul. The mosque was built by Architect Sinan upon the request of Mihrimah Sultan, the daughter of Süleyman the Magnificent, between 1562-1565.

Rococo. The almshouse, which is located in the middle of the mosque complex and is remarkable with its kitchen chimneys, has a Baroque charitable fountain and ablution fountain on its two sides. Selim III's sister Şah Sultan commissioned her own mosque complex made up of a charitable fountain and a school, in Eyüp. This first example of the Empire style was built in 1800 by the Architect İbrahim Kamil Ağa. Selim III had his mosque complex built in Haydarpaşa, made up of a mosque, bath, children's school and time keeping house, from 1801-1805.

When Selim III was dethroned with a rebellion and Mustafa IV was ascended to the throne, Alemdar Mustafa Pasha came to Istanbul only to see that Selim III was killed. Afterwards, he dethroned Mustafa IV, who had been ascended to the throne by the rebels, and gave the throne to Prince Mahmud. During the period of Mahmud II (1808-1839), Baroque style continued on one hand, while an evolvement towards the Empire style began. The school, ablution fountain and charitable fountain built in 1819 in the name of Cevri Kalfa, who had saved the life of Sultan Mahmud II, marked the beginning of the Baroque-Empire mixed style. The Nusretiye Mosque, which was commissioned by Sultan Mahmud II in 1822 and was completed in 1826, was a work of Architect Kirkor Balyan and its 7.5 m diameter and 33 m high dome has a Baroque appearance. On the 4 m high Baroque gate is an epitaph inscribed by the Calligrapher (Hattat) Rakım. The sultan's loge made up of four chambers is ascended via 24 steps. Within the mosque, the Surah Naba (the Chapter of Great Event) inscribed by Rakım is noteworthy. The time keeping house across the street was demolished, and the two charitable fountains facing one another were transferred to their current locations.

An aerial view of the Bayezid Külliye in Istanbul Bayezid Square. The külliye was built between 1501-1506 by the architect, Yakub Şah Bin Sultan Şah under the directives of Bayezid II.

Aerial view of Eyüp Sultan Mosque (1469). It was the first to be constructed since the conquest of Constantinople. It was restored during the reign of Selim III as it had suffered damage over the years.

The tomb of Sultan Mahmud II's mother Nakşidil Valide Sultan, which is made from white marble and located in the Fatih Mosque, is a successful example of Turkish Baroque architecture. Mahmud II died in 1839 and was buried in his Empire-style tomb, which is located on the Imperial Road and covered with marble. Following the death of Mahmud II, his 16-year old son Abdülmecid ascended to the throne. The new sultan commissioned the Dolmabahçe Palace from 1843-1853 and moved from the Topkapı Palace to this palace. Furthermore, the Sultan commissioned the Small Mecidiye Mosque (Küçük Mecidiye Camisi) at the entrance of Yıldız Park in Beşiktaş, in 1848, and in 1850, he had the Hırka-i Şerif Mosque built in Fatih. The Dolmabahçe Mosque initiated by the sultan's mother Bezmialem Valide Sultan in front of the Dolmabahçe Palace was completed by his son Sultan Abdülmecid in 1853 after her death. The mosque, the architect of which was Nikogos Balyan, is spectacular with its wide windows. It was built in a mixed Baroque-Rococo style and the interior is very well enlightened and decorated with engravings.

The Ortaköy Mosque, which was commissioned to be built by Sultan Abdülmecid in 1854 to the Architect Garabet Balyan, over a quay surrounded by sea on three sides, is remarkable with its rich decorations. The two-storey Sultan's Apartment, which is in front of the mosque, extends alongside the western facade. The mosque and the two minarets present a beautiful unity with the Bosphorus Bridge. Abdülmecid, who commissioned more palaces and kiosks than mosques, died at a young age in 1861 and was replaced by his brother Abdülaziz. During the reign of Abdülaziz, a hybrid style, which was a mix of everything ranging from the Gothic style to the Indian architecture and which became widely popular in Europe, became predominant. However, the Valide Mosque (Valide Camii) in Aksaray, which was commissioned by Abdülaziz's mother Pertevniyal Valide Sultan to Architect Montani and Serkis Balyan in 1871, cannot be attributed to any style.

During the reign of Abdülhamid II, architects such as the French architect Vallaury and Italian architect Raimondo d'Aronco worked in Istanbul, creating many works including the Archaeological Museum (Arkeoloji Müzesi) and the Museum of Ancient Oriental Arts (Eski Şark Eserleri Müzesi). Furthermore, Raimondo d'Aronco was appointed as chief architect by Sultan Abdülhamid and produced works of art. The Hamidiye Mosque in front of the Yıldız Palace, commissioned by Sultan Abdülhamid II in 1885, has an indefinite style as well. The Cihangir Mosque, which was built by Architect Sinan for Süleyman the Magnificent's son Cihangir, burnt and thus it was renovated in 1889 in the Baroque style. The Teşvikiye Mosque, which was built during the reign of Selim III in 1891, was firstly renovated by Abdülmecid and then by Abdülhamid II.

Examples of the late-era mosques are the Galip Pasha Mosque in Erenköy dating from 1898, Suadiye Mosque from 1908, and the Hobyar Mosque built by Architect Vedat Tek behind the post office in Eminönü from 1905-1909. Kemalettin the architect, who was the leading figure of the Neo-classical style, built the mosques of Bostancı, Bebek, and the mosque of Kemer Hatun in Bakırköy and included them among the historical mosques of Istanbul as well.

Along with the development of the art of tilemaking in the 16th Century, calligraphy also experienced a great advance. Tile panels with calligraphy were used in the construction of buildings. Written on this panel that decorates the upper parts of windows in the Kadırga Sokullu Mosque.

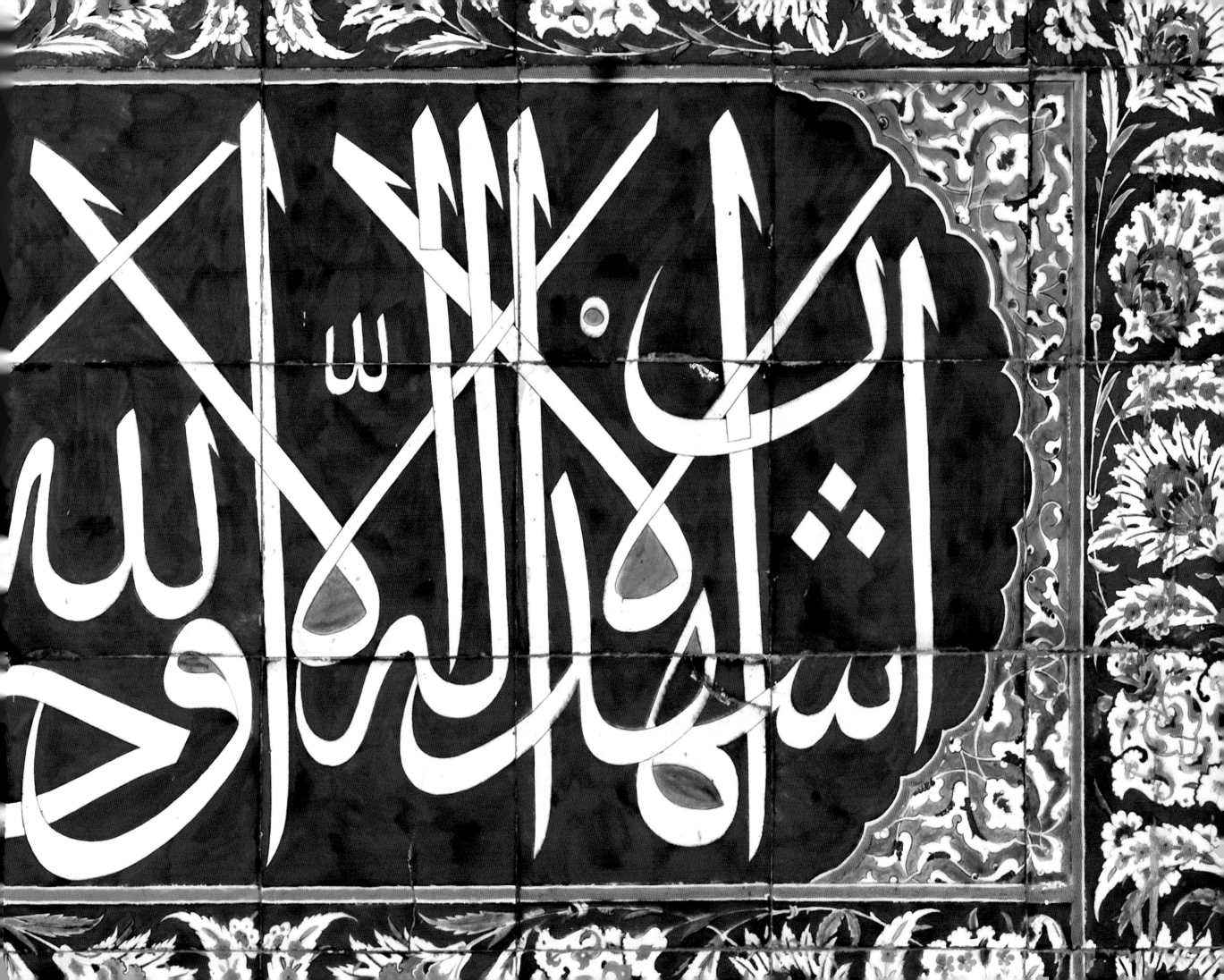

Süleymaniye Mosque

Referred to by historians as the "Magnificent" and by Turks as the "Lawmaker", Sultan Suleyman commissioned Architect Sinan to build a complex. Heeding the order he received from the famous sultan, Architect Sinan chose the third of the city's seven hills overlooking the Golden Horn on which to do so. Since the hill had a rather steep incline, it took quite some time to lay the foundation. In the meantime, stone and marble were brought in from quarries and timber from forests from the most far-flung regions of the empire.

On June 13, 1550, Sheikhul islam Ebussuud Efendi laid the first stone in the foundation-laying ceremony. Having completed the foundations, Architect Sinan waited until they all settled into place. Meanwhile, he had gotten involved in another construction project-that of the Ferhad Pasha Palace. His enemies took the opportunity to complain about Sinan to the Sultan, saying that he was not very interested in the mosque since he was doing something else at the same time. During the many years that went by after laying the foundations, Architect Sinan succeeded in completing the preparations to start the construction of the complex. He had even determined which columns he was going to place inside the building. He had one of them brought from Alexandria, another from Baalbek ruins, one from the Arcadius Monument in Istanbul and still another from Topkapı Palace.

Architect Sinan explained how he constructed Süleymaniye to his close friend, a poet and a calligrapher Sai Çelebi, who later recorded everything about it in a book he wrote called "Tezkeretül Bünyan (Book of Buildings), Sultan Süleyman the Magnificent is said to have arrived at the site while Architect Sinan was consulting with the marble workers. He severely reprimanded him, asking him why he was not working on his mosque, but rather, dealing with some less important work. He insisted that Sinan give him a completion deadline for its construction. Sinan, who, not used to being scolded like that, informed the sultan that he was going to finish the complex in just two months. The sultan, surprised at being told it would take only two months to complete, turned to those around him and said, " The Palace Architect said that he would finish in two months; I want you to be witnesses of what he has just said." But after he had returned to his palace, he ordered his officials back to the site to query once again, saying, "The Palace Architect has gone completely mad. Do you really think such a large complex can be completed in two months? You go and ask him..." But Architect Sinan told the same thing to all who asked. He had already completed the infrastructure of the complex and was ready to proceed. That is why he told them he planned to complete the construction of the complex in two months' time. He kept his promise by recruiting all the skilled workmen in the city, working them day and night to complete the complex by the deadline. The complex was to be inaugurated on October 15 1557. Architect Sinan had all its gates and doors locked and sent the key to the sultan to commence the ceremony. However, the sultan, having become so impressed with Sinan, sent him back the key and asked him to open the doors, telling him that it was he who was the most deserving of such an honor. So it

was that Sinan, who, having recently turned 67, proudly unlocked the gates of the mosque. The sultan lavished Sinan with gifts, showing how much he cared for him. Records show a total of 3,523 builders worked on the construction and 59,760,180 akçes, the Ottoman currency at the time, was spent. It was a complex that reflected the glamour of Sultan Süleyman the Magnificent. No matter how much Architect Sinan might have referred to this complex as a work of his apprentice period, it thoroughly reflects his architectural skills and genius since he was able to position the structures of the complex in an aesthetically pleasing manner over 60-acres of sloping land. Even today, the Süleymaniye Mosque, with its silhouette over Istanbul, continues to reflect the grandeur of the period. Architect Sinan placed the other buildings of that complex around its mosque so that they would not overshadow its magnificence.

Shops in what is known as the Tiryakiler Bazaar are at the side where the main entrance of the mosque is located. At the beginning of the shops was a primary school. This domed structure with an open anteroom is still used as primary school library. Behind these shops are the "Evvel" and "Sani" Madrasahs, the gates of which are connected to each other via an archway located on the street. The chambers and classrooms behind the domed porticoes are of the Classical Ottoman style. These madrasahs are currently utilized as the Süleymaniye Library. In addition to them, there was once a School of Medicine having an array of rooms. While only a few cells of that building are still intact, a maternity ward has since been built in its place. A charitable soup kitchen, guesthouse and a small hospital are found along the street to the west of the mosque, with the hospital located at the end of the street. This hospital once offered services to the sick and mentally ill in its mental asylum wing. This structure is in the shape of two consecutive courtyards with porticoed rooms situated around them.

Today, this building is used as a Qur'an school for girls. The building in the middle was a charitable soup kitchen where the elderly, students and the poor used to eat for free. It consists of domed rooms in a row around a courtyard. Once housing the Museum of Turkish and Islamic Arts, this building is currently being used as a restaurant called "Dar-ül Ziyafe." Besides this building, there was a hospice comprised of domed chambers around a courtyard with a pool in the middle. These were used as bread ovens, a kitchen, lodging for traveling merchants, stables for beasts of burden and warehouses to store their goods. A caravanserai was also located on the lower section. To the north of the mosque at the end of the street is the tomb of the creator of this complex, Architect Sinan. He was buried in this modest tomb when he died in 1588, at the ripe old age of 90. The inscription on his tomb belongs to Sai Çelebi and reads, "Sinan, the patron saint of architects passed through this world." Reflecting the Classical-Ottoman style, the "Rabi" and "Salis" Madrasahs are located in this area. The classrooms are situated independently on the western side of the entrance of the courtyard. Also built in the Classical style, the Dökmeciler Bath of the complex is on the corner, in front of these schools. The "Darülhadis" Madrasah is to the south of the baths. Consisting of a series

A sunset view of the Süleymaniye Mosque, a work Architect Sinan called his masterpiece. Along with the many other mosques built by this great architect, Süleymaniye helped change the silhouette of Istanbul.

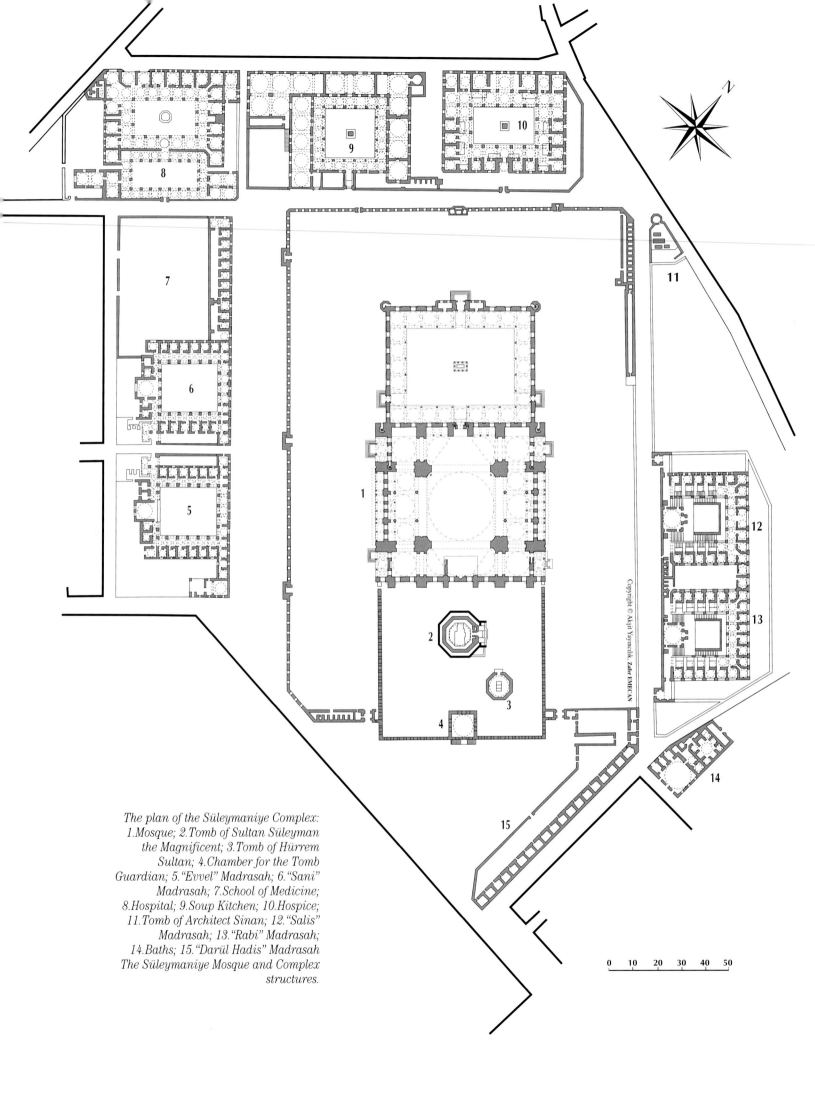

*The plan of the Süleymaniye Complex:
1.Mosque; 2.Tomb of Sultan Süleyman the Magnificent; 3.Tomb of Hürrem Sultan; 4.Chamber for the Tomb Guardian; 5."Evvel" Madrasah; 6."Sani" Madrasah; 7.School of Medicine; 8.Hospital; 9.Soup Kitchen; 10.Hospice; 11.Tomb of Architect Sinan; 12."Salis" Madrasah; 13."Rabi" Madrasah; 14.Baths; 15."Darül Hadis" Madrasah
The Süleymaniye Mosque and Complex structures.*

Copyright © Akşit Yayıncılık   Zafer EMECAN

0 10 20 30 40 50

of domed chambers, the building is accessible via a flight of steps. The Tombs of Sultan Süleyman the Magnificent and his wife Hürrem Sultan are situated behind the mosque. Here, another chamber called "Darülkurra" is also found. With its additional buildings, the complex is every bit as splendid as the mosque. The vast outer courtyard of the mosque is accessible through ten gates. The rectangular-plan inner courtyard is accessible through three gates, one of which is right in the center. Some fine stone masonry is displayed above the central main entrance gate. Its inscription bears the "Kelime-i Tevhid" Qur'anic verse. Twenty-four columns of porphyry, white marble and red granite are said to have been brought from the Imperial Loggia in the Hippodrome called "Kathisma," while its floor is paved with marble. A portico with 28 domes surrounds the courtyard. A decorated rectangular-shaped fountain lies right in the middle of it. Two of the four minarets are located in the corners of the northern facade, each with two balconies. Situated behind the mosque, the other two minarets with three balconies are higher than the first two. The minarets have a total of ten balconies, as Süleyman the Magnificent was the 10th sultan of the empire. Measuring 63 meters x 68 meters, the nearly square-plan mosque has a dome measuring 26.5 meters across and 53 meters in height. The mosque is accessible through two gates, one in the front and the other on its western side. In addition, there are two other gates that open into the Sultan's Loggia and a yard where a stone bier is located. Measuring 6.20 meters x 5.10 meters, the central dome is set upon four arches supported by four elephantine pillars on either side. In addition, semi-domes cover the niche and the main entrance. The area between the elephantine pillars covered with five smaller domes gives the devout ample room to pray. All gates of the Süleymaniye Mosque are made from ebony. Its niche and pulpit are elegant examples of marble etching. The mosque is filled with a total of 138 windows, which give the inside of the mosque an elegant and fresh look. Panels on either side of the niche are made from 16th Century Iznik tile and bear inscriptions on a dark blue background. The inner part of the domes is also covered with calligraphy. The acoustic setup of this mosque is another clear indication of Architect Sinan's mastery. He installed 255 small jars all around the mosque to achieve these acoustics and to prevent candle soot. Four porphyry columns were positioned inside the mosque between the pillars facing the northern and southern sides. Like the other material, these columns were shipped in from all over the empire. They measure 9 meters in height and 1.14 meters in diameter. The interior of the Süleymaniye Mosque measures 5,364 m². All calligraphic inscriptions belong to Ahmed Karahisari and his student Hasan Çelebi, whereas the stained window glasses are the work of İbrahim the Drunkard. Both the Süleymaniye Mosque and the tomb that Architect Sinan constructed for Sultan Süleyman the Magnificent can be considered two of the wonders of Ottoman architecture.

The Tomb of Sultan Süleyman the Magnificent

Sultan Süleyman the Magnificent suffered a lot of misery throughout his 46-year reign. He had to give orders for the execution of his sons Crown Prince Mustafa and Crown Prince Bayezid as they rebelled against the state. He also lost his other sons, Crown Prince Cihangir and Crown Prince Mehmed. On top of the sorrow of losing his sons, his wife Hürrem Sultan, with whom he was deeply in love, died in 1558. He outlived her by eight years and passed away while on his military campaign to Zigetvar (Szigetvár) on September 06, 1566. Grand Vizier Sokullu Mehmed Pasha hid his death from the army by secretly bringing his corpse to Istanbul to bury him in the tomb constructed by Architect Sinan. Eight columns support the dome of his octagonal-planned tomb on the inside. Another 29 columns support the tomb, which is

A view of the interior of and system of domes in the Süleymaniye Mosque, which reflects the architectural genius of Architect Sinan. The interior of the domes is embellished with engravings.

surrounded by porticoes, from the outside. Four green porphyry columns are located on either side of the main gate, where there are also strikingly beautiful Iznik tile panels. The gate wings of this monumental Classical style tomb structure have ivory inlays and engravings. One of the gates bears the verse "La ilahe Illallah," which means, "There is only one God," and the other "Muhammedin Resulallah," which means "Mohammed is his Ambassador." 16th-Century Iznik tiles bearing floral motifs decorate the interior of the tomb. Pendentive medallions made from tiles bear names in white calligraphic inscriptions against a dark blue background. Above the lower windows is a band of Qur'anic verse in white on a dark blue background. There are some Byzantine-type painted panels resembling marble above this band, and above this section, there are triple windows. Its dome was constructed using the "malachite" technique. The materials of the dome and the red and white stone arches complement each other. The tomb has seven coffins, with that of Sultan Süleyman the Magnificent lying in the middle. To his left, are those belonging to Sultan Süleyman II, who died in 1691, Sultan Ahmed II, who died in 1695 and the Favorite Wife of Sultan Ahmed II, Rabia Sultan, who died in 1712. To the right of his tomb are the coffins belonging to his daughter Mihrimah Sultan, who died in 1578, the Third Favorite Wife of Sultan Ibrahim, Saliha Dilaşup Sultan, who died in 1689 and the daughter of Ahmed II, Asiye Sultan, who died in 1695.

The Tomb of Hürrem Sultan

Beside the tomb of Sultan Süleyman the Magnificent is that of Hürrem Sultan. Hürrem, whose real name was "Roxelana," was the daughter of a Russian monk. She was taken prisoner as a child and sold to the Ottoman Palace. Later, this very intelligent concubine was given the Turkish moniker "Hürrem." She finally attracted the attention of Sultan Süleyman the Magnificent, becoming his wife as well as the First Lady of the Empire. Hürrem was to bear him many children. Simply adored by Süleyman, she would write him poems to express her deep love for him. The ordeal she went through to have her sons sit on the Ottoman throne, and the subsequent fratricidal infighting over the throne exhausted her and she fell ill. She was not able to withstand all the palace tragedies and passed away at the age of 54 in 1558. Sultan Süleyman the Magnificent buried her in a tomb he commissioned Architect Sinan to build in his complex. The tomb is octagonal on the interior, and has 16 sides on the exterior. Covering the ashlar stone tomb are twin domes that sit on a cylindrical drum. A portico with triple-arched vaults stands in front of its main entrance, on either side of which there are tile panels. This tomb is also adorned with beautiful 16th-Century Iznik tiles. Inscriptions containing Qur'anic verse are etched onto the panels and above the gate. Its doors and windows represent the finest examples of wood craftsmanship.

Iznik tiles cover the interior of the tomb up to the bottom of the top windows, as well as the niches between the windows. Pretty dark-blue, white, turquoise peonies and pointy leaves are used as decoration on the niches. The tops of the walls are crowned with "sulus"-style Qur'anic verse inscribed in white on a dark blue background. Three coffins lie in the tomb; the largest one belongs to Hürrem Sultan while the others belong to the son of Selim I, Crown Prince Mehmed and the granddaughter of Süleyman the Magnificent, Hanım Sultan.

The interior of the Hürrem Sultan tomb. Hürrem Sultan died in 1558 when she was 58 years old and buried in her tomb in the Süleymaniye Complex.

An interior view of the Tomb of Süleyman the Magnificent. A detailed view of the tile decorations on the walls of the Tomb of Süleyman the Magnificent. After having ruled for a long time, Sultan Süleyman died in 1566 and was buried in the tomb built inside his külliye. The interior of the tomb is decorated with choice Iznik tiles.

Sultanahmet Mosque

When Mehmed III suffered a fatal heart attack on December 21, 1603 at the age of 37, his son Ahmed I ascended to the Ottoman throne as the 14th Sultan. He was only 14 years old at the time, but in spite of his youth, he was devoutly religious. This led him to have a mosque built in his name.

In the meantime, the architect Davud Ağa had recently succumbed to the plague. One of Architect Sinan's students, Mehmed Ağa, was appointed Palace Architect as his replacement. Mehmed Ağa had been recruited from the Balkans in 1562 and brought up in the apprenticeship school. He was at first fond of music but then got involved in architecture and nacre "sedef" craftsmanship. That's why he was called Sedefkar Mehmed Ağa. He was also a student of Architect Sinan for 21 years, during which time he learned quite a lot from his master. Sultan Ahmed I commissioned Sedefkar Mehmed Ağa to construct a vast mosque for himself.

After meticulous studies and research, he was able to determine the place of the prospective mosque. However, there were some palaces on the site that belonged to Grand Vizier Sokullu Mehmed Pasha, as well as Mesih Pasha. He purchased the buildings, razed them and prepared the site for the mosque. In 1609, the sixth year of his reign, Sultan Ahmed I struck the first ceremonial shovel into the ground to begin work on the foundation. The mosque was finally finished after eight years. However, the inaugural ceremony of the mosque took place before the addition of the structures that would turn it to a complete complex was completed. Ahmed I died of typhoid at the age of 28 on September 07, 1617. He was buried in the tomb of his complex, which was finally completed in 1620.

We have learned the story of its construction from a book called Risale-i Mimari written by Cafer Çelebi in which he narrated the life of Palace Architect Sedefkar Mehmed Ağa.

Besides its mosque, the Sultanahmet Mosque Complex was comprised of a sultan's kiosk, tomb, primary school, madrasah, hospital, fountain, public fountain and a marketplace. The architecture of the madrasah next to the tomb is of the Classical Ottoman style. Situated behind the tomb is a white marble cloakroom consisting of a single chamber, which dates from the 18th Century. Public fountains and the primary school lie on both sides of the courtyard. A separate building to the north of the mosque was the sultan's

A view of the Sultanahmet Mosque from Hagia Sophia.
The mosque was initially built as a külliye by Sedefkâr Mehmed Ağa, who was commissioned by Ahmed I. Apart from the mosque, only some of the buildings of the original complex are extant today.

kiosk and is currently used as a carpet museum. Below this building are shops selling souvenirs. A bath was situated next to this "Arasta" (marketplace), once known as the Sipahiler Çarşısı. There were shops lining the Hippodrome which still doing a brisk business in souvenirs. The charitable soup kitchen and a hospital used to be on the semi-circular terrace on the side of the Hippodrome near the Sea of Marmara. The Classical style horseshoe-shaped hospital lies behind a structure belonging to Marmara University. However, the hospital and the printing house of that complex are not longer extant.

The mosque is surrounded on three sides by an outer courtyard, which is accessible through eight gates, three of which are in the front. Accessible from the outer courtyard through three gates, the floor of the inner courtyard is paved entirely with white marble. The inner courtyard is surrounded by a portico covered by 30 domes supported by 26 columns. Two of these columns are porphyry while the remaining are pink granite and marble. In the middle of the courtyard is an elegant fountain with an octagonal dome supported by six marble columns. This mosque is the only one in Istanbul with six minarets. Four of them have three balconies, with the remaining two having two each, for a total of 16. The Sultanahmet Mosque is comparable to Hagia Sophia in many ways but it is larger and more impressive than Hagia Sophia. Measuring 23.5 meters in diameter, its central dome is based on four enormous arches, the corners of which are pendentive.

The arches are supported by four round, grooved elephantine pillars measuring 5 meters in diameter. The main dome is surrounded by four semi-domes on each side. Its corners are also surrounded by small domes. Galleries are situated above and on both sides of the main entrance. Thus, it has an area measuring 64 meters x 72 meters. Next to the Sultan's Loggia, in the left corner, is the Ordeal Cell of Ahmed I. The plan of the Sultanahmet Mosque is similar to that which was incorporated by Architect Sinan into the Shehzade Mosque: a single main dome supported by four semi-domes. However, Sedefkar Mehmed Ağa worked on this masterpiece as if he was crafting nacre. His calculations on illuminating the interior of the mosque, as well as the harmony of the color of tiles both show the perfection of his masterpiece. Some 260 windows were used to illuminate the interior. Its stained glass windows were restored over time, erasing the mystic atmosphere of the mosque, but giving the tiles a brighter appearance as well. The marble niche is enriched with engravings. The gold leaf used on the pulpit gives it a more precious and imposing appearance. One-third of all walls and pillars are covered with magnificent Iznik tiles up to the upper cornices. 21,043 Iznik tiles were used to decorate the interior of the mosque. The Sultanahmet Mosque is known as "Blue Mosque" as the tiles and engraving work seen inside give it a bluish effect. More than 50 tulip motifs of various colored tulips, daffodils, carnations and other flowers were crafted on its tiles on a white background.

The wooden ceiling below the Sultan's Loggia is adorned with gold leaf embossed embroidery. The wood craftsmanship in the Sultanahmet Mosque is as beautiful and striking as its tiles. Sedefkar Mehmed Ağa adorned its doors and windows with beautiful tortoise shell and nacre artwork. The calligraphy decorating the interior was inscribed by Kasım-ı Gubari.

Interior views of the Sultanahmet Mosque.

Next page: Detail of 16th-Century Iznik panels decorating the Sultanahmet Mosque. The mosque, which was built by the Sedefkar Mehmed Ağa between 1609-1617, is embellished with magnificent Iznik tiles.

Tombs of the Sultans

Different civilizations had various burial traditions in Anatolia over the centuries. Some buried their dead under mounds of soil, some under rocks and still others in mausoleums. Having defeated the Byzantines, the Seljuks reached into Anatolia and built cupolas to show respect to their dead. Today, we can see their cupolas in Ahlat around Lake Van in the East as well as in central Turkey in places like Sivas, Kayseri and Konya. After founding their own state in Anatolia, the Ottomans developed the architecture style they derived from the Seljuks. In particular, the Ottomans took the tomb architecture of the Seljuks and enhanced it by introducing a variety of different plans. Naturally, the most splendid of the tombs were built for the Ottoman sultans.

The tombs of the first six Ottoman sultans are in Bursa. Istanbul became the final resting place for subsequent sultans, as the city was chosen as the capital of the Ottoman Empire. There are 15 tombs in Istanbul. Ottoman sultans did not have their tombs constructed during their lifetimes. That task generally fell to the successive sultan. Besides the sultans, mother sultans, grand viziers and pashas would have their own tombs in Istanbul. The majority of these tombs were built in complexes that had been constructed in their name. Sultans whose tombs are located in their own complex include Mehmed the Conqueror, Bayezid II, Sultan Yavuz Selim (Selim the Grim), Süleyman the Magnificent, Mustafa III, Ahmed I and Abdülhamid I.

Other Ottoman sultans, such as Selim II, Murad III, Mehmed I, Mustafa I and İbrahim, were buried in the sanctity of Hagia Sophia. There were also those who were entombed in the tombs previously built by their parents. For example, six Ottoman Sultans lie side by side in the Tomb of Hatice Turhan Sultan.

Some viziers, pashas and mothers of sultans wanted to be buried in another sacred place: Eyüp. Ebu Eyyüp Ensari, the Prophet's soldier and flag bearer, was buried there in his own tomb after the conquest of Istanbul in 1453. Other tombs were scattered in districts such as Laleli, Bahçekapı and Divanyolu. The tombs adorning Istanbul, the capital of a giant empire for 500 years, are considered great works of art. The tombs belonging to the sultans succeeding Sultan Yavuz Selim have a distinguished place in architecture, as these sultans held the position of Caliph of Islam at the same time. We are going to describe all of the Sultans Tombs below. We will also mention some important Grand Vizier and Mother Sultan Tombs. It is impossible for us to mention all the tombs in Istanbul, as the total number is over 600, 119 of which are maintained by the Official Directorate of Tombs, with 30 open to the public. Tombs located in complexes shall be mentioned in the section that discusses Complexes. The conqueror of Constantinople,

Sultan Mehmed II headed fresh military conquests, while beautifying Istanbul at the same time. One of his most outstanding accomplishments was to have his own complex constructed. The Fatih Complex was built over a Byzantine church The Fatih Mosque Complex was built over a Byzantine church by the architect Sinan-i Atik between 1463-70. After he died en route to Europe on one of his military campaigns, Sultan Mehmed the Conqueror was brought back to Istanbul and buried in his own tomb. The tomb of Grand Vizier Mahmud Pasha is near a mosque by the Covered Bazaar built in 1473 in his name. This octagonal tomb made of ashlar blocks is decorated with dark blue and turquoise tile inlays. The Tomb of Rum Mehmed Pasha in the mosque in Üsküdar dated 1471 is next to the Tomb of the Davut Pasha Mosque dated 1485. Bayezid II commissioned the architect Yakub Shah Bin Sultan Shah to build the Bayezid Complex in Bayezid Square between 1501-1506. His son Sultan Yavuz Selim later had his father's tomb built next to the mosque.

By deposing his father Bayezid II, Sultan Yavuz Selim ascended to the Ottoman throne in 1512 and reigned for a short period of only eight years. Sultan Yavuz Selim gave orders for his own complex to be built on one of the hills overlooking the Golden Horn. But since he died in 1520, his son Sultan Süleyman the Magnificent gave orders to the architect Acem Ali to construct his father's tomb in this place. On a tile of the entrance is an inscription saying the tomb was ordered by Sultan Süleyman the Magnificent in 1523.

This octagonal tomb is covered with a main dome and has a portico supported by four marble columns in the front. Engravings decorate the dome and the areas above the windows. Selim's coffin is embellished with nacre inlays. Two identical glazed tile panels decorate both sides of the main gate of the tomb.

The octagonal Tomb of the Crown Princes is situated across the Tomb of Sultan Selim. The 16th Century tile panels inside the tomb are adorned with engravings. Five coffins belonging to the daughters of Sultan Yavuz Selim and the sons of Sultan Süleyman the Magnificent lie at rest inside the tomb. Inside Sultan Yavuz Selim's complex are the tombs of Sultan Abdülmecid, who had Dolmabahçe Palace constructed, and Sultan Yavuz Selim's wife, Hafsa Sultan, whose tomb is in ruins. Also, a little further down the road is the tomb of the daughter of Sultan Yavuz Selim, Shah Sultan, who was the wife of Grand Vizier Lütfi Pasha. Sultan Süleyman the Magnificent, otherwise known as Sultan Süleyman the Lawmaker, commissioned Architect Sinan to construct the Süleymaniye Complex during his long-lasting reign. In 1566, he was buried in the tomb situated right in front of the niche of the mosque, which is inside this complex. We have already

The Tomb of Sultan Ahmed I was constructed by Sedefkar Mehmed Ağa on the side of the mosque overlooking Hagia Sophia. Based on a square plan, this trisectioned marble portico lies in front of the tomb. Tile panels are on both sides of the main entrance gate. The interior of the tomb is brightly illuminated by 52 windows. Its walls are decorated with 17th-Century Iznik tiles, with motifs of tulips, daffodils, flower bouquets and leaves in blue, green, red and turquoise on a white background. There is a band of inscription containing the "Surah Al Mulk" Qur'anic verse. The upper parts of the tomb along with the inside of the dome are adorned with calligraphy. The elegant craftsmanship of the doors and windows belongs to Sedefkar Mehmed Ağa.

described the tombs of Sultan Süleyman the Magnificent and Hürrem Sultan in the section concerning the Süleymaniye Complex. The plain tomb of Architect Sinan is located right behind the Süleymaniye Mosque. Architect Sinan also constructed the Tomb of Barbaros Hayreddin Pasha in Beşiktaş in 1541. The tombs of many several Ottoman sultans lie in the garden of Hagia Sophia.

The Tombs of Hagia Sophia

Selim II ascended to the Ottoman throne upon death of his father Sultan Süleyman the Magnificent. Selim II, who had commissioned the construction of the famous Selimiye Mosque in Edirne, died in 1574 after eight years as sultan. Architect Sinan constructed a tomb for Selim II in the courtyard of Hagia Sophia and buried him there three years later.

The entrance and walls of this octagonal white marble tomb are adorned with 16th-Century Iznik tiles. The tomb, which has four columns and a small dome with eaves, rests on eight marble columns. The inner part of the tombs dome is decorated with engravings. A glazing technique was used on the symmetrical tiled panels on both sides of the main entrance gate. Considered one of the finest examples of 16th Century tile work, one of these panels is original, while the other one is a copy, as the original is on display in the Louvre Museum in Paris.

41 coffins lie in the tomb, which is one of the most elegant examples of Turkish art. In the tomb, besides Selim II, his wife Nurbanu Sultan along with their daughters and many other crown princes lie side-by-side.

Murad III ascended to the throne upon his father Selim II's death. After he died in 1595, he was buried in his tomb in the courtyard of Hagia Sophia. The architect Davud Ağa constructed a hexagonal marble covered tomb for him in 1599. The dome of the tomb, which has two rows of windows, is supported by six columns. Its walls are adorned with Iznik tiles. Tiled panels are between the windows inside the tomb. A strip of Qur'anic verse is on top of the window, whereas the inner part of the dome is decorated with Classical-style engravings. Sultan Murad III, his wife Safiye Sultan, three crown princes and their daughter lie side-by-side in the tomb. Also buried in the tomb are the crown princes of Sultan Ahmed I and Sultan İbrahim along with the latter's two daughters, the 19 siblings of Mehmed III who were murdered on orders of Mehmed III so that he could ascend to the throne, and other members of the Imperial Family. This makes a total of 50 coffins in the tomb. We encounter the Tomb of Mehmed III, who ascended to the throne after Murad III, in the courtyard of Hagia Sophia. Ahmed I, the son of Mehmed III, who died in 1603, commissioned the architect Dalgıç Mehmed Ağa to begin the construction of his father's tomb. But, as this architect succumbed to the plague, another architect, Sedefkar Mehmed Ağa completed the task in 1608.

This octagonal tomb has an outer portico that was later rebuilt in Baroque style. Tiles adorn the walls up to the top of lower windows. The "Surah Al Jumah" Qur'anic verse is inscribed along a 120 cm-wide strip on top of the window. The dome is decorated with engravings. The coffin of Sultan Mehmed III is surrounded by those of his wife Handan

The malakari ("plaster reliefs") decoration inside the dome of the Tomb of Selim II. When Selim II, whom Architect Sinan had served for 14 years, died in 1574, Architect Sinan built a tomb for him in the garden of Hagia Sophia, where he was buried. (1576-1577)

Sultan, as well as Ahmed I's six sisters, three princes and 14 daughters. The daughter of Murad III, Ayşe Sultan, also lies in this tomb. There is a total of 26 coffins in the tomb. Constructed by Architect Sinan in 1570, the Tomb of the Crown Princes is right next to the Tomb of Murad III. While this tomb is octagonal from the outside, its interior is rectangular, with the dome resting on pendentives. The inside of the dome is decorated with engravings that were all done during the late period. In this tomb are the brothers and sisters of Murad III who died while still very young. Moreover, Hagia Sophia's baptism chamber was converted into a tomb where Sultan Mustafa I and Sultan İbrahim were buried.

Tombs belonging to other sultans

Ahmed I ascended to the throne after his father Mehmed III. He died in 1617 after reigning for 14 years. Ahmed I commissioned Sedefkar Mehmed Ağa to build the Sultanahmet Mosque during his reign. After his death, he was buried in his tomb overlooking Hagia Sophia, next to his mosque. We mention this tomb in the section covering the Sultanahmet Mosque. Mustafa I, who ruled after Ahmed I, was buried in the baptismal chamber that was converted into a tomb, in the courtyard of Hagia Sophia. Osman II and Murad IV, who ascended to the Ottoman throne after Mustafa I, both lie in the Tomb of Sultan Ahmed. Sultan İbrahim I, rising to power upon the death of Murad IV in 1640, was buried next to Mustafa I in 1648. Mehmed IV, who succeeded his father Sultan İbrahim I, was buried in the tomb of his mother Hatice Turhan Sultan in the New Mosque (Yeni Camii). Süleyman II, who followed Mehmed IV, as well as Ahmed II, lies in the Tomb of Sultan Süleyman the Magnificent. Mustafa II, who ascended to the throne after Ahmed II, as well as Ahmed III, Mahmud III, and Osman III, respectively, lie in Tomb of Hatice Turhan Sultan.

Mustafa III, who became Sultan upon the death of Osman III, was buried in his own tomb located in the complex he ordered the architect Tahir Ağa to construct during his lifetime. Built in 1763, the tomb has a single dome and 10 corners. This ashlar block tomb was built in Baroque style; its interior is adorned with 16th Century glazed tiles in coral-red and blue-white. There is a strip of Qur'anic verse on top of the windows and its dome is decorated with engravings.

This tomb holds the coffins of Sultan Mustafa III and Selim III, as well as eight other coffins belonging to the daughters of Mustafa III. Abdülhamid I, who ascended to the Ottoman throne after Mustafa III as the 27th sultan, was the 92nd Islamic caliph. He died a sad death upon receiving word that his army had been defeated by Russia on March 27, 1789. He was buried the following year in his own tomb-the one that the architect Tahir Ağa had constructed in Bahçekapı, Eminönü. Most of the buildings of the complex have been deteriorated over time but his tomb is still intact.

This marble tomb, the corners of which are rounded, was constructed in Baroque style with a dome on the top and a portico at the entrance. Its windows and doors are embellished with nacre inlay; the "Surah Al Mulk" Qur'anic verse is inscribed on the wall against a marble background. The coffin of Abdülhamid I as well as those of his son Mustafa IV, and 20 relatives lie side-by-side in the tomb.

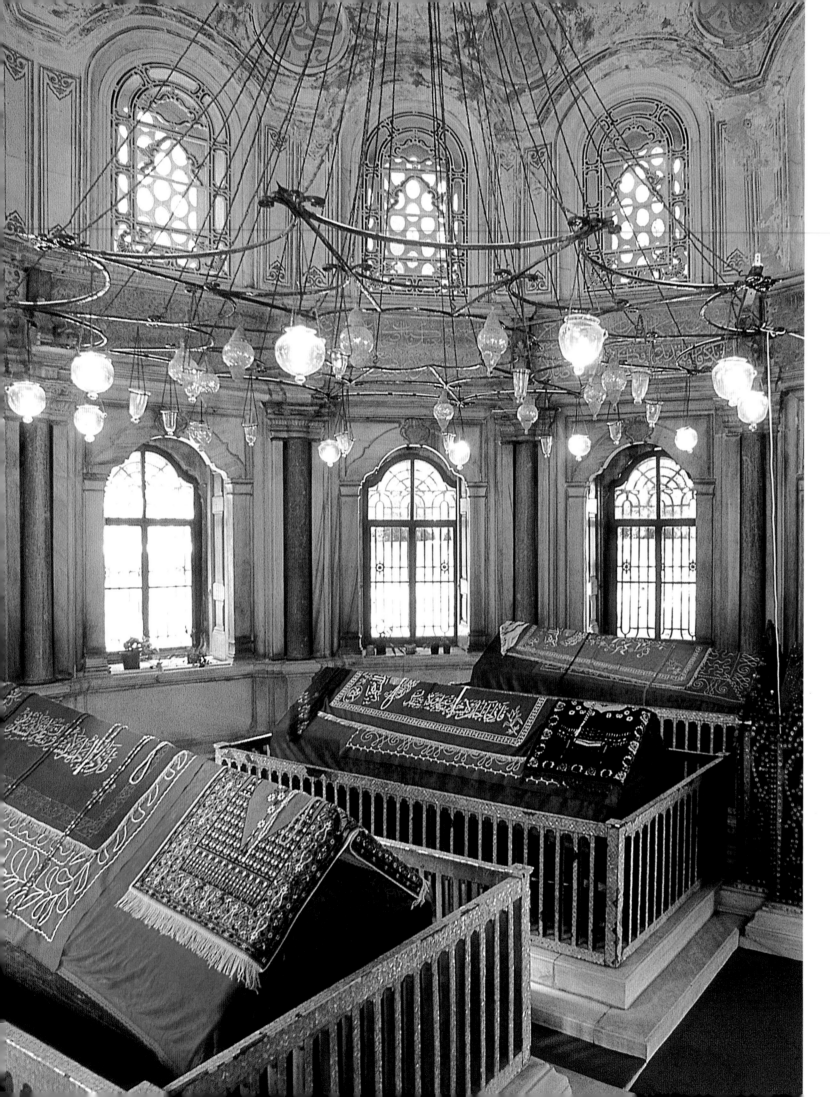

Selim III, succeeded Abdülhamid I, was deposed and executed during the Kabakçı Mustafa Rebellion of May 29, 1807 and was buried in the Tomb of Mustafa III, which is located in Laleli. Subsequent sultans who ascended to the throne were Mustafa IV and Mahmud II, respectively. Mahmud II, who ascended to the throne in 1808, ordered the construction of a tomb in the Fatih Complex in 1817 for his mother, Nakşidil Sultan. In addition to his mother's coffin, there are 15 others belonging to Cevri Kalfa and Mahmud II's children in this tomb. Upon Mahmud II's death in 1839, his son and successor, Abdülmecid had the architect Ohannes Balyan construct a tomb for his father along Divanyolu Street. Completed in 1840, this octagonal tomb was constructed in the Empire style. It is covered by a dome that is supported by its walls. The tomb has seven windows and a gate. Its walls are covered in marble on the outside. The Basmala (the opening verse in the Qur'an meaning "In the name of God, most Gracious, most Compassionate") is inscribed in "sülüs" calligraphic style on the outside of the main entrance gate, while the "Surah Al Rahman" Qur'anic verse is inscribed on the inner face. The inscription inside the tomb on a marble background belongs to the calligrapher Haşim. While the coffin in the middle belongs to Sultan Mahmud II, the ones on the right belong to Sultan Abdülaziz and Abdülhamid II. Those to the left belong to the wife of Sultan Mahmud II, Bezmialem Sultan, her sister Esma Sultan and their daughter Atiye Sultan. Behind the coffin of Mahmud II are those belonging to other members of the Imperial Family. There is a total of 17 coffins in this tomb. The coffins belonging to six wives of Mahmud II and the wives of Sultan Abdülaziz and Sultan Abdülhamid II lie at rest in the annex next to the entrance of this tomb, to the left. In the garden of the tomb, which is surrounded by high walls, are the tombs belonging to some important imperial statesmen as well as some of those from the Republican period, such as Sadullah Pasha, Said Halim Pasha, Fethi Ahmed Pasha, Muallim Naci and Ziya Gökalp. Abdülmecid ascended to the throne after his father Mahmud II. He had Dolmabahçe Palace constructed and moved from Topkapı Palace into his new premises. Abdülmecid died in 1861, leaving behind many works of art such as palaces and kiosks. He was buried in his bare tomb situated in the courtyard of the Yavuz Sultan Selim Mosque. He was succeeded by his brothers Sultan Abdülaziz and Abdülhamid II, who were buried in their father's aforementioned tomb in Cağaloğlu. Murad V, whose sultanate lasted a brief period of 93 days, was buried in an additional chamber in the Tomb of Hatice Turhan Sultan in Eminönü. Mehmed V Reşad, who came to the throne after Abdülhamid II, was buried in a tomb that the architect Kemaleddin had constructed for him in Eyüp. As the last Ottoman sultan, Mehmed Vahideddin was exiled; his tomb is in Damascus, Syria.

The Eyüp Tombs

The District of Eyüp is a part of Istanbul filled with tombs. The first of them to be built is the one belonging to Eyüp Sultan. Ebu Eyyüb Ensari, a friend of the Prophet Mohammed and his flag bearer as well, participated in such battles as the ones in Uhud and Hendek. He also took part in several of the Arab sieges against the Byzantines. He finally became a martyr in one such siege in 669. After the Ottoman conquest of Constantinople, Sultan Mehmed the Conqueror ordered a tomb to be constructed in 1458 in Eyüp for Ebu Eyyüb Ensari, whose real name was Halid Bin Zeyd.

Interior of the Tomb of Mihrişah Sultan.

The bronze-engraved hacet window of this octagonal tomb, which faces the mosque courtyard, was ordered built by Ahmed I. The tomb was thoroughly restored during the reign of Mahmud II. The panel bearing the footprint of the Prophet Mohammed, which is found in the cell inside the tomb, was a gift of Mahmud I. The silver grid work was donated to the tomb by Selim III. Both its interior and exterior are adorned with 16th-Century Iznik tiles. The interior tiles are adorned with verses from the Qur'an. Sokullu Mehmed Pasha commissioned Architect Sinan in 1568 to build for his children who died at a young age a complex in Eyüp consisting of a mosque, a madrasah, and a tomb. He was also buried there soon after he died in 1579. The tomb, the body of which is prismic in shape, is octagonal on the outside, with 16 corners in its interior. Its walls are made from coarse sandstone. Located right across from this tomb is the Tomb of Siyavuş Pasha, who served as grand vizier for some time. Embellished with alluring tiles that are fine representatives of 16th-Century Iznik tiles, it was constructed by Architect Sinan in 1584. This was the first of the polygonal-type tombs that were first seen at the end of the 16th Century.

Siyavuş Pasha and his sons lie at rest in this tomb. Constructed in 1589, the Tomb of Mirimiran Mehmed Pasha, which is quite near this tomb, has a plan based on 12 corners. Mirimiran Mehmed Pasha was a grand vizier during the reign of Murad III. In the same place is another tomb with 16 sides belonging to Ferhad Pasha, who was a grand vizier during the reign of Mehmed III and died in 1595. The tomb, which is the eternal resting place for 12 coffins, is thought to have been constructed by the architect Davud Ağa. The tomb of Zal Mahmud Pasha and the nearby Tomb of Nakkaş Hasan Pasha, both based on a square plan and date back to 1623, are in Eyüp as well.

Near the Golden Horn is the Tomb of Selim III, which is situated within the complex of his mother, Mihrişah Sultan, and dates from 1794. The architect of the tomb was Arif Ağa. The tomb is attractive, with marble covered interior and exterior walls and Baroque-style decoration. Selim III commissioned the architect İbrahim Kamil Ağa to construct a tomb on the Defterdar Road in Eyüp for his daughter, Shah Sultan, in 1800. Built in the Baroque-Empire style, the tomb is situated in a complex consisting of a public fountain and a school. In a group of tombs belonging to Hüsrev Pasha and Mahmud Celaleddin Efendi (Prince Sabahattin) at the Bostan Quay in Eyüp is another tomb dating back to 1860. Constructed in the Empire style, this tomb belongs to the daughter of Mahmud II, Adile Sultan.

The tomb of Prince Sabahattin is also in the Empire style and has a dome covering the building. One of the architects of the late-Ottoman era, Kemaleddin Bey, constructed the Tomb of Mehmed V Reşad, who was the 35th Ottoman sultan. This octagonal tomb lies on the banks of the Golden Horn. Its inscriptions were done by calligrapher Ömer Vasfi and its tile decorations were the work of Kütahyalı Hafız Emin.

Interior view of Hatice Turhan Sultan Tomb.
Hatice Turhan Sultan, the woman who had the mosque complex built,
is buried in the tomb decorated with tiles and engraving that is behind the mosque.
Also buried there is a total of six Ottoman sultans:
Mehmed IV, Mustafa II, Ahmed III, Mahmud I, Osman III and Murad V.

Aqueducts, Fountains and Baths

During the Roman and Byzantine periods, Constantinople was supplied with water from Halkalı, which was brought via aqueducts and stored in a number of cisterns. While the old cisterns were abandoned, the aqueducts were repaired and utilized during the Ottoman period. Today, there are three main networks that provide water for the European side of Istanbul: Halkalı, Kırkçeşme and Bahçeköy-Taksim. The water requirement for the Anatolian side is supplied by the Elmalı Dam. Halkalı was also Istanbul's sole source for water during the periods of Mehmed II, Bayezid and Sultan Yavuz Selim. However, Sultan Süleyman the Magnificent commissioned Architect Sinan to repair existing aqueducts and construct a new one from Kırkçeşme. Thus, water collected in the Belgrade Forest Dam was first conveyed to the Eğrikapı distribution station, then throughout the city via this waterway. Water flowed to all of the city's complexes, mosques and baths as well as to about 400 fountains.

The network which brought water in from Bahçeköy to Beyoğlu's Galata District was bolstered by dams and reservoirs constructed during the reigns of Mahmud I and Abdülhamid I. Mahmud II enhanced these aqueducts in order to distribute this water in a more efficient manner by adding a canal to the network and ordering a distribution station to be constructed in Taksim. Finally, water flowing in from the valley of Hamidiye, between Kemerburgaz and Cendere, was added to the network during the reign of Abdülhamid II and distributed to Galata and the Bosphorus region.

Water that flowed from Belgrad Forest was once collected in a number of historical reservoirs, such as those in Karanlık, Büyük, Topuzlu, Ayvat, Valide, Kirazlı, Şamlar, and Mahmud II, which were constructed in 1620, 1723, 1750, 1765, 1796, 1818, 1828 and 1839, respectively.

After adjusting the pressure in the "rock towers," otherwise known as "water scales," water conveyed from distribution stations was piped to fountains located on street corners. Today one can see examples of these "water scales," which were fashioned from Roman examples, next to the Shehzade Mosque, across from Hagia Sophia as well as in the courtyard of Topkapı Palace. Aqueducts constructed to carry water through the valleys and into town are considered to be distinctive works of art in their own right. Several were erected by Architect Sinan. One such aqueduct was the twin-level Mağlova Aqueduct (1554-64), which measured 35 meters in height and 257 meters in length with its four arches. He also constructed the Avasköy Aqueduct, with 120 arches and the 207 meters-long Kovuk Aqueduct, with 47 arches. Sinan built the latter in 1563 over the foundations of an older Byzantine aqueduct. He also constructed the 771–meter-long twin-level Uzunkemer Aqueduct, with 97 tapered arches, once again over the foundations of Roman and Byzantine works. Sinan also erected the Güzelce Aqueduct during the same year. Floods that hit the region in 1563 destroyed many aqueducts, whereupon Sinan undertook the task of repairing several of these between 1563-64. Those that could not be repaired, such as the Paşakemeri Aqueduct, had to be reconstructed. Istanbul's water network was operated by an organization called the "Water Travelers" up until 1926, when the municipality took over and renovated the system. As a consequence, though a great majority of the fountains no longer receive water, they still exist as colorful monuments of the past. Most of those still standing are products of the era of Sultan Süleyman the Magnificent. With their harmonious and well-balanced architecture, they are reflective of Classical-Ottoman style. There are also very interesting fountains which were built in the Baroque style during the Tulip Era. The Ottomans gave great importance to fountains and constructed numerous ones as well as "sebil," or charitable fountains, throughout Istanbul in the 18th-19th Centuries. They were named according to their function, as well as their location.

Fountains that were constructed at stopover points for caravans, army and "Sürre" (yearly processions to Mecca) were called "Ayrılık" (Separation) and "Namazgah" (Prayer Hall), whereas those constructed at stopover points for the commanding officer of the sultan's bodyguards were called "Bostancıbaşı." Fountains were also named according to the site at which they were constructed. For example, "Duvar" (Wall), "Köşe" (Corner) and "Meydan" (Square). Wall fountains built into the facades of structures were constructed in various styles until the 20th Century. Works found on the corners of streets and buildings were constructed single-faced in the earlier periods and double- or triple-faced in later years. Open-air fountains with engraved surfaces first appeared in the 18th Century and were essentially monuments that decorated public squares. Rather than mentioning all the fountains, we shall give you information regarding some of the more magnificent open-air fountains.

The Mağlova Aqueduct built by Architect Sinan. The six pillars of the two-storey, 260-meter-long aqueduct are under the water of the dam that is there today.

Square Fountains

These are considered the finest examples of the various types of fountains. The fountain in front of the Imperial Gate at Topkapı Palace that was constructed in 1728 by the architect Kayserili Mehmed Emin Ağa upon the orders of Sultan Ahmed III is the best example of a monumental square fountain. One of the most cultured examples of Baroque style art, this work has a vaulted fountain on each side and charitable fountains on each of its corners. Each of its faces is decorated with tiles and engravings. Lines of poetry from the famous poet of the period, Seyyid Vehbi, are inscribed at the top.

The Tophane Fountain, which is situated next to the Kılıç Ali Pasha Mosque in Tophane, is another square fountain gracing Istanbul. Sultan Mahmud I commissioned the architect Mehmed Ağa to construct it in 1732. The square-plan fountain is covered with a single dome topped by wide, overhanging eaves. It has marble facades ornamented with motifs of flowers, cypress trees and fruits.

Constructed in 1732 on the order of Grand Vizier Hekimoğlu Ali Pasha, the square fountain in Kabataş represents a fine example of the Turkish Baroque style. It was moved from its previous location at Setüstü and positioned next to the pier in 1955. Reflecting the transition in styles from Classical to Baroque is a fountain called Bereketzade, which was constructed by Defterdar Emin Efendi in 1732. This fountain was recently moved to its new home beside the Galata Tower. During the completion stage of the New Mosque, Mehmed IV's mother, Hatice Turhan Sultan ordered a fountain to be built as part of the complex. Sultan Ahmed III commissioned the architect Mehmed Ağa to construct both the fountain in Üsküdar's İskele Square in 1728-29, as well as the one in Sultanahmet Square.

The square-plan fountain in Üsküdar is covered with a four-cornered dome with engraved overhanging eaves. Though its architecture resembles the one in Sultanahmet, it does not have any charitable fountain windows. Its marble surfaces are engraved with inscriptions with lines from famous poets of the time. Constructed between 1731-32 for the mother of Mahmud I, Saliha Sultan, the fountain found in Azapkapı is based on a different plan. Here, one encounters a pair of overflowing charitable fountains in the middle with two fountains on either side. The other surfaces of the fountain were left unadorned.

The fountain situated between Beşiktaş and Maçka was constructed by Sultan Abdulmecid between 1839-40 on behalf of his mother, Mother Sultan Bezm-i Alem. One can see lines of poetry on the fountain belonging to two popular poets of the time, Şükri and Zevir as well as Empire-style reliefs. It is covered with a spire-like rock cone roof while its walls are unadorned.

The fountain in Eyüp, which was constructed in 1795 upon the order of Mihrişah Sultan, has an architecture that combines the fountain charitable fountain design. Its surface was ornamented with common decorations of that period. The Onçeşmeler

Fountain in Beykoz is striking for its distinct architecture. First constructed by Behruz Ağa, who was Sultan Süleyman the Magnificent's Keeper of the Privy Chamber, this fountain was renovated in 1746 by Istanbul's Chief of Customs, İshak Ağa. Thus, it is also referred to as the İshak Ağa Fountain. Water still flows from 10 faucets of the arched and domed fountain. Hamidiye water flows from the square Balmumcu Fountain, which has wide eaves. It was constructed in the neo classical style that emerged in the early 19th Century. In addition to this noteworthy fountain, there are others such as the Rukiye Kadın Fountain in Eminönü (1738), the Fleet Admiral (Kaptan-ı Derya) Hacı Hüseyin Pasha Fountain in Kasımpaşa (1732), the Süleyman Kaptan Fountain, also in Kasımpaşa (1748), the Mother Sultan Sineperver Fountain in Üsküdar (1780), the Süleymaniye Fountain (1792), as well as the Pertevniyal Mother Sultan Fountain in Eyüp. Although it is not a Turkish monument, one of the most attractive square fountains is the German Fountain in Sultanahmet Square. The fountain was constructed by Kaiser Wilhelm II on behalf of Abdülhamid II to celebrate his 25th year on the throne. It was constructed by the German architect Spitta in 1899 and assembled in its place in 1901. Its copper-plated dome is supported by green porphyry columns on an octagonal marble base. Its interior is embellished with a gold mosaic and with the monograms of both Wilhelm II and Abdulhamid II engraved on the mosaic.

Charitable Fountains

Water or sherbet used to be dispensed on certain days from the windows of charitable fountains in exchange for a prayer for the builder or the donor of the fountain, but this tradition has disappeared over the years. Today, Istanbul is decorated with almost 80 of these charitable fountains. First appearing in the 16th Century, these charitable fountains, with their polygonal and circular structures, enhance the appearance of street corners and buildings with their Baroque and Empire styles, and marble and wrought iron craftsmanship. The oldest charitable fountain dates back to 1587 and is found in Süleymaniye at the corner of the Tomb of Architect Sinan. Others that have survived to the present are Koca Sinan Pasha in Çarşıkapı (1593), Kuyucu Murad Pasha in Vezneciler (1606), Sultanahmet Mosque (1617) and Hagia Sophia (1640-48). Other significant charitable fountains include the one in the New Mosque Complex constructed on the order of Hatice Sultan (1663), Merzifonlu Kara Mustafa in Çarşıkapı (1691), Kaptan İbrahim Pasha in Beyazıt (1708), Damat İbrahim Pasha in Şehzadebaşı (1719) as well as Gazanfer Ağa at the bottom of the Bozdoğan Aqueduct. The Baroque-style Hacı Emin Ağa in Dolmabahçe (1744); the Turkish Rococo-style Seyyid Hasan Pasha in Vezneciler (1745); the Turkish Rococo-style Nuruosmaniye (1775); Mustafa III in Laleli (1763); Recai Mehmed Efendi in Vefa (1775); Koca Yusuf Pasha in Kabataş (1787), as well as many other charitable fountains bedeck the streets of Istanbul.

One encounters the 19th Century Empire style in charitable fountains located at the edge of Sultanahmet Square, at the bottom of the Cevri Kalfa School as well as the fountain next to the Tomb of Sultan Mahmud.

The Sultan Ahmed III Fountain. Situated at the outer gate of Topkapı Palace, this was built in 1728 by the architect Mehmed Emin Ağa (opposite).

*Next page:
The Cağaloğlu Bath, located in Yerebatan Street, was commissioned by Sultan Mahmud I in 1741 and is still functional today.*

Baths

There are no longer any baths belonging to the Roman or Byzantine periods in Istanbul, the capital of three empires. Nonetheless, it is known that the Romans did build some rather magnificent baths here. For example, historians mention the baths of Arcadius and Zeuxippus. It is known that there were also public baths such as Carosianae, which was completed by the daughter of Valens in 427. There were also baths inside large mansions. One can clearly see traces of Roman influence in baths which were built during the Byzantine and Turkish periods. Also, Turks were inspired to construct numerous baths in Istanbul in the Roman tradition. Just as there were baths built inside the grand complexes, there were independently operated baths as well. Foundations also constructed baths as a source of income.

Sadly, only a handful of the more than 150 baths built throughout the city are still operating today. The Balat Baths in the district of Balat were constructed by the order of Sultan Mehmed the Conqueror in the mid-15th Century. The same sultan was also responsible for the construction in 1460 of the baths next to the Rüstem Pasha Mosque. This structure was damaged in a fire in 1726 as well as in the earthquake of 1894. Utilized as a cold storage warehouse for many years after undergoing some repairs, it has since been converted into a market. Constructed by Grand Vizier Mahmud Pasha in Mahmutpaşa in 1466, only the men's section of the Double Baths (Çifte Hamamlar) is still in use today. In 1558, Hürrem Sultan commissioned Architect Sinan to construct the baths located south of Hagia Sophia, which consisted of both sections for men and women. After undergoing a thorough restoration, this bath is currently operated by the Ministry of Culture as a carpet shop. Situated in Çemberlitaş, the Çemberlitaş Baths were constructed in 1580 by the order of the mother of Murad III, Sultan Nurbanu. Originally constructed as a bath for men and women, only the men's section is open for business these days; the women's half has been converted into a shop. In 1741, Sultan Mahmud I ordered the construction of the Cağaloğlu Baths on Yerebatan Street in Cağaloğlu as a source of income for Hagia Sophia. It continues to function in this capacity. Apart from these baths, we can also count the Nişanci Mehmed Pasha Baths in Kumkapı, the Bayezid Complex Baths (1505), the Çardaklı Baths in Kadırga, which were constructed by the Head Servant of the Sultan's Palace, Hüseyin Ağa Baths (1503), the Barbaros Hayreddin Pasha Baths, constructed by Architect Sinan in Zeyrek, the Dökmeciler Baths inside the Süleymaniye Complex (1550), the Ağa Baths in Samatya (16th Century), and the Ağa Baths in Beyoğlu, (16th Century), the Hüsrev Kethüda Baths in Ortaköy (16th Century), Yeşildirek Baths in Azapkapı (1570), the Çukurcuma Baths in Beyoğlu, and finally the Galatasaray Baths (1715).

The Sultan's Baths of Dolmabahçe Palace.
They are covered with alabaster quarried in Egypt, while the taps are made of silver.

The Haseki Bath in front of Hagia Sophia.
Built by Architect Sinan for Hürrem Sultan in 1540, this bath has sections reserved for both men and women. The bath has been restored and has begun to be used for other purposes.

Apart from the protective walls in Istanbul, there are also a number of sites in and around the city where fortresses are found. One of them is the fortress situated in Anadolukavağı, which is a tourist attraction. Today, one can see the Byzantine Yaros Fortress in all its grandeur at the top of the hill. It was captured by the Genovesians as the Byzantine Empire was on its steady decline, which is why the fortress is referred to as the Genovese Fortress. The imposing fortress, along with its towers, is remarkably intact. Engraved onto its marble walls, are a coat-of-arms, and Classical-Greek inscriptions and epitaphs. The fortress was also used during the Ottoman era after extensive restoration. Sultan Mehmed the Conqueror was the first to have repaired the Anadolukavağı Fortress prior to building Rumelian Fortress. During the repairs, he had a mosque and some wheat granaries constructed on its premises. Armed with cannons, the fortress was strengthened to prevent aid from reaching Constantinople from the Black Sea. While we are on the subject of Anadolukavağı, let's mention Marco Pasha, who had a mansion in Anadolukavağı. The expression "Go and tell it to Marco Pasha" is still heard today. Marco Pasha was a doctor of Greek origin who was appointed to the rank of General during the Ottoman period. He had a famous reputation for patiently listening to complaints voiced by the public. Opposite Anadolukavağı is another touristic site. Known as Rumelikavağı, it was known in antiquity as the site of the Temples of Kybele and Serapis. One can find fortifications here from various periods. In 1642, the Kazakhs showed their displeasure with the Ottoman administration when they moved in front of Yeniköy and Tarabya.

As a consequence, a line of defense was considered against possible danger from the Black Sea. These shores were fortified by Murad IV and successive sultans. The fortress constructed on the shore at Rumelikavağı is rectangular in shape. Along with its counterpart on the opposite side, in Anadolukavağı, this fortress, with its iron gate facing Mecca, was the first line of defense of the Bosphorus. Sultan Murad ordered a mosque and two granaries constructed within the fortress, where the quarters for the fortress guards were also located. 100 cannons of various sizes were stored in the fortress in the past. It is understood that the fortress, which was constructed prior to the Ottoman period, was utilized after it was restored. In 1393, prior to the conquest of Constantinople, the Ottomans constructed the fortress of Anatolian Fortress, also known as "Güzelce Hisar" or "Yenice Hisar" during the reign of Yıldırım Bayezid. While the Rumelian Fortress, on the opposite shore, was under construction, Sultan Mehmed the Conqueror ordered this fortress to be enlarged and had a mosque erected in front of it as well. This mosque collapsed in later years; the one we see today was constructed in 1883. The main fortress is comprised of inner and outer fortress walls, and three towers. The rectangular-planned fortress was constructed over an outcropping of rock.

One enters the four-storey tower from the southwestern gate. The fortress was once surrounded by elegant houses, which also lined both sides of Göksu Stream. Flowing past the fortress and into the Bosphorus, the Göksu Stream once provided entertainment with the caiques that traveled up and down its shores. We shall mention in another chapter Rumelian Fortress, which was constructed by Sultan Mehmed the Conqueror and is currently operated as a museum. We only found it proper to do the same for the Yedikule Fortress, which is also a museum. We have already described the Leander's Tower and Galata Tower in the chapter dealing with the Byzantine Empire. Now it is time to mention something about the other towers in Istanbul.

Utilized as a fire watchtower during the Ottoman period, the 85 meter-high Bayezid Tower is situated in the garden of Istanbul University. First constructed from timber, Mahmud II had it built of stone in 1828 after it had suffered from one fire too many. The Bayezid Tower was renovated in 1889 and 1909 and is still intact. An inscription comprised of lines of poetry by the poet İzzettin was engraved by Calligrapher Yesarizade Mustafa İzzet.

Other lighthouses that can still be seen today are those of Ahırkapı, Yeşilköy and Fenerbahçe. The 36 meter-high Ahırkapı Lighthouse was constructed during the Ottoman Era by the Commodore of the Navy, Süleyman Pasha after a collision at sea. The 22 meter-high Yeşilköy Lighthouse entered service in 1856. The Fenerbahçe Lighthouse was constructed by Grand Vizier İbrahim Pasha in 1720 during the Tulip Era. The 25 meter-high lighthouse served sailors on the Anatolian shores.

In addition to these lighthouses, there are also many clock towers in Istanbul. These include the Dolmabahçe Clock Tower, the Yıldız Clock Tower and the Tophane Clock Tower. The Dolmabahçe Clock Tower was constructed by the Balyans in 1890, many years after the completion of Dolmabahçe Palace. The 27 meter-high tower was last repaired by this author in 1978 and it still runs like new. With inscriptions on all four sides, the Yıldız Clock Tower (1890) is 22 meters tall. The Tophane Clock Tower (1847), which is 15 meters high, is situated in the garden of the Tophane Summer Palace. We have already mentioned the more significant towers of the 16 found in Istanbul. Apart from those, we can count the 52 meter-high Topkapı Palace Justice Tower (1840), the Kandilli Observatory, and the Çubuklu Khedive Tower. Constructed by the Egyptian Khedive Abbas Hilmi Pasha in 1890, the tower of the summerhouse stands 14 meters and was constructed for its commanding panoramic view of the Bosphorus. There are also several other towers that grace the skyline of Istanbul, including the Atatürk Airport Control Tower, the Şişli Children's Hospital Clock Tower, and the Kasımpaşa Naval Hospital Clock Tower.

The Savarona yacht seen as sailing off the coast of the Rumelian Fortress. It was given as a gift to the great leader of Turkish nation Mustafa Kemal Atatürk but could only be used for a short duration during his illness.

Seven Towers Fortress

Situated along the protective walls of Istanbul is a fortress named Seven Towers Fortress (Yedikule Hisarı), which displays features of both the Byzantine and Ottoman periods. The 5,630 meter-long Land Walls that surround the old part of Istanbul start at the end of Marmara Walls. This was where the splendid ceremonial gate of the Byzantines was situated. Constructed by Roman Emperor Theodosius I in 390 AD. this gate was called "Porta Aura" because it was once gold-plated. Emperors would enter the city after their victorious military campaigns through this gate, which had the status of a victory arch. But in 413 Theodosius II constructed the protective walls that we see today, merging this gate into the walls.

Thus, the gate became one of the splendid gates of the protective walls. As a matter of fact, Michael Palaeologus entered the city on horseback through this gate after winning back the city from the Latins in 1261. Previously used as a triumphal archway, the gate had three arches and marble towers on both sides, as well as two statues positioned overhead; one was of Theodosius and the other was of Nike being pulled by an elephant cart.

These statues were destroyed by a pair of earthquakes that struck in 740 and 866. John V. Palaeologus had the gate repaired in 1389, adding figures in relief depicting Hercules' actions and some mythological scenes. These figures remained here until the 17th Century. Five years after conquering Constantinople, Sultan Mehmed the Conqueror ordered some additional buildings to be constructed here and turned this into an inner fortress separate from the protective walls.

Thus, a fortress called "Yedikule," which was comprised of seven towers including those remaining from the Byzantines, emerged here. Even though Sultan Mehmed the Conqueror first used this place to house his treasury, it was to be transferred to the Topkapı Palace later on.

Seven Towers Fortress was eventually converted into a dungeon where prisoners such as rebellious ambassadors and other influential people were locked up. For example, the Russian Ambassador Obrekoff and the French Ambassadors Jean de la Haye and Ruffin were a few of those who got on the wrong side of the sultans and ended up here in custody.

One of the most painful events to occur here was when the reformer Osman II, who was deposed when many people including Kösem Sultan provoked the Janissaries. He was subsequently brought here in 1622 and executed in the Eastern Tower. Apart from this, Grand Vizier Mahmud Pasha, Hasan Pasha and Deli Hüseyin Pasha were also executed here. Once past the narrow entrance gate at Yedikule Fortress, one reaches the old ceremonial gate of the Byzantines. The fortress, including the Golden Gate, Ahmed III Tower, Treasury, trunk walls and the entrance gate, was repaired between 1958-70. A minaret is all that remains of the mosque that was constructed for the fortress guards. It is possible to encounter traces of the dungeon inside one of the towers.

Aerial view of the Seven Towers (Yedikule).

Aerial view of the Anatolian Fortress. This fortress was commissioned by Yıldırım Bayezid in 1393, earlier than the Rumelian Fortress.

Rumelian Fortress

In 1393, Yıldırım Bayezid ordered the construction of a fortress called Anatolian Fortress, also known as Güzelce Hisar, on the site of the ancient Byzantine Temple of Jupiter. Prior to taking Constantinople, Sultan Mehmed the Conqueror ordered the construction of a fortress directly opposite Anatolian Fortress to prevent aid reaching the Byzantines from the Black Sea. Preparations made for the construction of the fortress were complete in the spring of 1452 while material and skilled workers were brought here from all over the country. Mehmed II arrived there on March 21 and set up camp on the site where the fortress would soon be constructed. In going over the plans one final time, he gave the command to commence construction of the fortress. He first decided to have a fortress constructed just at that point and started to prepare his plans to go further. The Byzantine Emperor protested the construction of the fortress, saying, "I will grant you a site as wide as the hide of a cow, but you can forget about building on land that is wider than that hide." It is said that Mehmed II cut up a cow's hide into a very thin (and long) thong, whereby he commenced building after marking off the stretched piece of cowhide on the ground. When the emperor sent his ambassadors to protest the action, the Conqueror presented them with this cowhide thong adding, "As per your zoning permission, we have only constructed the site as wide as this piece of cowhide. Let us know if we have exceeded your stated limitations, and we will gladly tear it down". Mehmed II appointed Saruca, Zağnos and Çandarlı Halil Pasha the task of building this fortress, ordering them to expedite the job, which they did. In this way, the slender ray of hope held by the Byzantines was extinguished as Mehmed II had carried out another one of his plans. It is said that between April 13 - August 31 1452, an architect named Musliheddin completed the construction of the fortress in just 139 days; but this hypothesis has never been proven. The task of constructing of the northwest cylindrical tower was given to Saruca Pasha. He built eight storeys into the 28 m high tower and covered the top floor with a brick dome. The northeast tower, which was 22 m high and had 12 corners, was built by the Grand Vizier Halil Pasha. Measuring 21 m in height, the southeast tower was constructed by Zağnos Pasha. An inscription indicating the name of the architect was engraved on the gate. Along its walls, the fortress is protected by turrets and narrow roads, the latter not connected to the towers.

The five gates inside the fortress are called Dizdar, Hisartepe, Sel, Dağ and İstihkam A collapsed minaret is all that remains of a masjid that was built during the period of Mehmed II. Situated on an area measuring 60,000 m², the fortress also has water facilities such as a fountain, a well and a cistern. While the Rumelian Fortress lost its strategic importance after the conquest of Constantinople, it continued to be used to monitor vessels that plied the Bosphorus, and as prison. Known as the "Black Tower," the Saruca Pasha Tower was converted into a national prison. One of Mehmed II's Grand Viziers, Gedik Ahmed Pasha, the Austrian Ambassador, as well as envoys from Venice and Erdel, were all imprisoned here. Guilty Janissaries were strangled here and their bodies tossed into the sea. The fortress lost its importance in the 17th Century, when the defense of the Bosphorus was moved up to the Black Sea coast. It was abandoned during the period of Mahmud II, with a new town quarter emerging from within it. The Rumelian Fortress underwent a complete restoration between 1955-58. The quarter that had placed itself there was removed and it was landscaped with a beautiful garden and inaugurated as a museum in 1958. Cannons and stone catapults as well as a part of the famous chain used to block the entrance of the Golden Horn are exhibited in this museum.

A view of the Rumelian Fortress and Bosphorus in spring.

156

Ottoman Palaces

After the Turkish conquest of Istanbul, Mehmed the Conqueror found the Byzantine Palaces to be run down; therefore he ordered a palace built for himself in Beyazıt (also Bayezid), where Istanbul University is located today. This palace proved to be too small later on and thus he had the Topkapı Palace built in 1475 and moved there. The wives, mothers and concubines of those sultans who left the throne began to stay in the old palace. For various reasons, many of the sea-side kiosks of Topkapı Palace could not survive to the present time. Süleyman the Magnificent had his sister Hatice Sultan marry his grand vizier Makbul İbrahim Pasha in 1524. As a gift for them, the sultan commissioned the İbrahim Pasha Palace in Sultanahmet, which is the modern-day Museum of Turkish and Islamic Arts. Another palace that does not exist today is the Summer Palace, located somewhere between Salacak and Haydarpaşa. The only thing remaining from this palace is the name 'Harem'. Another palace is known to have existed in Beykoz, as noted by a 17th Century traveler.

As early as the beginning of the 19th Century, especially during the period of Mahmud II, palaces along the Bosphorus began to be favored. In place of the palace which was consumed by a fire, Mahmud II had the timber coastal palace in Beşiktaş built in the 18th Century and he came to favor it over Topkapı Palace. Mahmud II's son Abdülmecid had the timber palace in Dolmabahçe demolished, which was commissioned by his father. In its place, he commissioned the current Dolmabahçe Palace by the Architect Garabet Balyan and his son Nikogos Balyan, spending five million gold coins. Abdülaziz, who took the Ottoman throne after his brother Abdülmecid in 1861, had the timber palace across the Bosphorus, which was commissioned by his father Mahmud II, demolished. In its place, he commissioned the Beylerbeyi Palace, which he envisaged as a summer palace, by Nikogos and Sarkis Balyan from 1861-1865. The palace was built with inspiration from French Baroque architecture, as three floors including the basement. The palace is completely marble. Sandstones brought from Bakırköy were also used. The palace has 24 rooms and 6 halls. The palace has a harem (quarters for women) and selamlık (quarters for men), which are separated from each other by the pooled hall downstairs. The Selamlık Hall on the second floor and the Reception Room are remarkable. The last room at the transition from the formal section (mabeyn) to the harem is the Formal Reception Room. In the formal reception (mabeyn) section, the upstairs rooms located towards the sea are remarkable with their wooden wall coating. The inner ornamentation at Beylerbeyi Palace is much different than the exterior. 19th Century European Baroque is seen on the furniture, mirrors, consoles and cornices, while Eastern style is presented on the ceiling and column capitals with a Western approach. Furthermore, verses written in fine sülüs (or thuluth) and talik script are remarkable on the ceiling and walls.

One of the largest halls of the Beylerbeyi Palace: the Pool Hall located downstairs.

The Beylerbeyi Palace, which was commissioned by Sultan Abdülaziz to Sarkis Balyan, between 1861-65.

The stairs leading upstairs from the entry hall of the Formal Section of the Beylerbeyi Palace.

A view from the Yıldız Palace, which is made up of many kiosks located in the Yıldız Park. Yıldız Palace, where the first construction began during the period of Selim III, was enlarged with the addition of new buildings during Abdülhamid II and used in his long-lived sultanate. Yıldız Palace has some important kiosks such as the Chalet Kiosk (Şale Köşkü).

The two gates with open-worked iron cast leaves, which are on the sea-side wall, lead from the quay into the palace garden. There are two little sea kiosks at the two ends of the wall. The garden, which is separated into sections, extends backwards and is decorated with rare trees, pools, and special marble and bronze sculptures created by artists. In the last section of the garden is a pool, and lined up around this pool are the Yellow Kiosk (Sarı Köşk), Serdab (or Sunken) Kiosk and Stable Kiosk (Ahır Köşk). This time, Sultan Abdülaziz commissioned the Çırağan Palace in Bosphorus from 1863-1871, in place of the old timber palace. This palace, created by Nikogos and Sarkis Balyan, is remarkable with its marble

workmanship. The palace, which was built with three floors and in two sections as the harem and the men's quarters, connects to the main road via two monumental gates. The ornate one is the Sultan's Gate (Hünkar Kapısı) opening into the garden of the formal section, and opposite that is the Coastal Gate (Sahil Kapısı). The other gate is the Mother's Gate (Valide Kapısı) opening into the harem section. After his 93-day regency, Sultan Murad V was dethroned and compelled to reside at the Çırağan Palace. The palace was used as the parliament building during the 2nd Constitutional Period. After burning in 1910, it remained in ruins for many years, and has recently been restored, with a hotel added to the side of it.

Since Abdülhamid II did not find Dolmabahçe secure, he moved to the Yıldız Palace and reigned there for 33 years. Later on, Yıldız Palace, which spans an area of 500 thousand m², was surrounded with high walls. With the addition of a theatre, museum, workshop, library, pharmacy and parks, this place turned into a living area that would meet every need. All of these buildings were gathered in three gardens and four large gates would provide entry into the buildings. Located in the first courtyard is the Large Formal Section (Büyük Mabeyn), which Sultan Abdülaziz had commissioned in 1866; to the north is the Chintz Pavilion (Çit Köşkü), where ambassadors were received, and to the east are the Offices of the Aides-de-

Camp to the Sultan (Yaveran Köşkü) and the Armory Building (Silahhane). Through a second large gate from here, a courtyard is reached, which then leads to the Little Formal Section (Küçük Mabeyn), commissioned in 1900 by Sultan Abdülhamid. A gate between the Chintz Pavilion and the Little Formal Section leads to a courtyard surrounded by high walls. This is where the kiosks for the sultans' wives, sultans and crown princes, and the theatre were located. The most significant building in the internal garden is the Cihannüma Kiosk with a dazzling view. The external garden is currently Yıldız Park, where palace women would take strolls. It includes the Chalet Kiosk (Şale Köşkü), Malta Kiosk and Tent Kiosk

Internal view of the Çırağan Palace. The palace, which was commissioned by Sultan Abdulaziz, was burnt in 1910 and has been restored loyally to its original in the recent years.

(Çadır Köşkü). The most well-groomed section of the Yıldız Palace is the Chalet Kiosk, which can be considered a large palace despite being called a kiosk. Chalet Kiosk was initiated to be built in 1889, in the honor of the first visit of the German Emperor Wilhelm II to Istanbul. The building was completed during his second visit. The Chalet Kiosk is made up of two stories over a basement, having a harem section and men's quarters. Today it is open to visits as a museum affiliated with the Department of National Palaces. In addition to these palaces mentioned, there were other palaces in Istanbul which do not survive to the present time. For example, there was the famous Sadabad Palace in the Golden Horn, commissioned by Damat İbrahim Pasha for Ahmed III. The palace was demolished during Patrona Halil Rebellion, which broke out in 1730. In place of this ruined palace, Mahmud II had a new palace built by Architect Kirkor Balyan. However, Sultan Abdülmecid did not quite esteem this palace, and so it went to ruins. Abdülaziz had it demolished and had the Çağlayan Summer Palace built in its place, which remains only to be seen on the canvases of artists today. The Tersane Palace, which was a glamorous building near Hasköy in the Golden Horn, was demolished in the 19th Century. Afterwards, Selim III ordered that a shipyard and a factory be established in its place. Only the Aynalı Kavak Kiosk was built over this broad land. From the Davut Pasha Palace, which was commissioned by the sultan back in the 16th Century to salute the army at the start of a military campaign, only some remnants survive presently.

Not many palaces belonging to the members of the dynasty remain today, and those that remain are used for different purposes. For example, Feriye Palaces, which were built for the services of the Çırağan Palace, are used as the Kabataş Highschool and Galatasaray Primary School today. The palaces commissioned by Abdülhamid in Ortaköy, for his two daughters, are used as a school and for other purposes. The building near the mosque in Ortaköy was the Coastal Palace of Esma Sultan, Mahmud II's sister. The coastal palace which Esma Sultan had commissioned by the Eyüp coast could not survive to the present time. The Coastal Palace of Hatice Sultan, Selim III's sister, was located in the place of the pier of the bridge in Ayvansaray, by the Golden Horn. We know about this palace only through the work of the famous artist Melling. A school stands in the place of the Fikirtepe Summer Palace today, where Murad V had spent his term as crown prince once. There were two palaces commissioned in Fındıklı by Sultan Abdülmecid, for his daughters Cemile and Münire Sultans. The one towards Beşiktaş belonged to Cemile Sultan. This palace was later allocated to Adile Sultan. In 1910, it was allocated to the Lower House and the Upper House of the Ottoman Parliament. It was used as Fine Arts Academy from 1926-48. The palace, which was burnt in 1948, was repaired and both of the buildings are allocated to Architect Sinan University today. Adile Sultan's palace on the Kandilli ridges was also transformed into a school but unfortunately, it was recently burnt and had to be repaired. Adile Sultan's kiosk in Koşuyolu is being used as a hospital now. The palace of the last caliph Abdülmecid is located on the Beylerbeyi ridges. It remains standing today thanks to a private bank. Another palace that is used as a hospital today is the Baltalimanı Bone Hospital.

A view of the Çırağan Palace from the sea, which was built between the years 1863-71 as commissioned by Sultan Abdülaziz to Nikogos and Sarkis Balyan.

Topkapı Palace

After the Turkish conquest of Istanbul, Mehmed the Conqueror found the Byzantine Palaces to be quite dilapidated. He initiated the reconstruction activities in this city which was to become the third capital of the Ottoman Empire. He ordered a palace built for himself on the Beyazıt Square. As this palace proved to be insufficient in time, a new palace was constructed in Sarayburnu from 1460-1478. This palace became a place where sultans from Mehmed the Conqueror until Sultan Abdülmecid resided with their wives, children and aides and was also where official governmental work was carried out, for 400 years.

Every sultan added new construction to the existing buildings which were gathered around four courtyards. When a harem section was added in, bringing the reflection of a totally different world, the palace almost became a small city with thousands of inhabitants. The palace buildings were surrounded by a wide rampart, which was known as Sur-u Sultani (Sultan's Rampart) and had many gates on it. There were cannons on one of these gates, which caused this palace to be named Topkapı (Cannon Gate) later on.

First Courtyard: The most spectacular entrance to the Topkapı Palace is through the Imperial Gate (Bab-ı Hümayun), which opens into the First Courtyard of the palace and has a triple entryway. This place was arranged as a kiosk to be used for important occasions and ceremonies but the upper floor is no longer existent. To the west of the first courtyard known as the Parade Square (Alay Meydanı), is the church of Hagia Eirene, which was used as the Armory Building of the palace, and located near that was the Imperial Mint Building (Darphane-i Amire) and wood and wickerwork storage. There was also a kiosk here, through which the public communicated their problems to the palace. Buildings such as the Palace Hospital (Enderun Hastanesi), Palace Bakery (Has Fırın) and Central Water Tank (Dolap Ocağı), which do not currently exist, were located on the square towards the palace. Kiosks surviving to date inside the Topkapı Palace Walls are the Tiled Kiosk, which is located in the garden of the Archaeological Museum today; the Parade Kiosk (Alay Köşkü) on the tram way, which has been known since the period of Murad III; and Sepetçiler Summer Palace (Sepetçiler Kasrı), which is being used today after being recently restored.

Second Courtyard: Used as the entrance to the Topkapı Palace today, the Gate of Salutation (Bab-üs Selam), which is the middle gate, leads into the second courtyard surrounded by porches on four sides. The second courtyard is also known as the Council Square (Divan Meydanı). On this ceremonial square, which represented the execution of the state administration, the imperial council would convene, coronation ceremony of the sultan would take place, and reception ceremonies for the ambassadors would be held. On the left side of the courtyard is the Tower of Justice (Adalet Kulesi), the shaft of which was built during the term of Mehmed the Conqueror. The tower was raised in 1820

during the period of Mahmud II, and during Sultan Abdülaziz, a kiosk was added to the tower. Located beneath the Tower of Justice is the Imperial Council Building (Divan-ı Hümayun), also known as Kubbealtı, which is one of the most important buildings. This building, which was ordered by Süleyman the Magnificent to the Chief Architect Alaeddin from 1527-29, is made up of three adjacent domed spaces. The first space is the Kubbealtı section, where viziers would convene. The other part belongs to the Imperial Council section. The last section was used as the archive chamber. Kubbealtı was damaged by a fire in 1665 and was repaired during the period of Mehmed IV. The epitaphs reveal that it also underwent repairs in 1792 and 1819 during the periods of Selim III and Mahmud II. The columned porch section in front of the Tower of Justice dates back to the 16th Century but it was reconstructed in the 18th Century with a wooden fringe with Rococo ornamentations. Sultans would follow the council meetings from the window above the chamber known as Kubbealtı. Here, grand viziers and council viziers and military judges from Anatolia and European territories of the empire would discuss the issues on the agenda and make decisions. Grand viziers would accept the ambassadors in this place where the state was administered from.

The building made up of eight domes, which was located to the east of the Imperial Council Building and was used by grand viziers, was the building of State Treasury (Dış Hazine) allocated to the expenses of the state. It dates back to the period of Süleyman the Magnificent and is used as a Weapons Museum today. The descending path next to Kubbealtı leads to the Palace Stables. This is where the palace horses were kept. On the northern end of the stables was the Harness Treasury (Raht Hazinesi), where opulent trappings were preserved. The Quarters for the Halberdiers with Tresses (Zülüflü Baltacılar) and the Beşir Ağa Mosque are also located in this section.

Behind the porch on the right side of the Second Courtyard are the palace kitchens, which extend alongside the courtyard and are made up 20 spaces. The kitchens, which are entered through three gates, are known to have been constructed together with the palace. Destroyed by a fire in 1574, however, they were repaired by the Architect Sinan and given a different look with their domes and chimneys. The confectionary section (helvahane) and fruit juice section (şerbethane) of the palace kitchens, which were added during the period of Süleyman the Magnificent, are made up of four parts. In these sections, Turkish kitchen utensils, Ottoman-style Yıldız Porcelains, and glassware can be seen, while European porcelains and Ottoman silverware are exhibited in what used to be the Cooks' Quarters formerly. Chinese and Japanese porcelains are shown in the main kitchen section.

Chinese and Japanese Porcelains: The Chinese porcelains, which began to be exported to the Middle East and Near East as of the 9th and 10th Centuries, reached as far

Tower of Justice and Kubbealtı (The Meeting Hall of the Imperial Council), Topkapı Palace.

Aerial views of Topkapı Palace

167

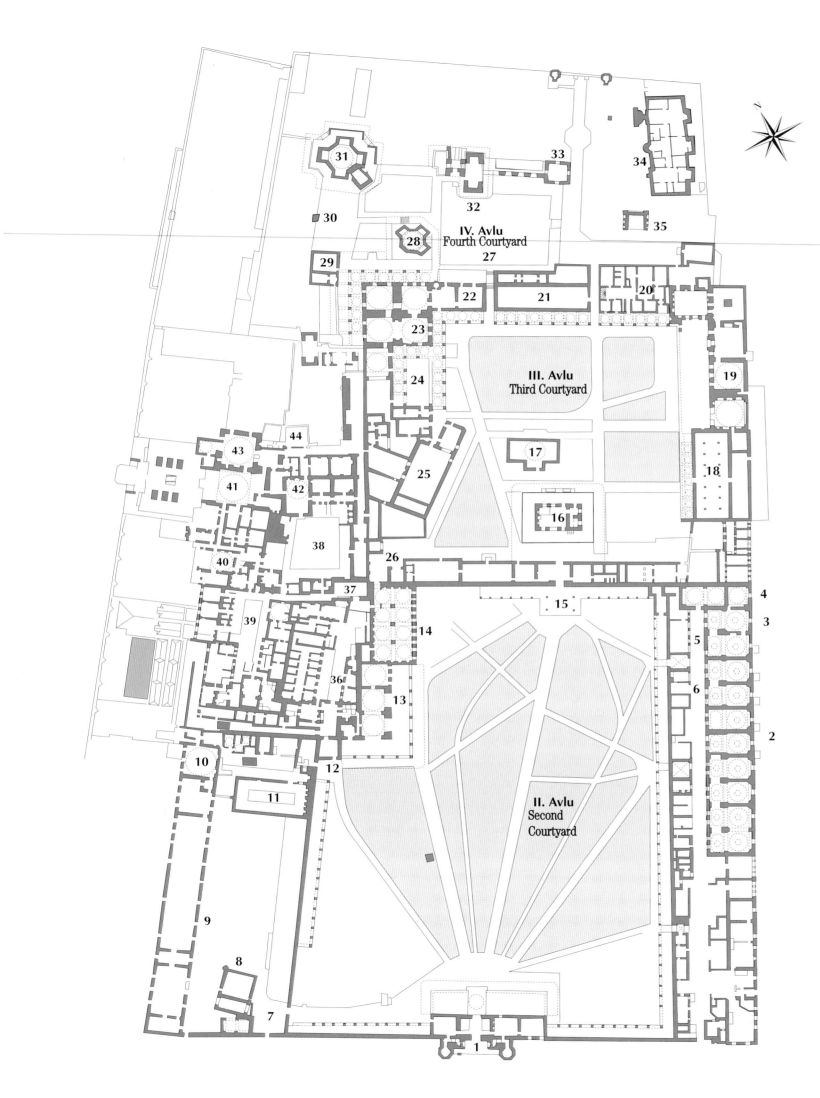

Plan of the Topkapı Palace:

1. Entrance to Topkapı Palace (Bab-üs Selam)
2. Kitchens (Chinese and Japanese Porcelain Section)
3. Confectionary Section (Helvahane)
4. Istanbul Glassware and Porcelain Section
5. Cooks' Quarters
6. Silverware and European Porcelain Section
7. The Funeral Gate (Meyyit Kapısı)
8. Beşir Ağa Mosque
9. Privy Stables
10. The Harness Treasury (Raht Hazinesi)
11. The Quarters for the Halberdiers with Tresses (Zülüflü Baltacılar)
12. Carriage Drivers' Gate to the Harem
13. The Council Apartments (Kubbealtı)
14. The State Treasury Section (Dış Hazine)
15. Gate of White Eunuchs (Bab-üs Saade)
16. Audience Chamber (Arzodası)
17. Library of Ahmed III
18. Textile and Caftan Section
19. The Treasury Section
20. Museum Administration [Pantry (Kilerli) Quarters]
21. The Chamber of the Treasury Servants
22. The Clock Section
23. Holy Relics Section (Hırka-i Saadet)
24. The Sultans' Portrait Gallery
25. Library (Ağalar Mosque)
26. The Aviary Gate (Kuşhane Kapısı), Harem
27. Entrance of the Fourth Courtyard
28. The Revan Kiosk
29. The Circumcision Chamber
30. The Iftariye Arbor
31. The Baghdad Kiosk
32. The Mustafa Pasha Kiosk
33. Tower of Head Doctor (Tower of Chief Lala)
34. The Mecidiye Kiosk
35. Dressing Room

Plan of the Harem:

36. The Black Eunuchs Stone Yard
37. Eunuchs' Waiting Spot
38. The Mother Sultan Stone Yard
39. The Concubines Stone Yard
40. Hall of the Mother Sultan
41. The Sultan Anteroom
42. The Fireplace Anteroom
43. Kiosk of Murad III
44. The Crown Prince Chambers

Baghdad Kiosk (1639)
This octagonal-planned kiosk was built by Murad IV to celebrate the Ottoman conquest of Baghdad. The central dome is flanked by vaulted extensions. They open out into a broad portico on the front covered by wooden eaves and supported by 22 marble columns. Between them run geometric-interlace carved balustrades. Looking from the garden below the kiosk, it is clear that it was originally a two-story building. The windows on the lower course are marble-framed and the facade is marble-faced at that level to the eaves. 17th Century tiles cover the area above the marble covered facade. The walls and dome are embellished with fine polychrome-traced gesso on the interior. Gilded geometric relief work on the coffered vaults is particularly well preserved. To the right of the entrance stands a copper fireplace. A decorative orb hangs from the dome. Closets and window shutters are inlayed with nacre and an inscription frieze in celi sülüs encircles the walls between the upper and lower courses. This frieze was done by the calligrapher Tophaneli Enderuni Mahmud Çelebi.

as Anatolia via the Silk Road later on entering the Ottoman Palace. The Chinese porcelain collection, which comprises 10,358 pieces, is one of the most significant Chinese porcelain collections in the world. Moreover, by providing an uninterrupted chronology from the 13th to 19th Century, this collection reveals the historical development of the Chinese porcelains. Belonging to Yuan, Ming and Qing dynasties, these porcelains are categorized as celadon, blue and white wares, mono-color series and multi-color series. Green-glazed celadons, which were believed to reveal the poison put inside, constitute an important part of the collection with 1354 pieces. Used by the sultans in the 16th Century, these Chinese porcelains were decorated by golden frames in the palace goldsmith workshop. Topkapı Palace also holds Japanese porcelains of about 600 pieces, which include large plates, vases, bowls and jars.

Third Courtyard: The third gate of the palace, the Gate of Felicity (Bab-üs Saade), was guarded by the White Eunuchs and thus known as the 'Gate of White Eunuchs' (Akağalar Kapısı) as well. It acquired its current Rococo-style appearance during the sultanates of Abdülhamid I and Mahmud II. Ottoman sultans would ascend to the throne in front of this gate, where state notables would extend their congratulations to them. Furthermore, exchange of bajram (religious festival) greetings, and funeral processions for sultans who had passed away would also take place here. This gate leads into the third courtyard, to the Inner Palace Square (Enderun Meydanı) where the internal organization of the palace is located. Found here are the residences of the Sultan and his privy officers, together with the dormitories of the palace school. From the White Eunuchs Gate, one passes into the Audience Chamber (Arz Odası), which was one of the first buildings of the Topkapı Palace. It served as a functional and ceremonial hall. Having survived to the present time with various repairs until the beginning of the 19th Century, the internal decoration of the building was last redone in the Empire style in 1856.

Located behind the Audience Chamber, in the middle of the courtyard is the Palace Library, which was built in 1719 during the period of Ahmed III, in the Tulip Era style. Having a fountain in front of it, the library is accessed via staircases on both sides. The interior walls are covered by tiles and the cabinets are with nacre and tortoise shell inlays. The Guardian Eunuch's Apartment (Kapı Ağası Dairesi) just to the right of the door, and the changing section of Selim II's bath which is located at the corner ahead from here, are still existent. This section is currently used as the first hall of the treasury. Next to the bath was the Barrack of the Campaign Pages (Seferli Koğuşu), where the servants who ceremoniously washed the sultan's garments and turban were found. Today, the garments of sultans are on display here. Since Ottoman sultans were Islamic caliphs at the same time, their garments were preserved in a bundle of clothing bearing their names and thus the collection of sultan caftans was formed. Besides the caftans, amazing talismanic shirts as well as infant garments also survived to the present time. Garments of the sultans have been preserved in a chronological order from Mehmed the Conqueror to Mehmed Reşad. The garments of the latest sultans took the form of jackets and trousers under European influence but traditional caftans continued to be used. Sultan caftans weaved in the palace workshops in patterns created by privy painters, and were made from precious fabrics such as kemha (brocade); çatma, a type of velvet with patterns higher than the base;

Ceremonial caftan and detail of Shehzade (crown prince) Bayezid (died 1562).
Long-sleeved ceremonial caftan, sometimes associated with Bayezid II (1481-1512) but more plausibly belonged to another of Süleyman the Magnificent's sons. It is thought to have been made with cloth specially woven in the palace workshops in finest "Gülistani" kemha.

seraser, very expensive silk woven from gold-silver alloy threads; diba, and atlas. Summer caftans were made from thin fabrics, whereas winter caftans were made from thick ones. Among the examples which are intact and currently exist are Sultan Selim I's serenk caftan, Prince Mehmed's embroidered atlas caftan, Selim II's kemha and seraser caftans, Mehmed III's and Murad III's furred çatma caftans.

There are also caftans made from silk such as those of Murad III and Ahmed I. In addition to the sultans' garments in this section, there are also around 40 carpets and prayer rugs of Persian design, as well as samples of Ottoman fabrics. The halls referred to as the Fatih Kiosk, near the Barracks of the Campaign Pages, is one of the earliest buildings of the palace and is used as treasury section today. Situated next to the treasury section is the administrative division of the palace, which used to be the Pantry Quarters (Kilerli Koğuşu). This is where those who prepared the sultan's meals and set his tables would stay. Next to this was the Imperial Treasury Ward (Hazine-i Hümayun Koğuşu). The clock collection of the palace is on display in the building known as the Treasury of the Sultan's Weapon Guards, which has a connection to the Privy Chamber. In this collection, it is possible to see the most interesting examples of Turkish, German, Austria, English, French and Swiss clocks. At the north eastern corner of the courtyard is a building known as the Section of Holy Cloak or Holy Relics (Hırka-ı Saadet or Kutsal Emanetler Dairesi). This was a private apartment for the sultans and contained the Throne Chamber as well. After the transfer of the Caliphate to the Ottoman sultans as of the 16th Century, it was allocated to the holy relics. The building adjacent to the Section of Holy Relics was the masjid of Privy Servants (Has Odalılar) who provided private service to the sultans. Currently, portraits of the Ottoman sultans are exhibited here. On the north western side of the Third Courtyard of the palace, also known as the Inner Palace Courtyard, the Aviary Gate (Kuşhane Kapısı) of the harem section is found. In the Ward of White Eunuchs (Akağalar Koğuşu) located next to the Gate of White Eunuchs, providing entry into the courtyard, there is a section where Ottoman palace embroideries and leather works are on display. There are three engaging sections of the Topkapı Palace in the Inner Palace Courtyard.

Treasury Section: The treasury collection of the Topkapı Palace is exhibited in the three chambers known as Fatih Kiosks in the Third Courtyard, and the fourth chamber added to them. This treasury, featuring priceless works, was the Sultan's Treasury (Enderun Hazinesi) and there were also State Treasury (Dış Hazine), Ambassadors' Treasury and Harness Treasury. Sultan Mehmed the Conqueror's treasury was highly enriched with the booty brought by Selim I from Iran and Egypt. The Treasury Section would be opened and closed by a group of treasury officers. Ottoman sultans would have this heirloom treasury opened when they ascended to the throne, observe it with a ceremony, and work towards enlarging it. Precious works and money would come into the treasury through various ways. The most precious pieces of the war booty would be taken to the treasury. The other largest sources of the treasury were the gifts given by ambassadors during their reception ceremonies, and gifts given during the coronation ceremonies. Moreover, very precious gifts would also be received on the birthdays of the members of the dynasty, and circumcision and wedding ceremonies of the crown princes. Artists would also create exquisite works and present them to the sultan, in return for his help. Possessions of the

The Spoon-maker's Diamond.
One of the most valuable objects in the treasury is the Spoon-maker's Diamond. The gem is 86 carats and 42x35x16 mm in size. The entire diamond, with setting, is 70x60 mm

executed or discharged statesmen would also be assigned to the treasury. Another source was works that were purchased for the treasury. Apart from these, Ottoman sultans also commissioned precious works for the tomb of the Prophet Muhammed and sent them to Kaaba. Since every sultan was sending these precious works, their number increased at the tomb of Prophet Muhammed. In fear that these precious items would fall at the hands of other nations during World War I, they were brought by Fahreddin Pasha and deposited into the treasury. Some of the precious works that can be seen in the treasury today consist of these items. Some items seen in the treasury were acquired, as a result of the reciprocal gift exchange between Sultan Mahmud I and the Nadir Shah of Iran. After the long-lasting Iranian wars, peace was established and thus Nadir Shah sent his world-famous throne as a gift, while Mahmud I commissioned rare items prepared by the palace goldsmith and sent them to Nadir Shah via his ambassadors. The ambassadors had barely arrived at the border when Nadir Shah was killed, and so ambassadors returned together with the gifts that were to be given to him and the gifts were deposited into the treasury. Such works as the Topkapı Dagger, which can be seen in the treasury today, and the quiver ornamented with extremely precious stones, are among these items. Gifts that were thus acquired were not the private possession of the sultan but were registered in the treasury and kept in the cabinets as treasury's property. Some of these items were exhibited during the period of Sultan Abdülmecid I, which also continued during the period of sultans who succeeded him. The majority of the items that are in the treasury today date to the 16th -19th Centuries. Additionally, there are also a few samples from the Byzantine, Seljuk and Memluk periods. Let us categorize and examine these precious items in the treasury.

The most spectacular group in the treasury section is the thrones. One of these thrones is the ebony throne with its back and side surfaces inlaid with ivory nacre in rumi, palmetto and chintamani patterns. Dating back to the 16th Century, this throne is thought to have been used by Murad IV (1623-1640) during his campaign to Baghdad. The second wooden throne, which was made by Sedefkar Mehmed Ağa, is also known as Sultan Ahmed I's Throne or Arife Throne. Representing the best of wood and nacre workmanship of the 17th Century, this throne has tortoise shell and nacre inlays over walnut, and there are precious stones on the nacre inlays. The Bajram Throne, which is one of the most important thrones in the treasury, is thought to have been presented by the Egyptian governor İbrahim Pasha to Sultan Murad III. During their accession ceremonies or bajram ceremonies, Ottoman Sultans would sit on this wholly wooden throne covered by golden plaques and receive greetings. There are 954 large chrysolite stones on the throne. The most intriguing and precious item of the treasury section is the throne of Nadir Shah. The throne, which was known to have belonged to Ismail Shah, turned out to have belonged to Nadir Shah as revealed by recent research. This wooden throne, which was covered by golden plaques and ornamented with emerald, ruby and pearls over its outer surface, was sent by Nadir Shah of Iran to the Ottoman Sultan Mahmud I (1730-1754) as a token of peace.

The Topkapı Dagger (1741)
This dagger, the symbol of Topkapı Palace, was made for Mahmud I in 1741 as a present for Nadir Shah of Persia. It was returned to the palace upon the outbreak of unrest in Persia. There are three 30-40 mm oval emeralds on one face of the handle, the other side being decorated with enamelled and nacre fruit motifs. A hinged lid to the hilt, which acts as a setting for an octagonal -cut emerald 30 mm in diameter surrounded by diamonds, opens to reveal a London -marked watch. The sheath is decorated with floral enamelled motifs on gold, and encrusted with diamonds towards the tip and hilt. Baskets of fruit in enamel are worked on both sides of the sheath. L.35 cm

One of the other intriguing groups of objects in the treasury is the aigrettes, which were attached by the Ottoman sultans or princes to their turbans. They were almost the symbol of the dynasty. These precious jewels, which were ornamented with emerald, ruby, diamond and pearls together with huma bird, heron and peacock feathers, were worn on the turbans or fezzes. Another group of objects were made up of the pendants, which would mark the place of the sultan. Complementing the decoration of thrones and important places, these were ornamental elements symbolizing the sultan. Many of the pendants found in the treasury today were created for the tomb of the Prophet Muhammed. The emerald pendants that were commissioned by Sultans Ahmed I, Mustafa III, Abdülhamid I and Abdülmecid are the most remarkable. Pendants of Sultan Selim III and Mahmud II, made from glazed silver and decorated with diamonds, are known for their epitaphs and monograms. Another interesting group of objects in the treasury are the war tools ornamented with precious stones. The ornate armor of Mustafa III (1757-74), which is made from steel threads, is partially covered with gold. Another precious work of art in this group is an ornate helmet. It is also decorated with precious stones. Swords, daggers, scimitars, yataghans and maces too are ornamented with precious stones. Many precious daggers such as the epitaphed yataghan of Süleyman the Magnificent, rock crystal-hilted dagger of Sultan Yavuz Selim and the emerald-handled dagger that was given to Mehmed IV by his mother Hatice Sultan are also on display in the treasury.

The dagger that is known as the Topkapı Dagger today is characterized as the major item in the treasury. It was commissioned by Mahmud I to the palace goldsmith, to be given to Nadir Shah, and turned out to be one of the most exquisite works representing Ottoman jewelry. The dagger has three large emeralds on its hilt and an emerald-lid clock at the top of it. Its sheath is ornamented with diamonds over gold. The most important group of objects is those that were made from rock crystals. These include small but very precious items, in various forms, such as canteens, long-spouted ewers, pencil cases and cups. Pendent oil lamps, censers, gulabdans (perfume flasks), ornate pendants and candelabrums made for Kaaba, as well as golden candelabrums commissioned by Abdülmecid, are the most spectacular items in the treasury. Another group, many examples of which we see in the treasury, are jeweled book cases. These works, which mostly date to the 16th Century, are covered with gold and embellished with emerald, ruby and turquoise. Included among these works, which were mainly produced as Qur'an cases and which showcase the Ottoman art of jewelry, is the golden case of Murad III's divan (book of collected poems).

The treasury does not include many women's jewelry. They were not placed into the treasury because they were personal items of women. Diamonds such as Kevkeb-i Durri and Şebçırağ, and branch pin brooches with diamonds are among the rare samples of women's ornamental jewelry. The Spoonmaker's Diamond is undoubtedly the most precious item of this group. This diamond, which was found in Eğrikapı during the period of Mehmed IV, was bought for the palace. This 86-carat diamond was encircled with emeralds in the 18th Century. It is not possible to display all the pieces in the extremely rich Ottoman treasury, at the same time. Therefore, some samples are selected and exhibited alternately in time.

Section of Holy Relics: The four-domed Holy Cloak or Holy Relics Section, which is located on the northern corner of the Inner Palace Courtyard, was constructed as the Privy Chamber of the sultan during the period of Mehmed the Conqueror. The first hall at the entrance is known as the Anteroom with Fountain. The first chamber to the right of this anteroom is the Audience Chamber where those coming to meet the sultan would be

received. Attached to this is a second room at the corner, the Privy Chamber, where the Sultan's Throne was. To the left of the Anteroom with Fountain is the Privy Chamber Ward known as the Destimal Chamber. The walls of all of these chambers are embellished with Iznik tiles dating to 16th-18th Centuries. The holy relics which Selim II brought from Egypt were kept here and this place was called the Holy Cloak Section because Prophet Muhammed's cloak was among the holy relics.

In this section, the Holy Cloak Chest, the banner of the Prophet, his two swords and bow are exhibited, while personal belongings such as a letter by Prophet Muhammed, his tooth, beard, foot print and seal are on display in a window in the Audience Chamber. The golden protection of Hajr-e-Aswad, and the Qur'an that Caliph Osman (the third of the major caliphs) was reading when he was martyred, can be seen here. Furthermore many items such as the Prophet Moses's staff, Prophet David's sword, seven hairs from the beard of Prophet Muhammed, swords of the major caliphs, Bekir, Ömer, Osman and Ali, the timber embossment from the Masjid al-Aqsa, the cover of Kaaba, keys of Kaaba, and golden Kaaba troughs are also included in the holy relics. To the left of the Holy Relics Section is the single-domed Ağalar Mosque, which was built during the period of Mehmed the Conqueror and is used as a library today.

Fourth Courtyard: A gap leads from the Inner Palace Courtyard into the Fourth Courtyard. The terrace of this courtyard, which is in the direction of the Golden Horn, was expanded during the first half of the 17th Century during the sultanates of Murad IV and İbrahim, with new kiosks built on top of it. There is a pool with a fountain in front of the porches on the marble terrace. Surrounding this pool are the Revan Kiosk to the south, the Circumcision Chamber to the west, and Baghdad Kiosk further ahead. The Circumcision Chamber on the marble terrace is embellished with 16th and 18th Century Iznik tiles and it is thought to have been built during the period of Süleyman the Magnificent. It acquired its current appearance after the changes made during Sultan İbrahim.

Revan Kiosk, which is opposite the Circumcision Chamber and was commissioned in 1636 to Architect Koca Kasım Ağa, to commemorate Murad IV's campaign to Revan, has an octagonal plan. Its exterior is covered with marble plaques up to a certain spot, and with 17th Century tiles further above that spot. There are wide wooden fringes on two facades of the three-balcony kiosk. The walls of the kiosk are covered with tiles up to the skirt of the dome, and the interior of the dome is embellished with engravings of plant motifs. From the two sets of windows, the top row is decorated with stained glass, window shutters are decorated with nacre and tortoise shell inlays. The kiosk was also known as the "Turban Chamber" (Sarık Odası) because the sultan's ceremonial turbans would be preserved here. Situated in the corner of the stony yard with pool, overlooking the Golden Horn is Baghdad Kiosk which Murad IV commissioned in 1639 to commemorate his campaign to Baghdad. This octagonal-plan kiosk has four recesses on the inside and four projections on the outside. It is surrounded by a wide timber fringe, which rests on twenty two marble columns. Its exterior is covered with marble up to a certain point above the lower set of windows and decorated with 17th Century tiles further above. The interior of the dome covering the kiosk is fashioned in the malakari technique, reflecting the most successful examples of the period. Nacre and tortoise shell inlays were used on the doors, cabinets and window shutters of the building, while Ayat-al Kursi (Qur'anic verse) inscribed by Enderuni Mehmed Çelebi in white color against a dark blue background surrounds all the walls between the lower and upper windows.

A gold and enamel sherbet service encrusted with precious stones and signed by Rinzi. The tray is covered with medallions that have the monogram of Sultan Abdülaziz (1861-76).
45x27x29 cm

There is the Iftariye Arbor between the Baghdad Kiosk and the Circumcision Chamber. This arbor, which was also known as the Moonlight Arbor, was built during the period of Sultan İbrahim in 1640. Made entirely from metal, the Iftariye Arbor would be decorated during bajrams and exchange of greetings would be held here. Furthermore, sultans would break their Ramadan fasts, or in other words have their iftars here, during summer. This is why the arbor must have been named the Iftariye Arbor. Sofa Kiosk is also located in the Fourth Courtyard, on the western section of the stone yard with pool. When exactly the kiosk was built is unknown; however, it came to be associated with Koca Mustafa Pasha, who served as grand vizier between 1670-1683, and survives to the present time intact due to multiple repairs. On the right side of the kiosk is the building known as the Chamber of Head Doctor or Tower of Chief Lala (servants in charge of princes' education). This is a tower on top of the walls of Mehmed the Conqueror which surround the palace. The reason why it is called the Chamber of Head Doctor is that the head doctor of the palace would examine his patients and prepare his medicines here. Through the tulip garden via a marble staircase, one arrives at the section where the Mecidiye Kiosk, Garment Chamber (Esvap Odası) and the Sofa Mosque are found. The last kiosk to be constructed in the palace was the Mecidiye Kiosk commissioned by Sultan Abdülmecid. The Garment Chamber was built simultaneously with this kiosk. With these buildings, which were constructed facing the extraordinary view of the Marmara Sea and the Bosphorus, we complete the architecture of Topkapı Palace. Let us also discuss the harem section here, which is an intriguing and mysterious complex of buildings, and learn of the Topkapı Palace in its entirety.

Harem: The Harem, where sultans would spend their time apart from their official life, with their family, concubines and crown princes, was famous in the Ottoman times but it is known to have existed before, during the Abbasids and Seljuks as well. Early on, Ottoman sultans married the princesses of the neighboring principalities or states; however, this procedure changed after Bayezid II and selection of the sultans' wives became more institutionalized, which became the basic principle in Topkapı Palace. The Harem section of the Topkapı Place is made up of complicated one or two-storey spaces surrounding small open-top courtyards, which were surrounded by walls on four sides and usually had stone-paved floors. The first core of these buildings was built during Mehmed the Conqueror. The sultan's mother, wives and children of the sultan, all lived at the harem together with their female servants and thus many annexes were added and changes were made to organize the spaces accordingly. The first change in the harem was made during the period of Süleyman the Magnificent and this structuring continued until Murad III. In 1587, Murad III moved the harem in the old palace, thus making harem functional. With the additions continuing until the period of Mahmud II, the harem continued to expand. The sultan was absolutely the chief actor in the harem. Following the sultan in rank were the mother of the sultan and wives of the sultan (when a favorite of the sultan, a haseki, gave the sultan a child, she would become an official wife and thus would be referred to as Haseki Sultan or Kadınefendi). The most colorful figures in the harem were undoubtedly the concubines. The Harem Eunuchs, who ensured the security of the harem, constituted an integral class of people within the harem. They were led by the Head Eunuch, who followed the grand vizier and Sheikhul Islam (chief religious official) in rank, which reveals their importance.

View of the Sultan's Anteroom, the ceremonial hall of the Harem.
It was built in 1585 and restored twice, once during Mehmed IV's sultanate and again in the 18th Century.

The entry into the harem is through the Carriage Gate (Arabalar Kapısı), which is located near the Tower of Justice and has an epitaph on it belonging to Murad III, dated 1587. This gate opens into an antechamber where the external services of the harem were carried out. This square-planned space, which is covered with a dome, was called the Dome with Cabinets due to the cabinets placed on all four sides. This place leads to the Anteroom with Fountain, the entryway into the harem, which was guarded by the Harem Eunuchs and was renovated after the fire in 1665. This rectangular-planned place, the walls of which are covered with 17th-Century Kütahya tiles, was divided into two with an arch and the first section was covered with a vault.

The Harem Eunuchs Masjid (Harem Ağaları Mescidi), which is located ahead from the Anteroom with Fountain, beside the Music School Gate (Meşkhane Kapısı), is square-planned and flat top. It must have been renovated after the fire in 1665. The walls of the masjid are covered with 17th-Century tiles and the ceilings are decorated with engravings. There is a picture of Kaaba seen in its shrine, and light green pictures of Madina and Arafat on its side walls. Located opposite this building is the Section of the Gentlemen-in-Waiting of the Sultan (Musahipler Dairesi), where the gentlemen-in-waiting of the sultan who were close to the sultan, treasurers who organized the finances of the harem, and palace dwarfs who entertained the sultan would reside.

The Ward of Harem Eunuchs (also known as the Black Eunuchs), was a considerably long three-storey building located in the Black Eunuchs Stone Yard (Karaağalar Taşlığı). As is known, harem eunuchs were castrated at a young age and recruited to the harem to serve as the guardians of the harem. They were headed by the most senior-level Harem Eunuch known as the Head Eunuch or Master of the Girls. The Apartments for the Master of the Girls (the leader of the Harem Eunuchs) was located on the left side of the Black Eunuchs Stone Yard. The doorway, walls of the chambers and the fireplace were covered with 17th-Century tiles and there was also a bath belonging to this section. The School of the Crown Princes was on the upper floor of this two-storey section. The Main Gate was located to the east of the Black Eunuchs Stone Yard. This iron-leaved gate would lead into a stone yard with large mirrors on its walls, which was known as the watching post where Black Eunuchs would mount guard. From the three gates here, the one to the left opens into the Concubines Stone Yard, the one in the middle to the Sultan's Mother Stone Yard, and the other into the Golden Way measuring 46 m long and 4 m wide. The gate opening into the Golden Way was used by the sultan and crown princes. The sultan, after ascending to the throne and completing the ceremony of sword girding, would arrive at the mounting block in the Sultan's Mother Stone Yard, and would dismount the horse and enter into the Golden Way through a door, arriving at the throne chamber. The second gate in the middle would open into the Sultan's Mother Stone Yard, and was surrounded by the Apartments of the Sultan's Mother and Apartments of the Wives.

On the left side, through a gate used by women that were outside the sultan's family, concubines, masters and assistant masters, provided entry in to a stone yard where the Ward of Concubines and the Apartments of the Sultan's Wives were located. Apartments of the second, third and fourth wife were located to the right of the stone yard. The Apartments of the First Wife (Baş Kadın Efendi Dairesi) was located near the Fireplace Anteroom in the Sultan's Mother Stone Yard. These apartments were known as the Haseki Sultan Apartments. Ascending the staircase in the corridor, one would arrive at the bedrooms on the upper floor, belonging to the wives of the sultan. The small chamber has

a flat-top ceiling made in the malakari technique, while the main chamber has a dome and colored engravings. Built for the wives of the sultan at first, these apartments are thought to have been allocated to the harem assistants later on.

Passing through two small hallways near the Apartments of the Sultan's Wives, one would arrive at the Apartment of the Sultan's Mother. The sultan's mother would ceremoniously arrive at this palace from the old palace, after her son had become the sultan, and settle in these apartments. The Sultan's Mother Courtyard, which is in front of the Apartments of the Sultan's Mother, was in the form of an open-top central courtyard. The center of the harem was constituted by this stone yard, with the other harem buildings developed around it. To the south of the stone yard is the Golden Way, which is thought to date to the period of Mehmed the Conqueror. Located to its west are the wards belonging to the palace assistants and masters, and the pharmacy of the harem next to them. The buildings located near the Golden Way, towards the east of the Sultan's Mother Stone Yard, belonged to the haseki sultans.

The Apartments of the Sultan's Mother is reached after passing a chamber just to the right of the Sultan's Wives Stone Yard, passing through two hallways. The first chamber to be seen here, which has a fireplace, tile-covered walls, and a nacred, embedded cabinet, belonged to the chief servant of the Sultan's Mother. One would pass into the Apartments of the Sultan's Mother from here. The real entrance to the Apartments of the Sultan's Mother is in the direction of the Sultan's Mother Stone Yard. There are two chambers here; one was used as the waiting room for guests, the other served as the entrance. On the gate of the Apartments of the Sultan's Mother, there are repair epitaphs dated to 1667, which were placed after the fire in 1665. First, the large hall, which was used as the dining hall, is entered into. The lower sections of the two-storey hall are covered with 17th-Century tiles. Decorations on the upper sections of the hall and the interior of the dome were created in 1817, during the period of Mahmud II.

The bedroom is accessible from the left side of the dining hall, through a nacred and double-leaved door. The bedroom with walls covered with 17th Century tiles was covered by a cavetto vault. Below a carved, gilded baldaquin on the left side is the place of the bed, which would be closed with a curtain. The prayer room of the Sultan's Mother, located opposite the bedroom, was connected to the bedroom through two bronze-lattice windows and a door. Seen on its walls is a light green depiction of Makka dating to 1667. The Apartments of the Sultan's Mother underwent many repairs from the 16th to 20th Centuries and has lost its authentic appearance. Its dome was repaired at the end of the 18th Century and decorated with ornamentations reflecting that era. The floor on top of the Chamber of the Sultan's Mother is the Apartment of Mihrişah Sultan, which Selim III commissioned for his mother Mihrişah Sultan to the palace architect Melling. This square-planned space is made up of two flat-ceiling chambers. The ceilings and walls of both of the chambers have gilded, Baroque and Rococo decorations. In the internal chamber, there is a marble Baroque-style fireplace, covered by European faiences with white and blue floral patterns. Landscape pictures with European influence can be seen on both sides of the fireplace. In the second chamber, same pictures decorate the sides and the top of the window inside a large niche, which faces the dining hall of the sultan's mother.

The bedroom of Abdülhamid I is located near the Apartments of the Sultan's Mother, opposite the Sultan's Bath (Hünkar Hamamı). Until the period of Osman III (1754-1757), Ottoman sultans would sleep at the Murad III Kiosk. In the 16th Century, this section

The first room.
The Chamber of the Crown Princes.
It was built by two different sultans
in the 17th Century and used by
the crown princes of
the Ottoman Dynasty.
In the first room of the chamber
there are panels with cypruss motifs
and Venetian blinds covered
with nacre.

bearing the style of chief architect Davut Ağa, was decorated in a highly Rococo style and used during the periods of Osman III and Abdülhamid I, after its covering system was turned into a flat ceiling. Sultans after Osman III also used this as a bedroom. Since it was Abdülhamid I who repaired and used the room, it came to be known by his name. This is a flat-top rectangular-plan chamber, made up of three sections. The walls and the ceiling are embellished with gilded Baroque and Rococo ornamentations. There is also a marble Baroque fountain in the chamber. The interior of the fountain is covered with gilded European faiences with blue and pink floral design against a white background. The place of bed is seen beneath the carved, gilded baldaquin. Passage was ensured from here into the Apartments of Selim III and Mihrişah Sultan, and the Osman III Kiosk. The Music Chamber of Selim III is accessible from the bedroom of Abdülhamid I. This is known to have been built during the period of Osman III, and decorated and used by Selim III. These apartments are made up of two chambers known as the Chamber of Selim III and Music Chamber of Selim III. Chamber of Selim III, which was built in 1790, is square planned and has a wooden ceiling. The walls and the ceiling are wholly embellished with gilded Baroque and Rococo ornamentations. In this chamber, which reflects all the characteristics of the Turkish Rococo, there is a marble fireplace within an arch. The interior of the fireplace is decorated with European faiences with blue floral pattern on a white background.

Osman III Kiosk is accessible through a long corridor from the Chamber of Selim III. This kiosk, which began to be constructed during the period of Mahmud I and completed in 1754 during the period of the succeeding sultan Osman III, is located in the Golden Horn direction of the hanging garden before the Sultan's Anteroom (Hünkar Sofası), on the inner palace rampart. There is a wide level area before the kiosk, which is made up of three nested rooms which project outwards. The ceilings of the walls are ornamented with wood and its walls have Baroque and Rococo decorations. Among them, brown and blue patterned European tiles against a white background were placed. Moreover, western-influenced pictures can be seen within the niche in the middle chamber, and within a rectangle on the wall in the other two rooms. The large chamber, namely the hall, is the most opulent chamber of the kiosk. This hall was formed by four big and four small octagonal cantilevers.

On the way from the Apartments of the Sultan's Mother to the Sultan's Anteroom, located to the right are the Sultan's Bath and Sultan's Mother's Bath. The Sultan's Bath, which was the most beautiful bath in the harem, was built from white marble by Sinan the Architect in the 16th Century and redecorated in Rococo style in mid 17th Century. Next to this is the Sultan's Mother's Bath, which was renovated by Mehmed IV's mother Turhan Sultan. This too is the same as the Sultan's Bath as far as planning goes. The fact that the two baths were side by side helped both baths be heated by one furnace. The Sultan's Bath was planned as three sections, where the first chamber was planned to be used as resting and massage chamber. The remaining traces in this section reveal that the walls were covered with engravings. The sofas with white canopies on them give a feeling of serenity. In the changing section, the gilded wooden cabinet and a crystal mirror with a gilded frame add more beauty. The third section is the main bath. The caldarium is accessible after a small frigidarium. This place is enlightened by the windows of various sizes located on the small and large domes. The iron-lattice section seen to the left is where the sultans would take a bath. The main reason why this section was covered with

The Fruit Room of Ahmed III.
It is connected to the Ahmed I Library by a door.

metal railings was to protect the sultan from assassination while he bathed. After this highly interesting section with its dainty basins, faucets and small divisions, the Sultan's Anteroom, which is the most spectacular hall of the harem, is accessible through a small chamber. This place, where the sultan would spend his daily life, ceremonies and receptions would be held, and bajram greetings would be exchanged, is known as the Sultan's Anteroom (Hünkar Sofası). The Sultan's Anteroom was built in 1585, under the supervision of Architect Davud Ağa, right after the Murad III Kiosk. This domed hall went through fundamental change during the period of Mehmed IV after the fire in 1665, and during the period of Osman III in the 17th Century. During repair work, Osman III had the baldaquined balcony and the sofas underneath built, where the sultan would sit. This hall was used as a ceremonial hall after those years. The hall has a total of twenty six windows including the upper ones, and its dome is carried by four pointed arches ornamented in the Rococo style. The wooden parts of the dome such as the windows and cabinets were decorated with various embroideries. The original 16th-Century ornamentations which are apparent on the arches give a view as to the first decoration of the place.

In the Sultan's Anteroom, which is covered by Delft tiles with blue patterns against a white background, there is also a throne for the sultan opposite the entrance. Two large-size China vases were placed on both sides of the throne. On the left side are remarkable sofas with çatma velvet canopy, and above them is a balcony where the orchestra would be. The clocks, which are symmetrically placed, are the gifts of Queen Victoria. The wooden seat at the corner, which was made in the Empire style, was sent as a gift by the German Emperor Wilhelm to Abdülhamid II. It was placed here just to add touch. The mirrored cabinet at the left corner of the hall is in fact a door. If required, the sultan was able to pass through this secret door into the other section of the harem. The verse Ayat-al Kursi is written inside the tiled frieze, with large blue and white calligraphy. Furthermore, the date of repair 1666 and the name of Mehmed IV are also read on the frieze, above the seat of the sultan. The pendentives and the interior of the pointed arches carrying the dome are decorated with 16th Century engravings. They have been renovated loyally to the original.

One needs to pass from the Fountain Hall (Çeşmeli Sofa) to go from the Sultan's Anteroom to the Murad III Kiosk. The Fountain Hall was where the crown princes and sultan's wives would wait before going to the Murad III Kiosk or Sultan's Anteroom. The Fountain Hall, which is in the form of a rectangular hallway covered by a lacunar vault, was named the Fountain Hall due to a fountain on its wall. The name of Mehmed IV is read on the fountain. This hall, the walls of which are decorated with 17th-Century tiles, opens into the Fireplace Anteroom (Ocaklı Sofa) via a door. The walls of this place, which is decorated with a large fireplace, are covered with 17th-Century tiles. According to the tile epitaph surrounding its walls, it was renovated after the harem fire in 1665, by the command of Sultan Mehmed IV.

The Murad III Chamber (or Kiosk), which is accessible through the Fountain Hall and is one of the most beautiful chambers of the harem, was built by the Architect Sinan in 1578. The chamber, which reflects all the grandiose of the 16th Century, is enchanting with its coralline tiles which are scattered among blue tiles. The kiosk is covered by a magnificent dome decorated with classical motifs. The baldaquined seats which rest on four ornate posts symmetrically facing each other, on the right side of the hall, increase the splendor of the hall by many folds with the engravings on their interior and gilded covering system on their exterior. These fountains, which still run today and bring back many echoes from

the past, were used to prevent the conversations being heard from outside. The nacre inlaid cabinets, wooden embroidered doors, sofas and braziers here are remarkable as the other elements which complement the beauty of the place. The frieze which circles the chamber has the verse Ayat-al Kursi on it. There is a wide pool benath the kiosk. Sultans after Murad III used this as their privy chamber.

Through the gate located opposite the Murad III Chamber, Ahmed I Library commissioned to the chief architect Sedefkar Mehmed Ağa is accessed. This is a square-planned small chamber, which is remarkable with its exquisite Iznik tiles which were produced one period after the tiles in the Murad III's Chamber. Uniquely beautiful cabinets on the walls, with nacre and tortoise shell inlays, and nacred leaves of the windows add a distinct touch to this chamber. There is a fountain dated 1608, within the niche to the left of the entrance. Blue and white and green and white tiles with sülüs inscriptions, which surround the upper part of the walls, date to the 17th Century. The Fruit Chamber (Yemiş Odası), which is the smallest but is considered to be the most attractive places in the harem, is seen in this section.

The Apartments of Crown Princes (Şehzadeler Dairesi or Çifte Kasırlar), which came after the Murad III Kiosk, is made up of two nested chambers accessible via several steps. These chambers were each built as privy chambers during the periods of Murad IV and Mehmed IV, in the 17th Century. The first chamber which belonged to Murad IV is accessible through a narrow door. The chamber is almost square planned, and its dome has gilded ornamentations with various motifs on linen. This magnificent dome was concealed by a ceiling for many years, and its existence was only revealed after the last repairs, as a result of the removal of the ceiling.

The side walls of the chamber are covered by dazzling 17th-Century tiles, while the top of the fireplace to the right of the entrance is ornamented with engravings that are similar to tile motifs. There is a band of tile and inscriptions between the two windows. There are inscriptions inside the windows as well. From this place, which is very attractive with its exquisite stained glass, and faucets within the windows, a small door leads into the second chamber of the Apartments of Crown Princes. This chamber too is thought to have been built by Mehmed IV as privy chamber. The level difference on the floor of the chamber has been discovered only after the last repairs. These privy chambers, which are covered with tiles at the interior and exterior, were allocated to crown princes after the 18th Century.

After leaving the Apartment of Crown Princes, the buildings seen at the back of the Favorites Stone Yard (Gözdeler Taşlığı) belong to the Apartment of Favorites. This place is accessible via a staircase near the Golden Way. As one takes a right turn, the corridor considered to be one of the most renowned sections of the harem, known as the Golden Way (Altın Yol), is reached.

The 46 meter long Golden Way is reminiscent of a narrow street. This place was home to some historical incidents, such as the incident of the devoted assistant Cevri Kalfa stopping the rebels from assassinating Mahmud II by throwing ash into their eyes. The main reason why this not-so-attractive corridor was named as the 'Golden Way' was that the sultans would throw gold coins at the concubines from here, on the occasion of bajrams and military campaigns. The Golden Way is the last stop of the mysterious world of harem.

After leaving the Crown Prince Chambers, where the princes were once either full of hope or fearful of death, one encounters the "Courtyard of the Favorites" and the "Pool of the Favorites." Down the way is a place called "Şimşirlik." The chambers behind the courtyard are the Apartments of the Favorites, which are comprised of five separate rooms on the upper floors, which were built by Abdülhamid I.

Dolmabahçe Palace

Dolmabahçe Palace, which is located by the sea in the district of Beşiktaş today, is intriguing with its different architecture. This location, which was filled during the first half of the century, used to be an inlet where the captain pashas (admirals) would anchor their ships around the beginning of the 17th Century, Timber kiosks and waterside mansions were built over this location during the reign of various sultans. Mahmud II considered the Topkapı Palace to be very gloomy and thus he expanded the recently-built timber coastal palace to be renovated and the palace officials used this place as their formal residence. When Sultan Abdülmecid ascended to the throne, he resided in this palace for a while but he also continued the innovative movements of his father Sultan Mahmud II effectively and had the coastal palace in Beşiktaş demolished because he wanted to commission a European-style palace in place of it. Accordingly, he had Dolmabahçe Palace built by Garabet Balyan from 1843-1856, in a way to match the lavishly ornamental style of the century. With this palace, a European way of life was also adopted for the first time; the buildings were formulated and decorated in accordance with these principles, and a new order was created.

Even though the palace was built in the lavishly ornamental style of the 19th Century, some sections reflecting the old Turkish architecture can be sighted sporadically. A Turkish type of house plan, which is arranged around anterooms, seems to have been applied here separately for each section.

The palace, which is located on a 600 m quay, ornate with profoundly opulent railings, is made up of a basement and two floors. The main building is placed on an axis, with a considerably high ceremonial hall at the center, and selamlık and harem (quarters for men and women respectively) connected thereto with corridors. Located at the end of the harem quarters is the veliaht (heir) section, the facade of which is characterized as the continuation of the palace. The apartments for the valide (mother of the reigning sultan), which extends backwards perpendicular to them, measures 95 m in length. In addition to the main building, other buildings complementing the palace are hazine-i hassa (sultan's treasure), furniture section, the Glass Kiosk, quarters for the pashas in the sections extending towards Beşiktaş, quarters for Kızlar Ağası (master of the girls in the harem) and for harem gatekeepers, the Aviary Kiosk, two departure kiosks, as well as the pharmacy and pastry section extending across the Beşiktaş road. Apart from the buildings enumerated, the palace also has a woodcutters section, a palace almshouse, palace stables, a section for carriage drivers, and harem quarters for the shehzades (princes), which were located on a lane extending all the way from Kabataş to Beşiktaş. Today, some of them have been demolished, while some are being used as government offices for other purposes.

Another building referred to in the sources is the palace theater which was built by Sultan Abdülmecid I and later burnt.

Two of the gates on the wall of the palace yard are main gates and they appear as the best examples of the innovative practice. These gates, one of which is the Treasury Gate at the entrance to the clock tower, represent examples of metal founding besides their decorations. There is the tuğra (monogram) of Abdülmecid dated 1853 on its top and a two-line epigraph of the poet Ziver dated 1857. The other gate is the Imperial Gate (Saltanat Kapısı) facing Beşiktaş Street, on which there is only the monogram of Abdülmecid dated 1854. Other noteworthy gates of the palace include Valide Gate, Furniture Gate and Kitchen Gate. There are five waterside mansion gates at the seaside facade.

The exterior facades of Dolmabahçe Palace are in eclectic style with Baroque and Renaissance emphasis. Motifs predominantly used for decoration such as cartouches, rosettes, medallions, oyster shells, garlands, decorative vases and curves are all Western originated. These were used on the facades symmetrically. The interior ornamentation, where crystal, alabaster and onyx was used, is said to have been made by Italian and French artists.

Decoration and furniture is the work of Séchan-the famous decorator of the Paris Opera. Gilded mahogany and rosewood gates, windows and frames decorated with thin emboss-ments, and ceilings with fresco technique express influences from French palaces. Ceilings are the most ornamented sections in the interior decoration. These are generally divided into cassettes and were created with paint over grout. Furthermore, still lifes, landscapes and figural compositions must have been painted on a cloth and stretched over the surface of the ceiling.

The palace has 285 rooms, 43 halls, 6 balconies and 6 baths. In the formal (mabeyn) section and harem quarters, there are very large halls, each of which have been a scene to various historical events, such as the Entrance (Medhal) Hall, the Ambassadors (Süfera) Hall, the Staircase Hall, the Hall Facing Two Sides (the Zülveçheyn Hall), the Small Equestrian Hall (Küçük Binek Hall), the Holiday Reception (Muayede) Hall, and the Blue Hall. The gold leaf furniture, large sofa sets, curtains, lacquered cornices, stone inlay work in the furniture, porcelain and enameled fireplaces, crystals mirrors, and coffee tables with solid silver pedestals were placed in the rooms and halls, which are the harbinger of a completely new order.

Baccarat and Bohemian crystal chandelier and fireplaces are among the most distinct and beautiful elements decorating the palace. The most spectacular one among the existing 36 crystal chandeliers weighs 4.5 tons and decorates the 36 m ceiling of the Holiday

Aerial view of Dolmabahçe Palace, which was constructed on orders of Sultan Abdülmecid between 1843-1856.

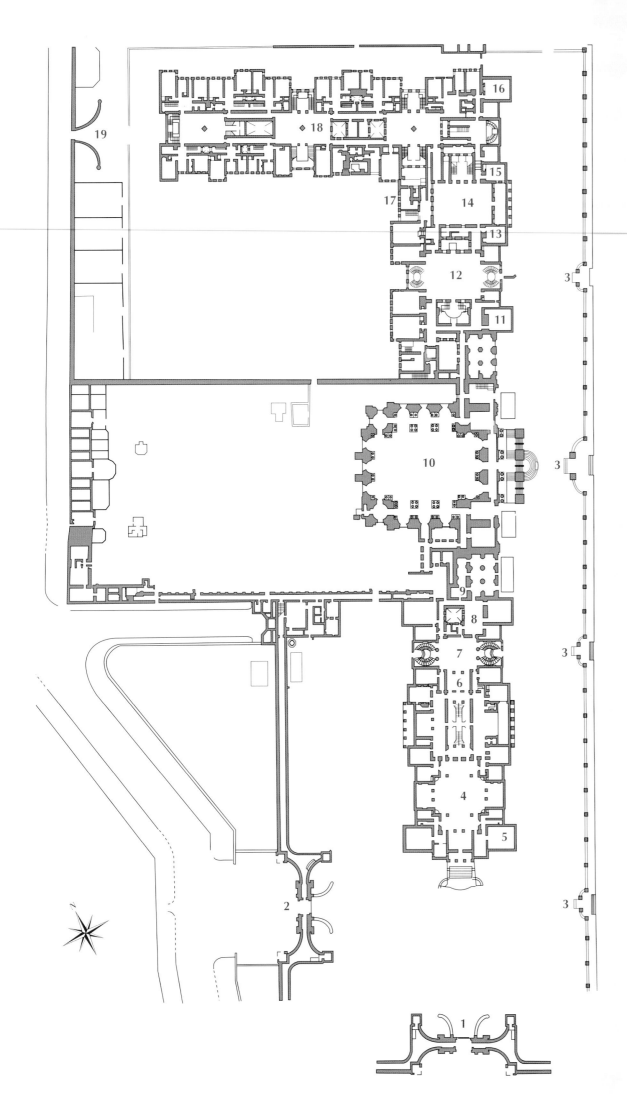

Reception Hall, and was reportedly given by the Queen Victoria. The records show that the chandelier was ordered from England in 1852 and was brought to Istanbul in 1853. It was hung in place with the help of two technicians coming from England. The chandelier was adjusted as a coal gas lamp. Its coal gas equipment was changed after 1910 when an electrical fixture was constructed in the palace and the 750 bulbs, which are still on it today, were attached to it. Illumination of the palace is known to have been ensured first by kerosene lamps, later by coal gas brought from the Gazhane (coal gas plant), and finally by electrical illumination.

The rich painting collection in the palace including the works of famous artists such as Zonaro, Fromentine and Aivazovski; the 280 vases made from porcelains of China, Japan, Yıldız, and Europe; the 156 historical and elegant clocks, 581 candelabrums made from silver, crystal and miscellaneous material, 11 braziers, décor sets, dining sets made from gold, silver and crystal impress the visitors extensively.

On the double Imperial Staircase (Saltanat Merdiveni), which connects the protocol entrance to the upper floor, a complex system of wooden structures were used and the railings are combined with crystal-covered metal posts. Apart from this stairway, the palace has five other stairways as well as a few service stairs.

The building was initially warmed with braziers and fireplaces. After Abdülhamid II, very large porcelain stoves, which were ordered from abroad, were used to warm it. During the reign of Mehmed V Reşad, central heating and electrical fixture were installed.

The diligently-made marquetry parquets in this palace, which decorate every room and hall especially in the formal (mabeyn) section, are beautiful and versatile enough to become a subject of study on its own.

Since the Ottoman sultans considered the valuable items in the palace the property of the state, after the abolishment of the Ottoman dynasty, with the Act no. 431 dated March 3, 1924, palaces were transferred to the nation. Dolmabahçe Palace is administered by the Department of National Palaces today, which is affiliated with the Turkish Grand National Assembly.

The Entrance Hall: The Entrance (Medhal) Hall, which is the formal entrance to the palace and the formal (mabeyn) section, is accessed via a footpath made from grey Marmara marble, with 11 steps and four columns. The ceiling of the hall, which rests on four big columns in the middle, is divided into cassettes and their interiors are ornate with colorful engravings. Among the four rooms located at the corners, the sadrazam (grand vizier) room is located to the right of the entrance, whereas the Sheikhul Islam (chief religious official) room is located to the left of it. The fireplaces, the upper sections of which are mirrors made from cut crystals, and large-size monogrammed vases produced by Yıldız Tile Factory enrich the hall further.

The plan of Dolmabahçe Palace:
1.Sultanate Gate 2.Ceremonial Gate 3.Waterside Mansion Gates
4.Ambassadors Hall 5.Reception Room for Ambassadors 6.Staircase Hall 7.Hall with two Sides (Zülveçheyn Hall) 8.Library 9.Baths 10.Holiday Reception Hall 11.Bedroom of the Mother Sultan 12.Blue Hall 13.Room where Atatürk passed away 14.Pink Hall 15.Bedrooms of the Sultan's Wives 16.Bedroom of Sultan Reşad 17.Harem Baths 18.Harem Section

The Palace Ceremonial Gate.

The Staircase Hall: The crystal stairway with two declivities and two ascents leads to the upper floor. Over the Staircase Hall is a vaulted glass ceiling and a magnificent chandelier hangs down into the footpath in the center. This hall has crystal balustrades and is surrounded by artificial marble columns with composite capitals. The mahogany doors ornate with gilded embossments create a warm atmosphere together with staircase coatings. At the four corners of the hall are 4 crystal candelabrums with pedestals, and at stairwells, there are 4 candelabrums with silver with pedestals.

The Ambassadors Hall: This hall, where governmental and diplomatic group receptions were held and especially foreign monarchs and princes would come to presence, had three projections towards the land, sea and garden. In this hall, which is suitably decorated for palace protocol, the four corners are adorned with fireplaces which are made from tile at the bottom and cut crystal and gilded embossments at the top. The lacunar ceiling, which is divided into cassettes, is decorated with gilded embossments.

This hall, where important decisions of Turkey's history were made and where the Alphabet Revolution was brought to life, is adorned with a magnificent (Baccarat) crystal chandelier at the center. Furthermore, the crystal and silver candelabrums with pedestals, which are placed on all four corners of the hall, are among the intriguing items.

In the yard section of the spectacularly decorated Ambassadors Hall, there is a waiting room for foreign ambassadors. After an entry room for translators, which is decorated in Gothic architecture, the waiting room adorned with the grand crystal chandelier is reached. The ceiling, which is divided into cassettes, is decorated with gilt and this decoration extends to the ceiling soffits.

At the sea-facing corner of the Ambassadors Hall are the rooms where the sultan would accept the foreign ambassadors to his presence. The smaller room in the front, which is the anteroom where the ambassadors and delegations would wait, is remarkable with its gilded cornice surrounding all three windows, as well as with the paintings of renowned artists. This anteroom leads to the reception room, which is predominately red. The cornices which are made from monolithic wood and are decorated with gilded engravings and embossments, the red crystal fireplaces and the mahogany coating on half of the wall give a distinct atmosphere to the room.

The Onyx Room: This room, which is located on the upper floor of the formal (mabeyn) section of the palace and faces the sea, was named the Onyx Room because its ceilings and walls were covered with imitation onyx grout. This room is one of the important ones where the last Ottoman sultans received some of their guests. When Murad V ascended to the throne, he received congratulations here. During the reign of Mehmed V Reşad, two Balkan monarchs and the Bulgarion King Ferdinand and the queen attended a concert here, which was organized in their honor. King Alexander of Yugoslavia, who came to Istanbul on October 4, 1933, had a face to face meeting with Atatürk in this room, and King Edward VIII of Britain, who came to Istanbul on September 4, 1936, had a meeting with Atatürk in the Onyx Room as well.

Also known as the "Crimson Room," the Reception Room for Ambassadors derives its name from the matching color of the drapes and furnishings. Dolmabahçe Palace.

Situated on the first storey of the palace beyond the Hall of the Crystal Stairs and over the entrance, the Ambassadors Hall was used as the Reception Room for Ambassadors. Dolmabahçe Palace.

The Hall with Two Sides: The small corridors of the Onyx Room lead to one of the larger ceremonial halls of the palace; the Hall with two Sides (Zülveçheyn Hall). At the right corner of this hall, which is characterized as a two-sided hall facing both the sea and land, there is a three-room section which was transformed into a library during the reign of Caliph Abdülmecid. As in the other large halls, this hall too is heavily ornamented. Complementing the splendor of the hall are a Bohemian crystal fireplace, crystal candelabrums with bronze pedestals and a grand chandelier. This hall used to be of religious nature where, mevlid recitals (poems celebrating the birthday of Muhammed) were held, marriage ceremonies were performed, teravihs (supererogatory night prayers during Ramadan) were performed, and peace lectures (lectures on Qur'an) were given. During Ramadan, prayer rugs would be laid in the hall, and a special room for women was created with cages. This hall is also one of the most appropriate halls for a large amount of visitors. During the first days of the Mehmed V Reşad's accession to the throne, feasts were organized in this hall for the Egyption Khedive (Ottoman governor) Abbas Hilmi Pasha and King and Queen of Bulgaria. During the reign of the last Caliph Abdülmecid Efendi, two feasts were given; one for the sultans and one for the princes, and a mevlid recital was held. During Atatürk's first year in Istanbul, this hall was arranged as a dining hall; when Atatürk ate dinner with his guests here, there would be a group of traditional Turkish musicians in the seaside section, and an orchestra towards the Staircase Hall. When the King Abdullah of Jordan was a guest at Dolmabahçe Palace, he received some of his visitors in this hall.

The Marble Bath: The Hünkar Bath (Sultan's Bath), which is accessed from the Ambassadors Hall through the internal formal (mabeyn) section corridor, was made from alabaster brought from Egypt and comprises three interconnected parts. The lacuna ceiling of the resting room at the front is decorated with gilded embossments. From this room, through a massive bath door with the monogram of Abdülmecid, the bath section is entered into. Inside are a small anteroom, tepidarium and halvet (seclusion) section to the right, and the toilet section to the left. Even though the Turkish tradition was retained in the style of the bath, the iron-framed glass vault of the three-basin seclusion section and large windows opening into the sea are encountered as novelties. This is a reflection of how eastern and western traditions were nicely imposed together in the palace.

The Harem: An iron gate at the end of the corridor which connects the selamlık (quarters for men) and the harem (quarters for women), ensures a passage into the entry corridor to the harem. The sea-facing rooms to the right of this corridor have double entries into the anteroom and corridor but do not have a closet. Therefore, they cannot be considered a bedroom. The corridor entry in this room, which can be described as the room where the Sultan's mother would receive her guests, was later closed and a bath for the Sultan Reşad was placed here. The adjacent room was defined as the bedroom of Sultan's mother, which was used as the bedroom of Afet Inan when Atatürk was in power, and Mevhibe Hanım when İnönü was in power. The documents report that these were the most spectacular rooms and decorated diligently by Séchan.

Caliph's Staircase.
This staircase, which is located in the Harem section of the Dolmabahçe Palace, opens into the Blue Hall upstairs.

View of the Blue Hall. This hall is predominated by blue and thus was named the Blue Hall. The room where Atatürk passed away is located at a corner, in this section of the palace.

The Blue Hall: The exit from the bedroom of Sultan's mother opens into the Blue Hall, which extends from the sea facade as far as the yard side and where bajram (holiday) greetings were received and large ceremonies were held. The hall, which reflects the Turkish house plan with a balcony, corner rooms and internal anteroom, is one of the largest anterooms of the palace which separates the Hünkar Section (Sultan's Section) from all the other sections and where formal ceremonies were held and the dynasty came together. It was named as such since the curtains of the hall and decorations on the walls and the ceiling are blue. The hall is lighted by three windows on each of the two facades in the form of projections. The ceiling is divided into cassettes, and each of the cassettes is decorated with frames ornate with gilded lavish engravings. This decoration is complemented by a red and white crystal chandelier. Crystal mirrors on the consoles located beside the doors must have been placed in a way to best reflect the light emanating from the crystal-column candelabrums located on the four corners. In this hall, which is decorated with grand Japanese vases with embossments and gilded descriptions of groups fighting against dragons, as well as Chinese and Yıldız Palace vases, an elevator was added in the middle of the opening for light during the course of Atatürk's illness.

This hall is where Sultan Abdülmecid exchanged bajram greetings with his women and children, where Abdülaziz received the greetings of women and sultans during his 15-year legacy, and where Abdülmecid II's ascension to the throne took place. Years later, tired Mehmed V Reşad was to be seen in this hall, with a blithe spirit due to his ascension to the throne. Girls, who comprised the music band of the harem, played marches.

At the land side of the Blue Hall, the room on the left-hand corner, which was the private room of the sultans in the harem, was lastly defined as the painting workshop of Abdülmecid Efendi.

A door at the sea-facing corner of the hall leads to an anteroom. There is a bathroom to the left, at the daylight section between the Blue and Pink Hall. Remaining from the time of Sultan Reşad, this bath was also used by Atatürk. From the two rooms opening into the anteroom, which are side by side, the first one has opulent ornamentation and two doors; one opening into the corridor, the other into the Blue Hall. Atatürk is known to have used this room as study. The adjacent room, which is larger, served an important function during the illness and death of Turkey's eternal leader. This room, which was used as winter quarters by the last Ottoman sultans, was used during the illness of Atatürk during the Republic period. Inside is a painting which Atatürk greatly admired, a walnut bedstead, a walnut closet, a mirrored console and a chaise lounge. The ceiling of the room is decorated with color engravings.

The room at the inland-facing corner of the Blue Hall is known as the bedroom of Sultan Abdülaziz. It is richly decorated, has a closet for bed linens and a porcelain fireplace. The large bed in this room, which is covered on three sides, is known to have belonged to the sultan.

The Pink Hall: The section which is know as the quarters for the sultan's mother (Valide Sultan Dairesi) and which has about 30 spaces is made up of lower and upper floors surrounding the Pink Hall.

Ceiling decorations of the Holiday Reception Hall.

The Pink Hall, which has sea-facing and inland-facing facades suiting the traditional order of the palace like the Zülvecheyn Hall, is the largest hall of the Harem quarters, and was given this name due to the color of the walls. On the wall to the left of the entrance, arrangements in the form of niches are seen. During the time of Atatürk, a door was opened through the mirrored closet leaning on one of these and a passage was created to the bathroom remaining from the Sultan Reşad period.

This hall, where the ceiling is decorated with pastel color engravings on top of grout and the floor is laid with parquet, has many consoles and mirrors which are ornate with gilded embossments. The 60-candlestick chandelier hanging down into the hall forms a unity with the footed crystal-column candelabrums placed on four corners of the anteroom. On the sea-facing facades of the hall is a balcony with columns and pediments, opening through arched passages.

The rooms which are lined up along a corridor after the Pink Hall connect to the Quarters for the First Wife (Başkadinefendi Dairesi) through other corridors. These rooms are known to have belonged to the wives of the sultan. The quarters for the sultan's mother in Dolmabahçe Palace were allocated for various people apart from Sultan Abdülaziz's mother, Pertevniyal Sultan and for a short duration, Murad V's mother, therefore its real identity became ambiguous in time.

Therefore, one could say, these rooms were allocated for the favorites in the harem during Pertevniyal, who used the quarters for an extended duration of 15 years. On this corridor, to the right, there is the bedroom which is said to have belonged to the first wife of the sultan. Its ceiling is decorated with colored engravings over grout.

The second room near it is reportedly the bedroom of the second wife. The bronze-ornamented, walnut-coated bedstead here showcases a fine example of ornamentation. The ceiling is ornamented with color engravings over gypsum plaster. Located at the end of this hall, on the corridor is the bedroom of the third wife. The walls of the room are covered with wallpaper until the ceiling soffits, and the ceiling is ornate with color engravings.

The large room near it is the bedroom of the old ruler Sultan Reşad. At the entrance, to the left, a bedstead with baldaquin, which is coated with a mixture of mahogany and walnut and covered on three sides, was placed. The M.R insignia, which is a rendering of the initials of the Sultan Reşad, is noticed at the bedstead's end. The same insignia is seen on the clock on top of the bedstand as well, which belongs with the bedstead.

The Harem Bath, which is located at the land-facing side of the Pink Hall isolated from the hall, is made up of a resting room, changing room, washing room and toilet. Inside the bath, the ceiling and the walls halfway up are coated with grey Marmara marble, and with European-pattern tiles made in Iznik up to the ceiling.

It has three basins with silver faucets in the washing room. The stove in the resting room, which was made by an Armenian craftsman, and its tray which is used as a table now, reflect the brightest period of the Kütahya tile art.

The Holiday Reception Hall: The upper floors of the Holiday Reception (Muayede) Hall, which is in the middle of the palace, are surrounded by a gallery with a balcony. In this gallery, sultans, women, ambassadors, foreigners and musicians who came to watch the ceremony would sit. Holiday Reception means exchanging of bajram (holiday) greetings. A few days before the bajrams, the throne of Murad III, which was located in the Treasury section of the Topkapı Palace would be brought here and placed in the section towards the yard. Located opposed to it would be the box of seats for foreign diplomats. The sultans would rest in the corner rooms following the bajram prayer and only the members of the dynasty and the ministers of the state would accept the greetings of men included in the protocol, they would come before the throne and kiss the gilded tassel held.

The actual entrance of the hall was through the large marble gate towards the sea. Out of all of the rooms located at the four corners, those towards the sea have flat ceilings, whereas the ones towards the yard are domed. These were the rooms where the sultan would take a rest before the greeting ceremonies. The room on the yard side, which is to the left, was repaired during the reign of Abdülhamid II in order that he could secretly leave the ceremony and a staircase was added to the yard side. This hall, which measures 40x45 m and is laid with parquet, is covered with a dome. The dome measures 36 m high and is supported by half domes and arches carried by composite-capital double columns. The interior of the dome was coated with lead and the whole surface was decorated in an architectural composition employing an illusive technique, with color engravings. On one of the staircase vaults leading up to the gallery are the names of three Armenian masters, which indicates that the decoration was done by these masters. The columns are imitated marble and were made by casting.

Candelabra with colored onyx marble bases and crystal bodies at the four corners of the hall, and silver-body candelabra placed opposed to one another as well as a chandelier weighing 4.5 tons ensures the illumination of the hall. The chandelier hanging down from the dome, with 750 candlesticks, was given as a gift by the British Queen Victoria II. In an earthquake which took place during a ceremony held by Abdülhamid II, the lower section of the magnificent chandelier fell down, which turned out to weigh 700 kg after a later measurement.

The heating of the hall was ensured through a system installed on the basement floor. In this system, 6 furnaces were built at certain parts of the basement, and they were covered by sheet domes and covers. The heated air was sent into the hall through the gaps between the meander-patterned sheet metals placed under the double columns. The furnaces would be ignited two days before the ceremony and would ensure 18 to 20 centigrade degrees of heat in the hall.

Apart from the exchange of bajram greetings, the Holiday Reception Hall was also scene to other crucial events in the Turkish history. In 1856, Sultan Abdülmecid held a major feast here in the honor of Marshal Pelissier. There was also a formal reception held here in the honor of the Hungarian Emperor Franz Joseph. Furthermore, during the last months of the World War I, a formal reception was organized here for the emperor of Austira -Hungary Karl and the empress. One of the most historic events taking place in this hall was the ceremonial opening of the first House of Representatives (Mecls-i Mebusan) on March 18, 1877 by Abdülhamid II. Atatürk came to Istanbul in 1927, which was his first visit to Istanbul as the President of the Republic, and addressed the members of parliament, generals and notables of the city here, honoring Istanbul. After the death of Atatürk, Istanbulites passed before his corpse again in this hall.

Holiday Reception Hall.
This wide hall was where receptions and holiday ceremonies were held. The women of the harem would watch the ceremonies from the upper galleries. A gift from Queen Victoria, the chandelier gives the room an atmosphere of imposing grandeur.

Kiosks and Summer Palaces

The Ottoman Sultans had several palaces, such as Topkapı, Dolmabahçe and Beylerbeyi, where they resided and administered the state. Besides these, they also had kiosks and summer palaces built, which they used temporarily or for going on the occasional hunt. Summer palaces are those described as slightly smaller than palaces and were built for sultans. Kiosks, on the other hand, were larger than residences but not as large as palaces. Kiosks situated along the shore are called "yalıs" or "waterside mansions." Though sultans commissioned kiosks and waterside mansions, they were mostly built and resided in by grand viziers, generals and statesmen. There are several kiosks found within the palaces of Topkapı, Beylerbeyi and Yıldız. They will be discussed, but for now, let's simply describe some of the places that are still around which were constructed as single units. As it is, most of these are open to the public as museums. Besides those in Topkapı Palace, there are only three surviving kiosks. The first of these is Tiled Kiosk, which dates back to 1472. This kiosk is found on the grounds of the Istanbul Archaeological Museum and is utilized as the Tile and Porcelain Museum. The Parade Kiosk, which is located on the edge of Gülhane Park over the light rail line, has four storeys, windows and is capped with a conical-shaped roof. Dating back to Mehmed the Conqueror, it was renovated during the 19th Century in the Empire style. It is called the "Alay" ("Parade") Kiosk, as sultans would watch religious processions, merchant and diplomatic processions as well as army parades from here.

The Sepetçiler Summer Palace is located on the seaside and was constructed by Sultan İbrahim in 1643. Renovated during the period of Mahmud I, it was constructed for the sultan and those of the Harem to watch naval ceremonies. Restored in recent years, it is currently used as the International Press Center. Küçüksu Summer Palace

Situated in Göksu on the shore of the Bosphorus, the Küçüksu Summer Palace is attractive for its beautiful stone masonry. Today's summer palace is found in place of previous buildings. Attracting attention during the period of Mahmud I as an excursion spot, Divitdar Emin Pasha had a kiosk built in 1752, which he presented to the sultan. This summer palace was expanded in 1792 by Sultan Selim III, who had a fountain with rich Rococo reliefs made there as well. After commissioning the architect Nikogos Balyan to construct the Dolmabahçe Palace, he had him erect a summer palace here on a plot of land 15 meters x 27 meters in dimension. This palace, which was constructed by pounding pilings into the seabed and positioning blocks of stone on top of them, has three storeys, including the basement. The

View of Küçüksu Summer Palace built during the reign of Sultan Abdülmecid in 1857. With its striking architectural style, Küçüksu is one of the most beautiful structures along the Bosphorus.

Decorations on the dome above the staircase leading upstairs in the Küçüksu Summer Palace. Küçüksu Summer Palace is three-storey together with the basement. The floor above the basement has four chambers around the anteroom with staircase.

basement is where the pantries, kitchen and servants' rooms are located. There are four rooms placed around the stairway anteroom on the other two floors.

The parquet, fireplaces, ceiling and wall decorations are all strikingly beautiful. On the sea facade outside, one sees a double set of baroque marble stairs. Between these stairs are reliefs of exuberant acanthus and hearts. The stone masonry on the outer walls consists of some fine examples of craftsmanship. This summer palace is administered by the Department of National Palaces as a museum and serves as a tourist attraction.

Aynalı Kavak Kiosk: The Shipyard Shore Palace, whose foundation was laid during the period of Sultan Ahmed I, was used until the end of the 18th Century.

The only part of it that remains is the Aynalı Kavak Summer Palace. The sultans would watch naval and circumcision ceremonies held on the Golden Horn from the Shipyard Shore Palace. Starting from the second half of the 18th Century, it began to be neglected. Sultan Selim III had a large section of it torn down in an effort to modernize the shipyard, giving the land to the shipyard. Selim III expanded his Sultan's Chambers here and began utilizing it in 1791. It is said that he composed

music and played with musicians here. The summer palace appeared to be two-storeys from the side facing the sea and a single-storey from the side facing the land. It receives plenty of light thanks to the wide rectangular windows.

Sultan Selim III had the interior décor furnished in the Rococo style. Yesarizade's "Eulogy to Enderunlu Vasıf," which he wrote in calligraphy, is found here. The Submission Room is next to the Council Apartment. They are decorated in the Rococo style. A eulogy to the sultan that the Sheikh Galib wrote is above the windows in the room. The Nacre Room is behind the Submission Room. It derives

its name from the nacre inlaid work. Musical instruments are also displayed on the bottom floor. Located within a wide garden in Hasköy, the Aynalı Kavak Summer Palace is administered by the Department of National Palaces as a museum serving as a tourist attraction.

Ihlamur Kiosk: Situated in Beşiktaş, Sultan Abdülmecid commissioned Nikogos Balyan to construct the Ihlamur Summer Palace as a place of rest having an archery range and hunting lodge. It was built between 1849-55. There are actually two kiosks, one of which is the Ceremony Kiosk and the other, the Retinue Kiosk, with

Sultan Abdülmecid commissioned Nikogos Balyan to build the Ihlamur Summer Palace (1849-1855), which was used as a hunting and leisure mansion.

the former being more decorated than the later. These kiosks have two rooms surrounding an anteroom. The two kiosks are located in an extensive garden. Both of the kiosks were built with two floors added to a basement. One goes from the basement to the floor above via two sets of curved symmetrical staircases. While the interior and exterior of the Ceremony Kiosk originally was decorated in elegant Empire style, it was redecorated in a Baroque style with exaggerated ornamentation during the reign of Sultan Abdülaziz. There are enormous statues on pedestals inside niches on the sides and under the entry arch. The exaggerated decoration of the kiosk is apparent from the windows, stairs and balustrades, heavy garlands, columns and grid balconies. The interior is decorated with gold leaf stucco borders and baroque reliefs. The Ihlamur Summer Palace was recently restored and is currently administered by the Department of National Palaces as a museum serving as a tourist attraction.

Maslak Summer Palaces: The first summer palaces that were built during the period of Mahmud II gained importance during the period of Sultan Abdülhamid II, who used it while he was Crown Prince. The group of Maslak Kiosks is made up of the following: Imperial Summer Palace (Kasr-ı Hümayun), Imperial Formal Section (Mabeyn-i Hümayun), Greenhouse (Limonluk), Tent Kiosk (Çadır Köşkü) and Pasha Apartments. The Imperial Summer Palace has two floors, the bottom of which is made of stone while the top is made of wood. Imperial Formal Section is to the northwest of this structure. It is an elegant single-floor stucture made of stone. The Limonluk is adjacent to this building. The Imperial Summer Palace is in a spot that dominates the woods on the northwestern side where the Tent Kiosk is found. The octagonal-shaped Tent Kiosk displays some of the finest examples of wooden decoration. The General's Apartments were built as a single-storey stone building. The Ihlamur Summer Palace was recently restored and is currently administered by the Department of National Palaces.

The Beykoz Summer Palace: The Egyptian Khedive Mehmed Ali Pasha commissioned the architects Nikogos and Sarkis Balyan to build the Beykoz Summer Palace next to the Sultan's Quay in Beykoz between 1855-66. This neo-classical style summer palace was to be presented to Sultan Abdülmecid but he passed away just prior to its completion, so Said Pasha presented it to Abdülaziz instead, who had recently ascended to the throne. Established over a wide terrace, this stone structure is covered with marble. Surrounded by trees, the gardens of the palace extend all the way down to the sea. The palace halls are wide and have lofty decorated ceilings, whereas the upper floor is reached via a wide staircase.

The Khedive Summer Palace: Egyptian Khedive Abbas Hilmi Pasha commissioned the Italian architect Delfa Seminoti to construct this summer palace in the extensive woodlands of Çubuklu in 1907. With two main storeys and a service attic, this stone structure has a commanding view of the Bosphorus. The curved dining hall on the lower floor opens out into a garden with a veranda having 24 columns. The floor above this was transformed into a penthouse suite belonging to the Khedive. There are also six bedrooms on the side overlooking the courtyard.

The Yellow Kiosk (Sarı Köşk) located in the Emirgan Woods was commissioned in the 19th Century by Ismail Pasha, the governor of Egypt.

The Malta Kiosk located in the Yıldız Park.
It was commissioned by Sultan Abdülaziz.

Aynalı Kavak Summer Palace, where Sultan Selim III studied music.

The floor terrace with its stairway on this side has a panoramic view on three sides. The tower belonging to the Khedive Suite with a private elevator gives the structure an intriguing appearance. Renovation of the building was recently completed and today the Istanbul Metropolitan Municipality operates the building as a tourist attraction. In addition to these, the Khedives had some kiosks such as those situated within the Emirgan Woods constructed as well. Sultan Abdülaziz allocated the Emirgan Woods to Egyptian Khedive İsmail Pasha. The Khedive had two ponds and three wooden kiosks-"Yellow," "Pink" and "White," constructed on the site

during the latter half of the 19th Century. These are currently operated by the municipality as tourist attractions. Among the other structures that the other Egyptian Khedives had constructed in Istanbul, are the Abbas Halim Pasha kiosks on Heybeliada (1897), and the Bebek Khediva Summer Palace, which was constructed at the start of the 20th Century. The Italian architect d'Aronco was commissioned to construct the palace in Bebek by the mother of Egyptian Khedive Abbas Hilmi Pasha, Khediva Emine. It is currently used as the Egyptian Consulate General. Let us briefly mention a few kiosks not previously covered. Sultan

Abdülmecid commissioned the Balyans in 1851 to construct the Tophane Summer Palace in Tophane. Nikogos Balyan built the Adile Sultan Summer Palace in Validebağı, Üsküdar in 1853. He also built the Hunting Lodge of Abdülaziz on the grounds of the palace garden. Abdülaziz commissioned Sarkis Balyan to build a Hunting Lodge in Ayazağa while he was still the Crown Prince. Sultan Abdülaziz commissioned Sarkis Balyan to construct the Kalender Summer Palace in Tarabya was in 1862-63; it is currently utilized as the Presidential Kiosk. Situated on the grounds of a 20-acre garden, the Yusuf İzzeddin Efendi Kiosk was constructed at

the bottom of Büyük Çamlıca Hill at the end of the 19th Century. This three-storey wooden kiosk was constructed in the neo-classical style for the son of Sultan Abdülaziz, Crown Prince Yusuf İzzeddin Efendi. The Men's Quarters Apartment is all that remains of a kiosk that was built for Crown Prince Abdülmecid Efendi in Bağlarbaşı in 1901. There is also the Crown Prince Vahideddin Efendi Kiosks situated within a 50-acre plot of land above Çengelköy. Sultan Abdülhamid allocated this kiosk to the crown prince. These palaces and kiosks make up some of the important historical structures in Istanbul.

Khedive Summer Palace was built by the order of Abbas Hilmi Pasha in 1907. Recently restored, this venue is currently operated by the Istanbul Metropolitan Municipality as a tourist attraction.

View of the Anatolian Fortress and Bophorus.

Waterside Mansions by the Bosphorus

There are many waterside mansions (also known as yalı), which have attractive architecture and décor, that were built during the Ottoman period. The word "yalı" means "shore" in Greek, but in Turkish it is expressed as a "house on the shore." Let's talk about some of the more important remaining residences. One of the oldest on the Anatolian side of the Bosphorus is the Amcazade Hüseyin Pasha Waterside Mansion. Constructed in 1699, it is unfortunate that only the pool and its "T"-shaped antechamber remain. Its construction was ordered by one of the grand viziers of Mustafa II, Amcazade Hüseyin Pasha. Painted a bright red color, this waterside mansion represents a mature example of Turkish decorative art. The gold leaf ceiling decorations and the engravings on the walls are priceless and are unique heirlooms of history. The recently restored waterside mansion looks as if it is about to slide into the water. The Count Ostrorog Waterside Mansion in Kandilli dates back to 1850 and is one of the most important waterside mansions along the Bosphorus. It was purchased from the Ottoman Foreign Minister Server Pasha by Polish ex-patriate, Lord Leon Valerien Ostrorog, while he was the law advisor to the Ottoman Empire at the turn of the 20th Century. This residence, painted in bright red, has always been associated with his name. It later passed into the hands of the Count's wife, who was originally from Czechoslovakia. There is yet another beautiful waterside mansion in Kandilli. It is called the Cypriot Mehmed Emin Pasha Waterside Mansion. Complemented by the extensive woods in the back, this residence has the longest facade of any building along the Bosphorus. Mehmed Emin Pasha from Cyprus, who worked in embassies and in governor's offices, was also a grand vizier and the Commodore of the Ottoman Navy. There is a fountain in the center of a grand ballroom of the residence, which was constructed in the 1840s. The columns of the mansion are fashioned from wood. The dome-fitted ceiling is decorated with pictures. A waterside mansion named the Ethem Pertev Bey Waterside Mansion (1860) was constructed in a neo-classical style and has exquisite woodwork. It, along with the nearby Nazım Pasha Waterside Mansion, make up two of the most important works of the period. The neo-classical style Rukiye Sultan Waterside Mansion, which is otherwise known as the Vecihi Pasha Waterside Mansion, lies in the gulf between Kanlıca and Anatolian Fortress. There are many such historical waterside mansions between the gulf and Anatolian Fortress, such as the Hekimbaşı Salih Efendi Waterside Mansion. This residence painted in bright red belonged to Palace Physician Salih Efendi. He lived here until 1895. Another residence is the Marki Necip Waterside Mansion, also known today as the Demirören Waterside Mansion. The first owner was a French Marquis who later took the Turkish name "Necip Pasha." The Amcazade Waterside Mansion and

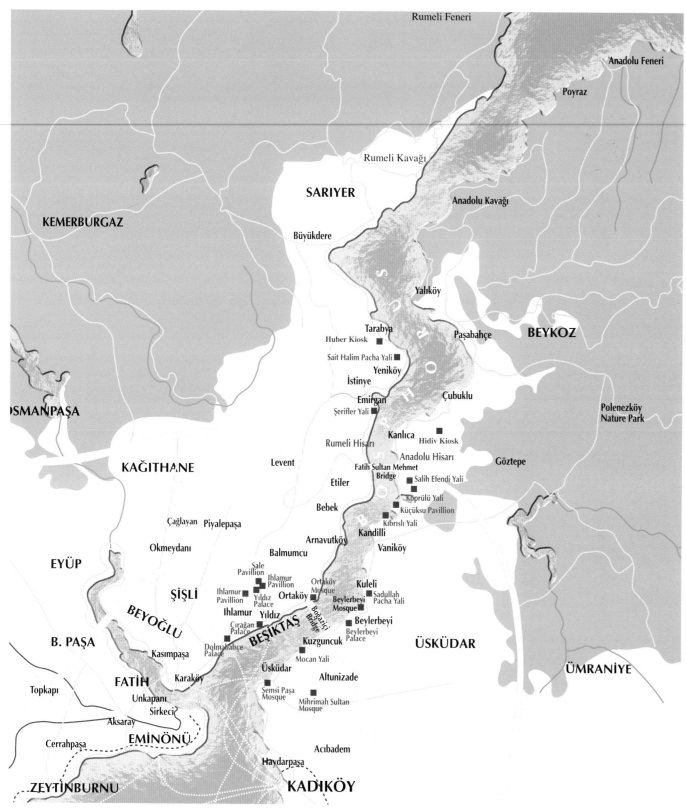

Map of the Bosphorus Straits of Istanbul.

Rumeli Feneri

Anadolu Feneri

Poyraz

Rumeli Kavağı

SARIYER

Anadolu Kavağı

KEMERBURGAZ

Büyükdere

BEYKOZ

Yalıköy

Tarabya
Huber Kiosk

Paşabahçe

Sait Halim Pacha Yali

Yeniköy

İstinye

Çubuklu

OSMANPAŞA

Emirgan

Şerifler Yali

Kanlıca

Hidiv Kiosk

Polenezköy
Nature Park

Rumeli Hisarı

Anadolu Hisarı

Göztepe

KAĞITHANE

Levent

Fatih Sultan Mehmet
Bridge

Salih Efendi Yali

Etiler

Köprülü Yali

Bebek

Küçüksu Pavillion

Kıbrıslı Yali

Çağlayan   Piyalepaşa

Kandilli

Okmeydanı

Arnavutköy

Vaniköy

EYÜP

Balmumcu

Şale
Pavillion

Kuleli

SİŞLİ

İhlamur
Pavillion

Ortaköy
Mosque

Sadullah
Pacha Yali

İhlamur
Pavillion

Yıldız
Palace

Ortaköy

Beylerbeyi
Mosque

BEYOĞLU

İhlamur

Yıldız

Çırağan
Palace

Yıldız

Boğaziçi Bridge

Beylerbeyi

B. PAŞA

Dolmabahçe
Palace

BEŞİKTAŞ

Kuzguncuk

Beylerbeyi
Palace

ÜSKÜDAR

Kasımpaşa

Mocan Yali

ÜMRANİYE

FATİH

Karaköy

Üsküdar

Altunizade

Topkapı

Unkapanı

Semsi Paşa
Mosque

Sirkeci

Mihrimah Sultan
Mosque

Aksaray

Cerrahpaşa

EMİNÖNÜ

Acıbadem

Haydarpaşa

ZEYTİNBURNU

KADIKÖY

*While the Istanbul Bosphorus divides Asia from Europe,
the Bosphorus and Fatih Sultan Mehmed Bridges connect the two continents.
The Bosphorus Bridge is seen in the foreground.*

207

Zarifi Mustafa Pasha Waterside Mansion, which are located in this area, are from the 18th Century. The Nazif Pasha Waterside Mansion was constructed in Vaniköy in 1870. A little further down the shore from the Nail Pasha Waterside Mansion is the Koç Waterside Mansion, which was constructed by Sedat Hakkı Eldem. Located next to it is the striking Grand Vizier Mahmud Nedim Pasha Waterside Mansion (1870).

The most well known waterside mansion in Çengelköy is the Sadullah Pasha Waterside Mansion. Sadullah Pasha was the Grand Vizier of both Murad V and Abdülhamid II. The bright red painted waterside mansion has two storeys. Its wonderfully decorative walls show the influence of Western styles on the architect. The Fethi Ahmed Pasha Waterside Mansion in Kuzguncuk is also an historical waterside mansion. Constructed in 1812, this waterside residence is known as the Pembe Waterside Mansion, or the Mocanlar Waterside Mansion, because the Mocans were his grandchildren. There are many other waterside mansions like these on the Anatolian side. These include the 18th Century Çürüksulu Waterside Mansion in Salacak, the Edip Efendi Waterside Mansion (1760) in Kandilli, the Abdullah Waterside Mansion (1815) in Çengelköy, the mid 19th-Century Recai Ekrem Bey Waterside Mansion in Vaniköy, the 19th-Century Ethem Ibrahim Pasha Waterside Mansion in Çubuklu as well as the Dehreli İsmail Pasha Waterside Mansion (1890) in Beylerbeyi. Many also dot the European side of the Bosphorus. The most famous of these is the Şerifler Waterside Mansion in Emirgan. The coastal road passes in front of this residence, which was constructed in 1872. Today, the only part that still exists of this historical waterside mansion is the Selamlık Kiosk, along with its pool. Illuminated by 20 windows, the dazzling ceiling décor of this residence, along with its 19th Century influenced wall ornamentation, is a sight to be seen. It is named "Şerifler Waterside Mansion" for it was once the summer residence of the Sheriff of Mecca.

The waterside mansion where the Egyptian Consulate is housed was constructed as a summer residence by the Khedive's family. Apart from this, the 18th Century Waterside Mansion with Snakes (Yılanlı Yalı) is situated next to the Aşiyan Tea Garden in the Rumelian Fortress area. The first waterside mansion in Yeniköy is that of the Firdevs Nuri Baras Waterside Mansion. Next door is the Atıf Pasha Waterside Mansion, which is attractive for its fancy décor and architecture. The Atıf Pasha Waterside Mansion was constructed by the Vallaury on behalf of Ahmed Atıf Pasha. After this residence comes that of Crown Prince Burhaneddin Efendi. This delightful palace was constructed using both timber and concrete. It is particularly striking because of the large balcony it has in the middle. Yeniköy resembles a city of waterside mansions. After the Beyazciyan Waterside Mansion and Karatodori Pasha Waterside Mansion, there is the Said Halim Pasha Waterside Mansion, which was recently destroyed in a fire. Said Halim Pasha was the grandson of Mehmed Ali Pasha, who served the Ottoman Empire as Grand Vizier between 1913-1917. He was murdered in Italy shortly after his arrival in the country. The Said Halim Pasha Waterside Mansion is currently undergoing restoration after the devastating blaze.

The Afif Pasha Summer Palace.
Situated between İstinye and Yeniköy, this Eclectic-style waterside mansion was built by the architect Vallaury for Ahmed Afif Pasha in 1910.

An interior view from one of the rooms in the Şerifler Waterside Mansion.
The waterside mansion, whose ceiling is gorgeously decorated, was initially built as a summer palace by the Sheriff of Mecca, Abdullah Pasha, in the 18th Century.

The waterside mansions of Faik Bey and Bekir Bey are situated right next to the quay. A little further down the road from here, one sees the Ali Rıza Pasha Waterside Mansion, the Hamapolas Waterside Mansion, which features Venetian-style architecture, while the Kalkavanlar Waterside Mansion is situated next door. A number of foreign embassies in Istanbul constructed their summer mansions here along the shore, giving Yeniköy a distinct ambiance. The first such residence seen in Yeniköy was the neo-classical style Austrian Embassy, which was built in 1898. It was bought from a rich Armenian named Mıgırdıç Cezayırliyan who was a relative of Mustafa Reşid Pasha. He lost all his wealth after the death of Mustafa Reşid Pasha and sold his residence to the Austrian Embassy. After Yeniköy comes Tarabya, where there are several waterside mansions as well. Particularly striking is the Huber Kiosk, which currently serves as the summerhouse of the President of Turkey. This place belonged to Herr Huber, who was the Krupp representative during the Ottoman period. The Finance Minister, Necmeddin Molla bought the Huber Waterside Mansion later only to sell it to Egyptian Princess Kadriye. This residence was donated to a charitable institution when the Princess returned to Egypt, whereby it became the summer kiosk of the President of Turkey in 1980. There is another whitewashed waterside mansion situated in the Tarabya Bay, which is particularly spectacular. During the period of Sultan Abdülaziz, Crown Prince Abdülhamid had his kiosk built on the grounds of this building, which used to belong to the German Embassy. Abdülaziz did not like the architectural style of this wooden structure and had it razed

The Count Ostrorog Waterside Mansion. The waterside mansion, which is located in Kandilli, was constructed at the beginning of the 19ᵗʰ Century. It got its name after being bought by Count Ostrorog.

Hekimbaşı Salih Efendi Waterside Mansion. Located between the Anatolian Fortress and Kanlıca, this waterside residence was built as a "harem" and "selamlık" in the second half of the 18ᵗʰ Century. The residence was named after a previous owner Salih Efendi, who was a physician during the sultanate of Mahmud II. Only the harem, with its three sections, is still extant.

to the ground. Then, when Abdülhamid II ascended to the throne, he granted the land, which was his personal property, to the Germans who later reconstructed the building as their embassy. Sailing past Tarabya Bay, one comes to the Italian Embassy in Kireçburnu. D'Aronco constructed the existing waterside mansion in the early 20th Century, next to a previously constructed building. The French Embassy can be seen a bit further down the way. This was the waterside mansion of Alexander Ipslante, whose family was once very influential in Istanbul. When it was discovered that he was spying against the Ottoman Empire, all his possessions were seized during the reign of Selim III, with this residence being donated to the French by Sultan Selim III. The English Embassy was constructed just beyond this mansion, but was subsequently destroyed in a fire. After Kireçburnu comes Büyükdere, where one can also see an abundance of waterside mansions. The first that comes into sight is the Azaryanlar Waterside Mansion, which is currently the home of the Sadberk Hanım Museum. Together with the adjacent building, it was recently acquired by the Koç family and converted into a museum. A little further down the road is the Kocataş Waterside Mansion, whose first owner was Abraham Pasha. In addition to this waterside mansion, the pasha is said to have owned much of the land from Beykoz to Riva. He also had a reputation for being quite a playboy during the period of Abdülhamid II. One day, he fell off his horse and died, whereupon Abdülhamid II nationalized all of his property. Famous for its many varieties of trees, the Abraham Pasha Woods is maintained today by the Beykoz Municipality.

Sadullah Pasha Waterside Mansion. Located in Çengelköy, this Baroque style mansion on the Bosphorus was built in 1783. It was bought by Esat Pasha in 1851. As his son Sadullah Pasha started to live there, it has always been remembered by his name.

View of Cypriot Waterside Mansion (Kıbrıslı Yalısı), (1755). Named after a Cyprus-burn Grand Vizier to Sultan Mahmud II, the Cypriot Waterside Mansion, one of the largest of the waterfront mansions, has been in the same family for seven generations.

211

Amcazade Waterside Mansion. Situated in the Anatolian Fortress area (Anadolu Hisarı), this waterside mansion was built by the order of the Grand Vizier Köprülü Hüseyin Pasha in 1699.

Prince Burhaneddin's Waterside Mansion.

Zarif Mustafa Pasha Waterside Mansion. Located in the Anatolian Fortress area (Anadolu Hisarı), this neo-classical waterside mansion was built in the late 17th Century.

Damat Ferit Pasha's Waterside Mansion.

The Huber Kiosk.

Yedisekiz Hasan Pasha's Waterside Mansion.

Kadri Pasha's Waterside Mansion.

Deli Fuat Pasha's Waterside Mansion.

Inns and Bazaars

Spaced roughly a day's distance apart from each other, inns were constructed to develop the trade routes of the Seljuks in Anatolia. Inns continued to function as such throughout the Ottoman Empire. The Ottomans altered the previous layout of lining up rooms around a courtyard, and built inns according to their own tastes. While the Seljuks constructed their inns with ashlar blocks, the Ottomans utilized bricks and stone. Also, the Ottomans preferred simple gates as opposed to the Seljuks, who built splendid victory gates.

A second courtyard was added to inns that were constructed in Istanbul after the city's conquest. They implemented features that differed from the inns of the Seljuk, such as stables in the basement and masjids in the courtyard. There aren't many examples from the 15th-16th Centuries. Inns constructed in the 17th Century were organized according to the layout of the land and roads, as we begin to see a more crowded city. Meanwhile, a third courtyard was added which separated the stables from living quarters, with the stables being introduced into this third courtyard. Three-storey inns that were mainly for guests appear in the 18th Century. In the 19th Century, these were transformed into an integral part of the city's commercial life. By then, inns were also starting to appear in arcades, which were initially built in Beyoğlu, then on down into Karaköy.

Istanbul's historical inns and caravanserais were for the most part situated inside complexes that were constructed as per orders of the sultan. Though the caravanserai in the Fatih Complex no longer exists, those seen today in the Crown Prince Complex, the Süleymaniye Complex as well as the Atık Valide Complex in Toptaşı, Üsküdar, built by Nurbanu Valide Sultan, all give us a fair idea about the classic Ottoman caravanserai. Constructed by Sultan Mehmed II's Grand Vizier, Mahmud Pasha, the oldest inn still intact in Istanbul is the Kürkçü Inn, near the Grand Bazaar. The two-storey inn has two courtyards, with stores and warehouses on the bottom floor and offices and lodgings on the upper floor.

The courtyard is surrounded with a vaulted gallery. The Galata vaulted bazaar in the Perşembe Pazarı-Galata district also dates back to the period of Sultan Mehmed II. With its four facades and nine domes, the structure has four pillars in the center that support the arches. The nine parts that emerge are covered with hoopless domes. The shops around the historic district of Perşembe Pazarı are no longer in business. Grand Vizier Rüstem Pasha commissioned Architect Sinan to construct the Kurşunlu Inn on the northern shore of the Golden Horn in the 16th Century. This inn possesses two stories and a courtyard. The Büyük Valide Inn was constructed on the Eminönü-Çakmakçılar Yokuşu by Murad II's mother Kösem Sultan in the mid 17th Century. This structure, which had two floors and three courtyards, is in ruins and has been greatly altered. Constructed by Köprülü Fazıl Ahmed Pasha in Çemberlitaş in the second half of the 17th Century, the two-

storey Vezir Inn was expanded with some additional wings and so is quite different from its original state. Constructed by Damat İbrahim Pasha in the 18th Century, the two-storey Çukur Inn in Nuruosmaniye has a courtyard as well as a basement. One of the inns that is still intact is the Hasan Pasha Inn, located in Beyazıt on Aksaray Street. It was constructed in 1770 by the architect Mustafa Çelebi on the orders of Seis Hasan Pasha. The two-storey inn has a courtyard, but does not have any stables or warehouses, a clear indication that it was built as a lodging inn. The inn has lost its original state because of the road construction and subsequent restoration work, which transformed it into an unrecognizable state. The Büyük Yeni Inn, which has three storeys and a courtyard, and is located on Çakmakçılar Yokuşu, was constructed by Sultan III during the second half of the 18th Century. Also built during the 18th Century is the Safevi Inn, which is one of the inns of the Grand Bazaar.

There are also some so-called "foundation" inns in Istanbul, the first of which is on the corner of Sultanhamam. Built by the architect Kemaleddin between 1911-18, this seven-storey inn has 50 rooms, including the basement. The Second Foundation Inn is also in Sultanhamam. The Third Foundation Inn, also built by Kemaleddin, has six stories, and is located in Beyoğlu at the intersection of Kuloğlu Sokağı and Turnacı Sokağı. Located in Bahçekapı, the construction of the Fourth Foundation Inn was begun in 1912 by Kemaleddin as well, but the various wars kept it from being completed until the year 1926. The Fifth Foundation Inn was built in Vefa to accommodate students of the Teacher's School, but was opened in 1923 as the Yüksek Muallim School.

Both the Narmanlı Inn in Beyoğlu and the Değirmen Inn in Eminönü are 19th Century buildings. The Rumeli, Anadolu and Africa Inns in Beyoğlu were all built by the Court Chamberlain of Abdülhamid II, Ragıp Pasha, at the end of the 19th Century. Istanbul is home to such other inns as the Abet Inn in Karaköy, the French Inn in Tophane, the Nordstem Inn in Karaköy, the Metro Inn, the Port Inn (Liman Han) in Sirkeci, and the Karaköy Palas in Karaköy. There are also a number of arcades situated next to these inns.

The Egyptian Bazaar: The Egyptian Bazaar is the second most important bazaar in Istanbul. The bazaar is within the New Mosque Complex and was designed in 1597 as a source of income for the mosque. The construction of the complex began in 1603 by the mother of Mehmed III, Safiye Sultan. It was halted because of her son's death and the fact that she was no longer the Mother Sultan. Construction on the site was to be postponed for 59 years, until the mother of Mehmed IV, Hatice Turhan Sultan completed the mosque and bazaar in 1663. The L-shaped Egyptian Bazaar is illuminated by 88 upper windows. It is called the Egyptian Bazaar because it sold goods from Egypt. The Bazaar has four main gates, two small gates and 86 shops. The two-storey bazaar was built with the main gates

An aerial view of the dome covering the Grand Bazaar. Lined up on more than fifty streets in this market place are 4400 stores, 40 inns and 2200 rooms in these inns.

at either end and the lower floor vaulted. The rooms on the top floor, which were once used as commercial courts, are accessed via a flight of stairs. In the early days, the bazaar was allocated to the cotton dealers and herbalists, but today the bazaar is better known for its spice shops. The Egyptian Bazaar burned down in 1691 but it reopened after restoration. It suffered heavy damage in a second fire that struck in 1940. Again, it was reopened after being restored in 1943.

The Grand Bazaar: We can certainly say that one of the most magnificent bazaars in Istanbul is the Grand Bazaar. The foundation of this great bazaar, which extended from Beyazıt to Nuruosmaniye, was laid after the conquest of Constantinople. While establishing the Grand Bazaar, Mehmed II first laid the foundations for the Eski Bedesten and then did the same for the Sandal Bedesten. The sultan had inns and shops built on streets for the wealthy class; then he had them covered. The Grand Bazaar consequently assumed its initial shape, which has survived until today, with several alterations.

Receiving light from the top windows, the upper part of the streets is covered with arches and roofs. Each street was turned into a trade center with quilt-makers, armchair and slipper-makers. There are 4,400 shops, and 40 inns with 2,200 rooms situated on more than 50 streets. With its workplaces, mosque, 10 separate masjids, 19 fountains and a bath, the Grand Bazaar has the appearance of a city. When the Grand Bazaar was first constructed, there were four gates situated in the Eski Bedesten's four facades. The "Sahaflar," "Takkeciler," "Zenneciler" and "Kuyumcular" Gates opened out into main avenues in the immediate vicinity called Çadırcılar, Yorgancılar, Fesciler, Kalpakçılar, Keseciler, Takkeciler and Nuruosmaniye, with a number of side streets merging into them.

The most important streets inside the 50 streets in the bazaar have such names as Kavaflar, Basmacılar, Sandal Bedesteni and Ağa Sokağı. The bazaar was badly damaged during fires that struck in 1546 as well as in 1660, 1695, 1701 and 1750. The Grand Bazaar was also badly damaged during the earthquakes of 1766, 1791, 1826 and 1894. The inns, in particular, were rendered useless. Moreover, subsequent to the 1894 earthquake, two gates with the monogram of Sultan Abdülhamid II embossed above them were built on the two corners of Kalpakçılar Street, which joins Beyazıt and Nuruosmaniye. Hit by two more fires, one in 1943 and the other in 1954, it has since lost much of its old atmosphere. However, despite this, it is continues to be a center where Turkish-jewelry making, carpet-weaving, embroidery and various handicrafts are displayed. Representing the nucleus of the bazaar, the Eski Bedesten is surrounded with 1.5 m thick walls and a roof covered with 15 domes. It was established over an area measuring 1,336 m². Its four gates open onto avenues named Keseciler, Takkeciler, Sahaflar and Kuyumcular. A second covered market, situated to the east, is called Sandal Bedesten.

In the past, the covered market had four gates but now it has two opening onto Nuruosmaniye Street. The Inner gate opens onto Sandal Bedesten Sokağı. Measuring 40x32 meters, the Sandal Bedesten is supported by 20 domes and 12 elephantine pillars.

Internal view of the Grand Bazaar.
External view of the Egyptian Bazaar.

Museums of Istanbul

The many works brought from beyond Turkey's frontiers, from such places as Egypt, Mesopotamia, Palestine and the Arabian Peninsula, are exhibited in three museums under the auspices of the Istanbul Archaeological Museums. They are 1) the Museum of Ancient Oriental Works, 2) the Museum of Classical Works, where one can see famous sarcophagi such as that of Alexander the Great, 3) and the Tiled Kiosk, with its famous Ottoman ceramic tiles and porcelain. Apart from these important museums, there is the imposing Byzantine Hagia Sophia Church, which is also open to visitors as a museum, and the Church of Hagia Eirene, which is also open as a monumental museum.

There are two museums in Edirnekapı-the Chora, and the Fethiye, both of which are world renown for their Byzantine mosaics and frescoes. Situated behind the Sultanahmet Mosque in the Arasta Bazaar, the Topkapı Palace Mosaic Museum exhibits some truly amazing Byzantine mosaics. Among other fabulous Ottoman and Seljuk works of art, one can see the finest examples of Seljuk-Ottoman carpets as well as exemplary Ottoman wood craftsmanship in the Museum of Turkish and Islamic Arts. Situated just opposite the Sultanahmet Mosque, the Columns and Obelisks in the Hippodrome are seen in front of this museum. Topkapı Palace is testimony to the splendor of the Ottomans. Constructed after this palace, Dolmabahçe Palace continues to enchant visitors. Besides these, there are palaces from the late-Ottoman period, such as Beylerbeyi and Yıldız, both of which are open to the public. Apart from these palaces, there are also Yıldız Chaled Kiosk, Aynalı Kavak, Ihlamur, Küçüksu and Maslak Summer Palaces, which are administered by the Department of National Palaces. The Khedive Summer Palace and the kiosks in the Emirgan Woods are open to the public and are administered by the Istanbul Metropolitan Municipality. Also worth a visit is the the Şerifler Waterside Mansion in Emirgan, which is a mansion administered by the Ministry of Culture. The Military Museum in Harbiye is worthy of attention because of its paintings and the military works remaining from the Ottoman Era. In addition to other works on display at the Naval Museum in Beşiktaş, one

Nejad Melih Devrim's Abstract Composition exhibited at Istanbul Modern Art Museum.

The Turtoise Trainer. Osman Hamdi Bey's oil painting on 221.5x120 cm canvas, exhibited at Pera Museum.

Next page: Felix Ziem's painting "Paddle and Sail Boats on the Bosphorus", exhibited at Pera Museum.

must see the splendid caiques that were once used by the Ottoman sultans. Right next to this museum, the Painting and Sculpture Museum, which is located inside the Dolmabahçe Palace Crown Prince Apartments, houses the paintings of many famous artists. In addition, there is also the Aviation Museum located in Yeşilköy, behind the airport. It houses the world's only existing example of a Polish P. Z. L. P-24 pursuit aircraft.

Located in Hisarüstü, there is the house of the famous poet, Tevfik Fikret, which is known as the Aşiyan Museum and is operated by the municipality. Other museums in Istanbul include the Atatürk Museum in Şişli, as well as the Fire Department Museum in Fatih, where obsolete fire fighting equipment is on display. Constructed under the orders of Sultan Mehmed III's Head Palace Servant, Gazanfer Ağa, the Gazanfer Ağa Madrasah in Saraçhane is situated beneath the Bozdoğan Aqueduct. Today, it houses the Caricature and Humor Museum. The famous Byzantine Yerebatan Cistern is open to the public as a museum. So is the Carpet Museum, which is located below the Sultanahmet Mosque. Operated by the General Directorate of Foundations, there are many examples of priceless historical carpets, kilims and straight-woven ground cloths. The madrasah in Fatih, constructed by Grand Vizier Hüseyin Pasha in 1697, is utilized today as the Museum of Turkish Art and Architecture, which houses monograms and inscriptions, tile coverings, wooden architectural pieces and lighting tools.

The Turkish Foundation of Calligraphic Arts Museum is housed in what used to be the madrasah of the complex constructed by Bayezid II in 1507. Here one can see such works of Ottoman sultans as Qur'ans, pamphlets, manuscripts, signboards and calligraphy. The building constructed by Ottoman Foreign Minister Saffet Pasha along Divanyolu Street in 1856 currently houses the Press and Media Museum. Not far from here, on the same avenue, is the Health Museum. Located on Yüksek Kaldırım, just south of Tünel, the Galata Mevlevi Lodge continues to serve as a museum called Divan Literature. ("Divan Edebiyatı"). The Feshane and Weaving Factory was re-organized and converted into the Museum of Industrial Structures. Named after the wife of the late-Vehbi Koç, Sadberk Hanım, this museum was opened after the restoration of Azaryan Water Mansion in Sarıyer. It is one of the museums that should be visited because of the very old Seljuk and Ottoman monuments on exhibit there. Some shoreline structures in Hasköy, which were once used as the Ottoman Empire's Shipyard and Iron Foundry, were recently opened to the public as the Rahmi M. Koç Industrial Museum. This is truly a world-class museum that has antique motor vehicles, steam engines, an interactive section, railroad cars, maritime engines and boats, and so on. Apart from these, there are also such collections in Istanbul as Şişe Cam Factory, and Yapı Kredi Bankası Vedat Nedim Tör in Galatasaray.

A Western Anatolian carpet with animal figures.
15th Century. Istanbul Vakıflar Carpet Museum.

Part of the kiosk of a 16th or 17th Century sultan's galley.
From the inscriptions on it, it is believed to have belonged to either Mehmed III or IV
Embellished with nacre and tortoise shell, it has a combination of floral
and geometric designs. Naval Museum.

Istanbul Archaeological Museums

The three museums collectively known as the "Istanbul Archaeological Museums" are considered to be among the most important museums in the world. Founded as the Imperial Museum during the Ottoman period, the collection includes a number of artifacts from various parts of the Ottoman Empire and Mesopotamia, such as the Tomb of Alexander the Great, the Tomb of the Weeping Maidens, and the Lycian Tomb, found in 1891 at Sayda, in Syria. Originally, the museum collection was exhibited in the Tiled Kiosk, a wing of the Topkapı Museum, but that building is now in use as the Museum of Tile and Ceramics. It houses items that date as far back as the period of Mehmed II. As the collection grew, the present building was erected (1892-1908) to which a wing has been added in recent years. Stylistically speaking, the late-19th Century museum building was inspired by the Tomb of the Weeping Maidens. The museum collection includes 60,000 archaeological findings of various kinds, nearly 800,000 coins and medallions, and nearly 75,000 cuneiform tablets, making it one of the greatest collections in the world. The collection can be seen in three separate sections: in the Museum of Ancient Oriental Works, which is situated opposite the main building; in the Classical section housed in the main building; as well as in the Tiled Kiosk. In the Museum of Ancient Oriental Works, the first hall houses Egyptian artifacts, including tombs and mummies. Halls III and IV display work from Mesopotamia, including findings from Aleppo, Ninevah, the periods of Early Sumerian, classical and Late Sumerian, and the Gudea statues.

In the section containing works of the Assyrian period are the statues of Puzur lshtar, governor of Mari, his son and Salmanasar III, and reliefs of winged spirits from the walls of the palace of King Tiglat Pileser at Nemrut. Other parts of the museum display seals and hieroglyphic tablets from Mesopotamia, and works of the Urartu and Phrygian periods. The Hittite period in Anatolia (2000-1200 BC.) is well represented, and the works on display include those of the Hittite Imperial period, and of the later Hittite city-states (dating after 1200 BC.). Among the most notable works of the period are vessels of various kinds, bronze axes and a hieroglyphic tablet inscribed with the text of the famous Kadesh Treaty. Late-Hittite works of note include the Zincirli reliefs, the Maraş findings, as well as the famous Babylonian reliefs, which are decorated with bull, dragon and lion figures in brickwork. They were originally part of the walls of the ceremonial pathway and the Ishtar Gate at Babylon.

The classical section of the museum was rearranged and opened to visitors in 1992. The triangular pediment of the Classical Section is supported by four pillars and is reached by white marble stairs. These stairs lead to a hallway where the statue of the god Bes of the Roman period stands. In the galleries on both sides of this hallway, masterpieces of the world are on exhibit. In the halls on the right hand side are ancient statues. The works in the first gallery are of the Archaic period. Works dating from the period of Persian dominance of Anatolia (546-333 BC.) are in the second gallery, whereas Attic tomb stelae and reliefs of the 6th-5th Centuries BC. are in the third gallery. Works of the Hellenistic period (330-30 BC.) adorn the hall in the following gallery.

Beautiful busts and a statue of Alexander the Great, whose reign initiated the period, are in this hall. One of these busts, found in Pergamon, draws attention because of the hair in the form of a lion's mane. Based on a portrait made by Lysippus in the 4th Century BC., this type of hair is peculiar to Alexander. This statue was made in a Pergamon sculpture workshop in the 2nd Century BC. Also in this hall is a statue of Marsyas, a work from the Roman period copied from the style of similar statues from the 3rd Century BC. According to mythology, Apollo punished Marsyas for daring to enter into a music contest with him by flogging his backside. This statue depicts Marsyas tied upside-down from a tree for punishment.

The most remarkable statues in this hall are those of Zeus, and a large divine statue found at the Temple of Hera in Pergamon most probably belonged to Pergamon King Attalos II (2nd Century BC.). Statues found in the Magnesia of Meander (today's Menderes River) and the Tralles (Aydin) are on exhibit in the fifth gallery. Across the hall is the Statue of the famous Ephebos, a young athlete. This statue, which was found in Tralles and belongs to the Early-Roman period, depicts a child athlete of about 12 years old at rest, exhausted from athletic activity. The boy wears a cloak thrown over his short garments. On the right hand side of the door is the statue of Apollo, goddess heads, and a statue of a half-naked Nymph. On the left hand side, is a statue of a woman named Balbia (1st Century BC.), a statue of Athena, as well as statues of a number of anonymous dignitaries. On the left side of the passageway, there is a striking statue of a woman, found at Tralles and used as a pillar. In the style of examples encountered with the Nereids Monument in Xanthos near Fethiye, and at the monument of Limyra near Finike, these statues have been used in place of pillars in various locations. Examples of Roman sculpture art are displayed in the next hall. In the center of the hall is a bust of the poetess Sappho, sculpted in the Roman period. On the right are statues of Aphrodite and Kybele. On the wall are the relief made in honor of Euripides, author of Greek tragedies and a relief of the Muses playing lyres. To the left of the hall are examples of Roman portrait art. Here are the busts of Emperors Augustus, Tiberius, and Claudius, and the statues of Nero and Hadrian. In addition, the statue and the bust

Reliefs of a lion. Made from glazed bricks, these were found on the walls of the ceremonial route leading to the Ishtar Gate in Babylon. 16th Century BC. Museum of Ancient Orient Works, Istanbul Archaeological Museums.

Tomb of the Weeping Maidens, 350 BC.

of Marcus Aurelius, the bust of Empress Faustina and busts of anonymous citizens adorn the hall. On the right hand side of the Aphrodisias Hall named for Prof. Kenan Erim, who conducted excavations for many years at Aphrodisias before he passed away in 1990, statues of Roman judges and the statue of a woman are on exhibit. Aphrodisias is near the provincial district of Karacasu in the province of Aydin in Western Anatolia. When Attalos III, King of Pergamon bequeathed his territory to Rome in 133 BC.,

sculptors here migrated to Aphrodisias, then the capital of the Carian region, and created marvelous works from marble obtained from rich marble quarries here. Statues that emerged from this Aphrodisias School of Sculpture were exported to Greece and Rome. Reliefs illustrating the war between the gods and giants are depicted on the walls of this hall. Works that have been uncovered in excavations at Aphrodisias are on display in the local museum whereas those found in Ephesus are on exhibit in the

A 5th Century BC. Lycian tomb, found in Sidon.

center of this hall. On the floor is a statue of the River God Oceanus, and next to it, the statue of Polemaeanus, the Prefect of Asia Minor, which was found in the Celsus Library of Ephesus. Artifacts found in Miletus, and, on the opposite wall, statues found in the Faustina Baths, are displayed on the left hand side of the hall. These statues from Faustina are of a Muse playing the flute, of Melpomene, and of Apollo playing the lyre. Next to the works found in Anatolia are works found within the former borders of the Ottoman Empire. The busts of Poseidon and Artemis, statues of Zeus and the Goddess of Good Fortune Tyche are among the works displayed in this hall. In the gallery, on the left hand side of the entrance, is an exhibit of sarcophagi, each more beautiful than the next, including that of belonging to King Tabnit of Sidon, which was sculpted from basalt. From the inscription on the sarcophagus, it has been concluded that it once belonged to General Peneftah, who lived during the time of the 26th dynasty of Egypt, and was later re-used for King Tabnit of Sayda. Surrounding this sarcophagus are Egyptian and Greek sarcophagi. Situated behind these is a magnificent 5th Century BC. Lycian sarcophagus, which was found in the necropolis of the King of Sidon. Called the Lycian Sarcophagus due to its resemblence to the sarcophagi of the Lycian region, it was found at Sidon by Osman Hamdi in 1877 and subsequently brought to Istanbul. One side depicts a lion hunt and two chariots, each drawn by four horses, while the other side is an illustration of a boar hunt. On the narrow surfaces are carvings of the fight of Centaur and Lapith and a scene of a struggle over a deer between two Centaurs. Also brought from Sidon is another late-5th Century sarcophagus behind this, depicting the life of a satrap of Persia. Made from white marble and bearing beautiful reliefs, the so called Sarcophagus of Alexander the Great, did not in fact belong to Alexander, but carries his name due to the war and hunt scenes which decorate it. Measuring 2.12 meters high, 3.18 meters long, and 1.67 meters wide, this sarcophagus is carved with the following images; Alexander's battle against the Greeks is depicted on the narrow surfaces; on the left end is an illustration of Alexander; while scenes of lion and deer hunts cover the other end. The wounded lion in the center of the hunting scene is illustrated in the act of biting. The cavalier to the left of the lion is Alexander himself, wearing the royal symbol on his hand. This 4th-Century BC. sarcophagus is covered with beautifully painted, delicate stonework. Behind this sarcophagus is that of the Weeping Maidens. Made for a Sidonian in 350 BC., there are 18 separately carved women mourning on this sarcophagus. Two identical funeral processions are depicted on the top cover. Some of the halls in this section of the museum are in the process of being restructured. On the upper floor of the newly opened section of the museum is an exhibition of Anatolian Civilizations. The "Through The Ages" exhibit is also on display. On the left side of the second floor are artifacts from the ancient city of Troy. Located

Previous page:
Tomb of Alexander the Great.
Measuring 3.18 m in length, 1.67 m in width, and 2.12 m in height, this tomb really belonged to the Phoenician King Abdalonymus, but was called the Tomb of Alexander due to the depictions of Alexander chiseled into its sides. One side shows Alexander and the Greeks fighting against the Persians while the side pictured here depicts a lion hunt.

Statue of Young Athlete. Standing 1.48 m high, the work was found at the Tralles site in Aydin. Late 1st Century BC.

30 kilometers from Çanakkale, Troy was razed and rebuilt nine times. As the site of the first archaeological excavation in Anatolia, Troy was the subject of one of Homer's legendary works. The city of Troy was continuously inhabited from 3500 B.C to AD. 300., making it possible to trace its cultural evolution through the ages. First excavated Heinrich Schliemann in 1870, the story of these excavations and the tremendously colorful personality of Schliemann has made Troy an even more interesting and important site to visit. The works on exhibit here are those found during the excavations conducted by Schliemann and Dörpfeld, whereas the gold decorative objects from Level II Troy and double-handled ceramic pots peculiar to Troy are seen in the first display case. Schliemann found these objects near the ramped gate of Troy in 1873 and thought that they belonged to the Treasury of King Priam of VI Level Troy. However, it was later proven during subsequent excavations that these works belonged to Level II Troy between 2500-2200 BC. The Troy beneath the second layer started in the third millennium BC. and terminated quite suddenly with heavy destruction around 2500 BC. Again, in this hall, ceramics uncovered from Levels III, IV and V (2200-1800 BC.) of Troy works, as well as works belonging to Level VI and Level VII Troy, just prior to the major war (1800-1275 BC.). One can also see artifacts displayed from the works from Levels VIII and IX, the latter of which was the period when Troy was under Roman domination. Moreover, the head of Zeus uncovered in the Troy excavations is displayed next to these exhibits. A reproduction of the Temple of Athena, which was located in an ancient city behind Troy, called Assos, conforms exactly to its original. Dating back to 530 BC., this was the oldest Doric-style temple in western Anatolia. After the Troy exhibits, Anatolian works from throughout the ages are exhibited in chronological order in the opposite cases. Palaeolithic, Neolithic and Chalcolithic period works uncovered at sites located on the outskirts of Istanbul, such as Yarımburgaz, Fikirtepe and Pendik, are also displayed in this gallery. Moreover, the cultures of Kumtepe, Karaağaçtepe, Babaköy and Yortan, which produced the first Bronze Age works in the third millennium BC. in Western Anatolia, as well as works found in Bozhöyük, are also on display. Ceramics and bronze works from the Early Bronze Age are seen side-by-side in these showcases. Findings of Boğazköy and Kültepe dating to the Middle Bronze Age (1900-1500 BC.) can be viewed here as well. Numerous cuneiform tablets uncovered at Boğazköy and Kültepe, which contain historical, religious and legal matters, as well as private letters, are on display in the same section. Works of the Anatolian Iron Age (1200-546 BC.) are found in the succeeding display cases. Works of the Urartu civilization, which thrived in Eastern Anatolia between the 8th-6th Centuries BC., are displayed separately from the works of Phrygian civilization, which existed in Central Anatolia during the same period. After examining the large vessels found in Kargamuş and Boğazköy and pots and ceramics found in the Phrygian city of Yazılıkaya (City of Midas), let us proceed to the upper floor to look at the works displayed there. Works that were brought from beyond Anatolia, such as Palestine, Cyprus and Syria, are on display here. The section displaying Byzantine artworks that were uncovered in excavations in the Istanbul area is on the museum's lower floor.

Statue of Marsias. He is shown nailed to a tree with an expression of suffering on his face after being flogged by Zeus. According to the legend, he entered a flute-playing contest with Apollo and lost. Found in Tarsus, this incomparable Hellenistic Era-statue is currently on display at the Lourve Museum.

Museum of Turkish and Islamic Arts

The Museum of Turkish and Islamic Arts is not only the first museum in Turkey devoted to the display of Islamic art, it is one of the few museums in the world to have an extensive collection of Islamic art covering all periods and types of art. For many years, the collection of art was displayed in the Soup Kitchen of the Süleymaniye Complex. But because of its expanding size and the lack of modern facilities, the need for a new museum building grew. It was with the restoration of the 16th Century İbrahim Pasha Palace, located on the grounds of the Byzantine Hippodrome, that the museum found its new home in 1983.

While it is not clear just when the palace, which was made with stone and brick in spite of the fact that wood was generally used in Turkish civilian architecture was built, it is known that it was repaired by Sultan Süleyman the Magnificent and given to the Grand Vezier İbrahim Pasha as a gift. İbrahim Pasha had married the daughter of the Sultan, Hatice Sultan, and settled in the palace. After his death, the palace, which became known by his name, continued to be used up until the present. A number of miniatures from 1528 that contain scenes of celebrations picture the building exactly as it is today. On them, for example, can be seen the balcony where the sultan and his entourage would sit, the Divanhane, as well as the painted columns and latticework of the building. The Museum of Turkish and Islamic Arts contains a great variety of works ranging from the earliest period of Islam right up to the 20th Century. For example, those of the Umayyad, Abbasid and Fatimid period are some of the earliest found at the museum. Following the death of the Prophet Muhammed, Osman became chosen as the Caliph. His clan, known as the Umayyads, subsequently grew in size. They became the first dynasty based on inheritance of political power from father to son. Pages of the Qur'an, written with Kufic letters, that were brought from the Umayyad Mosque in Damascus, are among the important documents reflecting the art of that period

The Abbasids, who were descendents of the uncle of the Prophet Muhammed, established a dynasty that ruled between 749-1258. They played an important role in art during the time of the Caliph Harun el Reşid. The pieces of art on display at the Museum, which were brought from archeological digs in Samarra, are examples reflecting the art of that period. The Fatimids, who were of the Shiite sect of Islam, created a philosophy and understanding of art in North Africa, where they established their rule, that was different from that of the countries of Eastern Islam. Establishing Cairo as their capital, they ruled other areas. The pages from the Qur'an, painted and wooden works, and the ceramic and ivory works found at the Museum are symbols of Fatimid art. The Great Seljuk State exercised hegemony over Asia between 1037-1194. This state, which had accepted Islam, also founded the Anatolian Seljuk State, which was subservient to them. It is possible to find tiles, ceramic and metallic works from this period at the Museum. Having accepted Islam, the Great Seljuk State undertook to act as the protector of the

Caliph. In order to do this, it was necessary to dominate Anatolia. When the Byzantines were defeated by the Great Seljuk Sultan Alparslan at Malazgirt in 1071, the Turks overran Anatolia. Wherever the Turkish cavalry got the upper hand, it established what have come to be called the "early emirates." One of the first of these was the Artuks, who established their emirates in the region of southern Anatolia. Drums, candleholders, and mirrors of the Artuks, who built the first mosques and madrasahs in Anatolia, as well as

the doorknocker of the Ulu Mosque in Cizre are on display at the Museum. After the period of the early emirates, the Seljuks continued to advance in Anatolia under the leadership of Kutalmışoğlu Süleyman. In 1096, they established the Anatolian Seljuk State, with Konya as its capital. They subsequently assumed sovereignty over all of Anatolia. The Anatolian Seljuks, who were first subject to the Great Seljuk State, continued to exercise sovereignty independently even after the latter collapsed. They

Left: Transylvania-type carpet. 18th Century.
Middle: Kuşlu (Bird motif) carpet, 17th Century.
Right: Konya Ladik Seccade (Prayer Rug), 18th C.

*Carpet with
dragon figure.
Central Anatolia or Western
Anatolia, 17th or 18th Century,
87x52 cm*

bequeathed the Turkish inheritance upon all of Anatolia by extensively building such edifices as mosques, madrasahs, caravanserais and tombs all over Anatolia. Metal and wooden works, and especially carpets, left by them are worth seeing. Being defeated by the Mongols in 1243, the Seljuks became subject to the Anatolian Mongol State. But with its collapse, the İlhanid State, established by the son of Cengiz, Hülagu, came to dominate Anatolia. When the Anatolian Seljuk State collapsed in 1308, the previously established emirates began declaring their independence from place to place, which ushered in the Anatolian Emirates Period. The fact that the Karamanoğuls, one of these emirates, continued the traditions of the Seljuks, is important. The window shutters of the Karamanoğlu İbrahim Bey Soup Kitchen, a wooden sarcophagus and wooden minber wings are among the major works of the Karamanoğuls on display at the Museum. Another emirate that declared its independence was the Ottomans. Having been established in 1299, it increasing grew to a point where it had begun to roam the European continent. However, when Yıldırım Bayezid defeated Timur in 1402, there began a 10-year period of chaos in Anatolia. Süleyman Çelebi, Yıldırım's son, once again established the state. There are works on display at the Museum from the Yıldırım period. The Ottomans, reestablishing their sovereignty over Anatolia, took Istanbul, thereby breathing life into the Ottoman Empire, which came to exercise its sovereignty over three continents. There are many works from the Ottoman period on display at the Museum. These include carpets from Uşak, Gördes, Pergamon, and Ladik, tiles, metal candlesticks, silver oil pots and hangers. Moreover, in addition to such manuscripts as edicts and Qur'ans, there are Qur'an protectors and Qur'an reading tables there, too.

Each of the many sections of the Museum of Turkish and Islamic Arts is so rich as to be able to form a separate museum all by itself. In the manuscript section of the Museum, there is a manuscript collection spanning the whole of Islam, from the Early Islamic Period to the Ottomans. In addition to these, there are nearly 3000 unsurpassed works produced by the Ottoman Sultans themselves, which include deeds of trust of pious foundations, edicts and acquittals. In the carpet section of the Museum, there are 1700 historical carpets. This is why the Museum has been called the "carpet museum." In addition to famous examples from the Seljuk period, all groups of carpets, extending till the Ottoman period, are represented. These include the large-sized Uşak carpets, for example, as well as the prayer rug from the Edirne Selimiye Mosque. Carpets from such famous carpet centers as Pergamon, Ladik and Gördes are on display at the Museum. Metal works exhibited at the Museum are important from the point of view of metal working of the Middle Ages. Among the metal works found at the Museum are the Artuknid drums, the doorknockers from the Cizre Ulu Mosque, and candlesticks from the Artuknid and Seljuk periods. The wooden forms of art at the Museum are extremely interesting. Those from the Seljuk Emirate Period are particularly exquisite. Door and window shutters, sarcophaguses and Qur'an reading tables are among the works on display. Works of genius reflecting superior workworking craftsmanship include Qur'an reading tables belonging to the Seljuk Period, window shutters of the Karaman İbrahim Pasha Mosque, from the emirates period, and the sarcophagus brought from the Mahmud Hayrani Tomb. Furthermore, the side-wings of wooden minbers of mosques can be seen at the Museum. Qur'an protectors and Qur'an reading tables with nacre inlays belonging to the Ottoman period are example of the superb Ottoman art of woodworking.

The tiles and bas-reliefs of Seljuk and Ottoman edifices that are no longer standing make up a completely separate section of the Museum. The tiles from the palace in Samarra, which was the capital of the Abbasids, tiles from Seljuk palaces, and tiles from the Ottoman period on which there are designs of the Kabe are particularly fascinating.

A gold-gilded copper oil lamp. The oil lamp, which belongs to the period 1481-1512, is from the Bayazid Mosque. The facades of lamp are decorated in latticework with Rûmî and Hataî motifs.

An enameled silver hanging oil lamp. It is decorated with motifs consisting of branches and flowers and colorful gems against an enamel base. The 17th Century oil lamp is from the Tomb of Sultan Ahmed.

Istanbul
in the 21st Century

Istanbul in the 21st Century

Today, Istanbul has become a European city that keeps up with the modern world, even setting trends in it, as a result of the rapid urban development process it entered into in the recent years. Adding the riches of the modern world to its historical and cultural accumulation brought from the past, the city has become more colorful and charming. In addition to its attractions, the city is also home to numerous places for delicacies, shopping and entertainment.

Istanbul has become a shopping center with its ever-increasing number of large shopping malls as well as its historical markets. A great deal of shopping complexes such as Akmerkez, Istinye Park, Kanyon and Cevahir enable keeping abreast with the world fashion. The largest-capacity shopping mall in Europe is in Istanbul. There are also select stores located in different districts of Istanbul, where world-famous brands can be found.

Istanbul, a city more highly populated than some small European countries, has a dense population of young people, which brings about an increase in both the number and variety of cultural, artistic and entertainment spots. Music festivals and concerts help world-famous musicians and their fans meet in this city. Theatres, musicals, opera, ballet and dance shows are held by not only state and municipality theatres but also private theatres and show centers.

Another well known characteristic of Istanbul is the liveliness and attractiveness of the night life. Night clubs and bars that are lined up along the Bosphorus open their doors to the city's visitors, offering them unforgettable fun, while a myriad of different restaurants with a spectacular Bosphorus view provide service on both sides of Istanbul. Other hot spots for bustling night life are Beyoğlu and Taksim Square (Taksim Meydanı). Delicious fish from the Sea of Marmara and the Black Sea can be tasted in the restaurants at the Flower Passage (Çiçek Pasajı) in Beyoğlu, as well as in Kumkapı, Bosphorus and many others scattered across all

Numerous tall buildings rose in Istanbul in the recent years.
Having changed the s ilhouette of Istanbul, skyscrapers are mostly centered in Maslak and Levent area. Some of the skyscrapers serve as the executive headquarters of large corporations, while some are used as shopping malls.

A night view of Istanbul from the Çırağan Hotel.
There are many five-star hotels in Istanbul which host congresses, meal meetings and weddings.

A view of Republic Festival ceremonies by the Boshporus.

Akmerkez - one of the modern shopping malls in Istanbul.

The first traces of opera and ballet in Istanbul
dates to the 16th Century.
The process was initiated by Ottoman ambassadors,
who informed the palace of the art performances
they watched in European countries and staged
the shows of these foreign groups at the palace theatre,
rapidly developing during the Republic Period.
Today, in addition to the State Opera and Ballet under
the Ministry of Culture, classical and modern dance ensembles
of individuals and private organizations too serve the development of
the opera and ballet culture in Istanbul. World-famous groups
meet art fans in Istanbul every year. In 2008,
the first Istanbul International Ballet Contest
was held in the city.

corners of the city. Restaurants serving rich varieties of Turkish cuisine can be found in every district of the city. Strolling the spacious gardens of the summer palaces such as Emirgan Summer Palace, Yıldız Summer Palace, Maslak Summer Palace and Khedive Summer Palace, and sipping your Turkish coffee in their cafes are distinct pleasures.

Istanbul hosts many national and international sporting competitions every year. Istanbul also made its mark on the world maritime map as a water city. Watching international yachting, canoeing and rowing competitions from the Bosphorus and Golden Horn coasts is exceptionally amusing for passionate sea-loving people. The Turkish home of Formula-1, the most famous annual world-wide sporting event, is also in Istanbul. Istanbul Park has a distinctive and special place among Formula-1 circuits due to its circuit structure, which increases the challenge of the competition and exhilaration of the spectators. National and international games of soccer, which is one of the favorite pastimes in Turkey as in many other countries, are followed in a festive mood with a high degree of involvement and excitement from the public. Istanbul hosts world-scale competitions not only in soccer but also in basketball.

In Istanbul, which is one of the largest cities of the world, intra-city transportation is carried out via land, sea and railway. Ferries affiliated with the Istanbul Sea Buses Company (İstanbul Deniz Otobüsleri İşletmesi) serve Istanbulites with more than 1200 sailings a day. Besides Bosphorus tours, these ferries also operate sailings to Princes' Islands, and the Marmara Sea Islands that are in the vicinity. Thanks to the tours organized by ferries and private tour boats, it is possible to see closely the wonders of the most beautiful strait on earth, with historical waterside mansions lined up on both sides.

As far as inter-city transportation is concerned, in addition to the public and private busses, there are other options such as the metro, metrobus and tram, which have rapidly expanded the transportation network in the city and relaxed the traffic to a significant degree. There are two airports on both sides of the city, serving on domestic and international routes. Atatürk Airport on the European side is one of the best European airports in terms of service quality. While the Sabiha Gökçen Airport on the Asian side is relatively new, it holds an important share both in domestic and international air transportation of the country. Both airports are accessible from many points of the city via bus.

For a unique experience in Istanbul, where every corner is as precious as treasure, the time in the city can be enjoyed with a versatile approach, without ignoring what modern Istanbul has to offer.

The Bosphorus Bridge, connecting the two continents, is the first choice for social events and organizations because of its enchanting atmosphere.

Emirgan Woods.
Parks and woods lined up along both sides of the Bosphorus merge green with the blue sea, thus giving Istanbulites tranquility and peace.

Sea gulls are an integral part of the panorama of Istanbul.